Karoline von Günderrode

OXFORD NEW HISTORIES OF PHILOSOPHY

Series Editors
Christia Mercer, Melvin Rogers, and Eileen O'Neill (1953–2017)

*

Advisory Board
Lawrie Balfour, Jacqueline Broad, Marguerite Deslauriers, Karen Detlefsen, Bachir Diagne, Don Garrett, Robert Gooding-Williams, Andrew Janiak, Marcy Lascano, Lisa Shapiro, Tommie Shelby

*

Oxford New Histories of Philosophy provides essential resources for those aiming to diversify the content of their philosophy courses, revisit traditional narratives about the history of philosophy, or better understand the richness of philosophy's past. Examining previously neglected or understudied philosophical figures, movements, and traditions, the series includes both innovative new scholarship and new primary sources.

*

Published in the series

Mexican Philosophy in the 20th Century: Essential Readings
Edited by Carlos Alberto Sánchez and Robert Eli Sanchez, Jr.

Sophie de Grouchy's Letters on Sympathy: *A Critical Engagement with* Adam Smith's The Theory of Moral Sentiments
Edited by Sandrine Bergès and Eric Schliesser. Translated by Sandrine Bergès.

Margaret Cavendish: Essential Writings
Edited by David Cunning

Women Philosophers of Seventeenth-Century England: Selected Correspondence
Edited by Jacqueline Broad

The Correspondence of Catharine Macaulay
Edited by Karen Green

Mary Shepherd's Essays on the Perception of an External Universe
Edited by Antonia Lolordo

Women Philosophers of Eighteenth-Century England: Selected Correspondence
Edited by Jacqueline Broad

Frances Power Cobbe: Essential Writings of a Nineteenth-Century Feminist Philosopher
Edited by Alison Stone

Korean Women Philosophers and the Ideal of a Female Sage: Essential Writings of Im Yungjidang and Gang Jeongildang
Edited and Translated by Philip J. Ivanhoe and Hwa Yeong Wang

Louise Dupin's Work on Women: Selections
Edited and Translated by Angela Hunter and Rebecca Wilkin

Edith Landmann-Kalischer: Essays on Art, Aesthetics, and Value
Edited by Samantha Matherne. Translated by Daniel O. Dahlstrom

Mary Ann Shadd Cary: Essential Writings of a Nineteenth-Century
Black Radical Feminist
Edited by Nneka D. Dennie

Slavery and Race: Philosophical Debates in the Eighteenth Century
Julia Jorati

Maria W. Stewart: Essential Writings of a Nineteenth-Century Black Abolitionist
Edited by Douglas A. Jones Jr.

Slavery and Race: Philosophical Debates in the Sixteenth and Seventeenth Centuries
Julia Jorati

The Emotions of Nonviolence: Revisiting Martin Luther King Jr.'s "Letter
from Birmingham Jail"
Meena Krishnamurthy

Susan Stebbing: Analysis, Common Sense, and Public Philosophy
Edited by Annalisa Coliva and Louis Doulas

Seizing Citizenship: Frederick Douglass's Abolitionist Republicanism
Philip Yaure

The Fugitive Blacksmith and Other Essential Writings by James W.C. Pennington
Edited by Jan Stievermann, Caitlin B. Smith, and Eddie Glaude Jr.

James W.C. Pennington: Essays Toward Rediscovering a Great African American
Intellectual and Reformer
Edited by Jan Stievermann, Caitlin B. Smith, and Eddie Glaude Jr.

Frederick Douglass: The Philosophical Writings
Edited by Nick Bromell

Slavery in Early Modern Philosophy 1500–1765: Essential Readings
Edited by Julia Jorati

Slavery in Early Modern Philosophy 1765–1800: Essential Readings
Edited by Julia Jorati

Women and Republicanism
Edited by Sandrine Berges and Alan Coffee

Karoline von Günderrode: Philosophical Writings
Edited and translated by Anna Ezekiel

Karoline von Günderrode

Philosophical Writings

Edited and translated by

ANNA EZEKIEL

OXFORD
UNIVERSITY PRESS

OXFORD
UNIVERSITY PRESS

Oxford University Press is a department of the University of Oxford.
It furthers the University's objective of excellence in research, scholarship,
and education by publishing worldwide. Oxford is a registered trade mark of
Oxford University Press in the UK and in certain other countries.

Published in the United States of America by Oxford University Press
198 Madison Avenue, New York, NY 10016, United States of America.

© Oxford University Press 2026

Library of Congress Control Number: 2025042287

ISBN 9780190089146 (pbk.)
ISBN 9780190089139 (hbk.)

DOI: 10.1093/9780190089177.001.0001

Paperback printed by Marquis Book Printing, Canada
Hardback printed by Lightning Source, Inc., United States of America

The manufacturer's authorized representative in the EU for product safety is
Oxford University Press España S.A. of Parque Empresarial San Fernando de Henares,
Avenida de Castilla, 2 – 28830 Madrid (www.oup.es/en or product.safety@oup.com).
OUP España S.A. also acts as importer into Spain of products made by the manufacturer.

MIX
Paper | Supporting
responsible forestry
FSC
www.fsc.org   FSC® C103567

To my Doktorvater *George di Giovanni, who taught me to philosophize in a spirit of mischief*

Contents

Series Editors' Foreword   xi
Acknowledgments   xiii

Introduction   1

PART 1. WORKS

1. Idea of the Earth   45

2. Letters of Two Friends   52

3. The Manes   66

4. The Malabarian Widows   74

5. "An Apocalyptic Fragment" and "A Dream"   77

6. The Wanderer's Descent   83

7. The Adept   91

8. The Frank in Egypt   95

9. Immortalita   102

10. Story of a Brahmin   112

11. Fragments on Ethics and Aesthetics   127

12. Fragments on Music   140

13. The Aeronaut   146

14. Once I Lived Sweet Life   151

15. Mora   158

16. Udohla   166

PART 2. NOTEBOOKS

17. Introduction to Günderrode's Notebooks   205

18. Notes on Philosophy of Nature   208

19. Notes on Chemistry   226

20. Notes on the Early German Romantics   230

21. Notes on Schleiermacher   239

22. Notes on Hemsterhuis   244

23. Miscellaneous Notes   247

PART 3. LETTERS

24. Günderrode's Letters   259

Appendix: Sources for the Translations   289
Bibliography   293
Index   299

Series Editors' Foreword

Oxford New Histories of Philosophy (ONHP) speaks to a new climate in philosophy.

There is a growing awareness that philosophy's past is richer and more diverse than previously understood. It has become clear that canonical figures are best studied in a broad context. More exciting still is the recognition that our philosophical heritage contains long-forgotten innovative ideas, movements, and thinkers. Sometimes these thinkers warrant serious study in their own right; sometimes their importance resides in the conversations they helped reframe or problems they devised; often their philosophical proposals force us to rethink long-held assumptions about a period or genre; and frequently they cast well-known philosophical discussions in a fresh light.

There is also a mounting sense among philosophers that our discipline benefits from a diversity of perspectives and a commitment to inclusiveness. In a time when questions about justice, inequality, dignity, education, discrimination, and climate (to name a few) are especially vivid, it is appropriate to mine historical texts for insights that can shift conversations and reframe solutions. Given that philosophy's very long history contains astute discussions of a vast array of topics, the time is right to cast a broad historical net.

Lastly, there is increasing interest among philosophy instructors in speaking to the diversity and concerns of their students. Although historical discussions and texts can serve as a powerful means of doing so, finding the necessary time and tools to excavate long-buried historical materials is challenging.

Oxford New Histories of Philosophy is designed to address all these needs. It contains new editions and translations of significant historical texts. These primary materials make available, often for the first time, ideas and works by women, people of colour, and movements in philosophy's past that were groundbreaking in their day but left out of traditional accounts. Informative introductions help instructors and students navigate the new material. Alongside its primary texts, ONHP also publishes monographs and collections of essays that offer philosophically subtle analyses of understudied topics, movements, and figures. In combining primary materials and astute philosophical analyses, ONHP makes it easier for philosophers, historians, and instructors to include in their courses and research exciting new materials drawn from philosophy's past.

ONHP's range is wide, both historically and culturally. The series includes, for example, the writings of African American philosophers, twentieth-century Mexican philosophers, early modern and late medieval women, Islamic and Jewish authors, and non-western thinkers. It excavates and analyses problems and ideas that were prominent in their day but forgotten by later historians. And it serves as a significant aid to philosophers in teaching and researching this material.

As we expand the range of philosophical voices, it is important to acknowledge one voice responsible for this series. Eileen O'Neill was a series editor until her death, December 1, 2017. She was instrumental in motivating and conceptualizing ONHP. Her brilliant scholarship, advocacy, and generosity made all the difference to the efforts that this series is meant to represent. She will be deeply missed, as a scholar and a friend.

We are proud to contribute to philosophy's present and to a richer understanding of its past.

Christia Mercer and Melvin Rogers
Series Editors

Acknowledgments

The translations of Günderrode's notebooks are based on hand-written manuscripts held at the Universitätsbibliothek Johann Christian Senckenberg Frankfurt am Main and the Frankfurter Goethe-Museum at the Freies Deutsches Hochstift. I am grateful for the kind assistance from these institutions in producing English translations from these manuscripts.

Preparation of this book was partly funded by the American Society of Eighteenth-Century Studies Women's Caucus Editing and Translation Fellowship 2022.

Once again, I must express my enormous gratitude to Dr. Katerina Mihaylova for her generous help with the translations.

Writing this book while dealing with chronic illness has made the help I receive from others more obvious than ever. Thank you to my family and friends who have supported me through these difficult years. Thank you also to Lucy Randall and Meredith Taylor at Oxford University Press, who have been flexible and kind about unpredictable health-related delays. To Sunita (Pinky) Rajput: I am so grateful you have come into my life; I could not do my work without you. Most of all, thank you to my partner Zac, who had to pick up everything I dropped.

Enormous gratitude to Dr. Kenny de Meirleir and all the staff at Himmunitas, without whom this book would not have been finished.

Introduction

In 1804, the "philosophical poet"[1] Karoline von Günderrode published her first volume of poetry, short stories, and dialogues, *Poems and Fantasies*, under the pseudonym "Tian." Reviews praised "The grace and purity of the language"[2] and claimed the collection presented "The most important problems of reason [. . .] in vivid images and with harmonious tones."[3] The most famous German literary figure of the time, Johann Wolfgang von Goethe, described the book more ambiguously as "really a strange phenomenon."[4] In 1805, Günderrode followed *Poems and Fantasies* with a second volume of poems and plays titled *Poetic Fragments*. During these years, three of her plays and one short story also appeared in journals. In 1806, the publication of Günderrode's third and final collection, *Melete*, was suppressed in response to her scandalous suicide; it remained unpublished for a century.

Despite her early success, Günderrode's accomplishments as a writer and thinker were soon eclipsed by her intriguing biography and a public persona as a mystical, tragic embodiment of feminine poetry. She became, in the words of one writer, "a tragic figure, beset by the shadow of death."[5] This picture of Günderrode and its use as a lens through which to interpret her work has persisted until recently. Partly as a result, for over two centuries, there were few serious studies of Günderrode's contributions to literature or philosophy. This is at last beginning to change. New editions and translations

---

[1] Lucia Maria Licher, *Mein Leben in einer bleibenden Form aussprechen. Umrisse einer Ästhetik im Werk Karoline von Günderrodes (1780–1806)* (Heidelberg: Winter, 1996), 398.

[2] Anon., "Literarische Beitrag aus Frankfurt am Mayn," *Der Freimüthige oder Ernst und Scherz* 97 (15 May 1804): 385, cited in Karoline von Günderrode, *Sämtliche Werke* [hereafter "SW"], ed. Walter Morgenthaler (Frankfurt and Basel: Stroemfeld/Roter Stern, 1990–1991), vol. 3, 62.

[3] Christian Nees von Esenbeck, Review: "Hamburg u. Frankfurt a. M., in Commiss. d. Hermannschen Buchh.: *Gedichte und Phantasien*, von Tian. 1804. 137 S. 8," *Jenaische Allgemeine Literatur-Zeitung* 163 (9 July 1804): 49–52, cited in SW 3:64.

[4] Goethe, Letter to Heinrich Carl Abraham Eichstädt, 28 April 1804, in *Goethes Briefe an Eichstadt. Mit Erläuterungen*, ed. Woldemar Freiherrn von Biedermann (Berlin: Gustav Hempel, 1872), 87, see also 130.

[5] Maria Peter, "Zwischen Klassik und Romantik: Karoline von Günderrode," *Das Goldene Tor. Monatsschrift für Literatur und Kunst* 6 (1949): 466.

Karoline von Günderrode. Anna Ezekiel, Oxford University Press. © Oxford University Press 2026.
DOI: 10.1093/9780190089177.003.0001

of Günderrode's writings have been published, her work features in main-stream journals and conferences, and her writings are taught in university courses. Scholars argue that Günderrode provides original alternatives to the philosophical ideas of her more famous male contemporaries, including Friedrich Wilhelm Joseph Schelling (1775–1854), Johann Gottlieb Fichte (1762–1814), and members of the philosophical and literary movement known as early German Romanticism, especially Friedrich Schlegel (1772–1829) and Friedrich von Hardenberg (1772–1801), better known by his pen name Novalis. Philosophers have begun to explore Günderrode's unique accounts of personal identity, agency, free will, gender, friendship, the human vocation, and environmental ethics, which she situates in the context of her uniquely strange and compelling metaphysics.

Although Günderrode's philosophical thought has historically been neglected, she has had a persistent following as a poet and Romantic personality. Her work influenced prominent German writers including the poet and novelist Johannes Bobrowski (1917–1965), Nobel Prize in Literature nominee Anna Seghers (1900–1983), and the East German novelist Christa Wolf (1929–2011). However, rather than her ideas or her writing, it is Günderrode's biography that has tended to draw the most attention. Following her suicide, a "Günderrode mythos" emerged, focusing on the mysticism, otherworldliness, pathology, and orientation to death that, it is often claimed, are revealed in both her suicide and her work. This focus manifested in interest in Günderrode's suicide, works of art and literature about her life and death, numerous biographies, and a secondary literature primarily focused on her supposedly morbid interest in love and death. Another stream of interpretation has connected Günderrode's suicide, as well as her writing, to an irreconcilable conflict between "masculine" and "feminine" identities that supposedly characterized her personality.[6] Other readers interpret Günderrode's life, death, and writings as responses to a social environment that restricted women's activities and identities.[7]

---

[6] E.g., Roswitha Burwick, "Liebe und Tod in Leben und Werk der Günderode," *German Studies Review* 3.2 (1980): 207–223; Christian Schärf, "Artistische Ironie und Fremdheit der Seele. Zur ästhetischen Disposition in der Frühromantik bei Friedrich Schlegel und Karoline von Günderrode," *Deutsche Vierteljahrsschrift für Literaturwissenschaft und Geistesgeschichte* 72.3 (1998): 433–462.

[7] E.g., Michaela Schrage-Früh, "Subversive Weiblichkeit? Die Frau als Muse, Geliebte und Künstlerin im Werk Friedrich Schlegels und Karoline von Günderrodes," *Subversive Romantik* (2004): 365–390; Patricia Anne Simpson, *The Erotics of War in German Romanticism* (Lewisburg: Bucknell UP, 2006), 104–127.

Due to the intense focus on Günderrode's biography, especially her suicide, as a framework for interpreting her writing, other interesting aspects of Günderrode's work were ignored for many years. These include her original perspectives on philosophical questions of the time, her reinterpretations of popular historical topics and literary themes, and her reimagining of gender roles. With renewed interest in Günderrode's writings and, at last, serious attention to her philosophical thought, it has begun to emerge that Günderrode's work contributes original solutions to problems in nineteenth-century German thought. As the pieces collected in this volume testify, Günderrode developed a new model for the nature of the world, human identity, and the relationship between these, while reconceptualizing agency and death. She critiqued various moral systems and views of religion, established a novel basis for conceptualizing friendship, and rethought the gendered grounds of early German Romantic ideas of love, personal development, and community.

At the time of its publication, reviews of Günderrode's work noted the philosophical potential of her writing, and this volume highlights this aspect of Günderrode's work. The rest of this introduction aims to make Günderrode's philosophical thought accessible to newcomers to her ideas and orient readers to the texts translated in this collection. After a first section on Günderrode's life and works, the introduction provides an overview of Günderrode's philosophical claims, considering her metaphysics, theories about selfhood, identity, and death, epistemology, social and political theory, remarks on ethics and aesthetics, and views on gender. Günderrode's philosophical work tends to be couched in literary forms such as dialogues, fragments, dramas, short stories, and poems. The introduction therefore includes a section on the role of these genres in Günderrode's work and the relationship of Günderrode's use of literary forms to the philosophy of her contemporaries, especially the early German Romantics. The last section of the introduction outlines the structure of this collection.

Günderrode's Life and Works

Karoline Friederike Louise Maximiliane von Günderrode was born in Karlsruhe on February 11, 1780, to an aristocratic family, the oldest of six children. Her four sisters were born in 1781 (Louise), 1782 (Wilhelmine), 1783 (Charlotte), and 1784 (Amalie), and her brother, Hektor, in 1786.

Although Günderrode died at the age of only 26, three of her sisters died before her: Louise in 1794, Charlotte in 1801, and Amalie in 1802, all from tuberculosis. Her father also died early, when Günderrode was just six. Günderrode's last surviving sister, Wilhelmine, died in 1819; of the siblings, only Hektor reached old age and died in 1862 with nine children.[8]

Günderrode's parents prized education and literary achievement. Her father, Hektor Wilhelm von Günderrode, was a civil servant and, in his spare time, a writer of historical biographies and "idylls." Her mother, Louise Sophie Victorine August von Günderrode, wrote stories and essays. One of these, titled *What is the Transition from Life to Death? Who Solves the Great Riddle?*,[9] anticipates the philosophical interests of her daughter, and it was Günderrode's mother who first introduced her to the work of Fichte.[10] Günderrode and her siblings had a personal tutor, read extensively, and were encouraged to write poems, short stories, and plays to be shared at home.[11]

Throughout her life, Günderrode enjoyed discussing philosophy and literature with family members and friends. The latter included other educated women such as Günderrode's friends Karoline von Barkhaus, Claudine Piautaz, Elisabetha (Lisette) von Mettingh, and Susanne von Heyden, as well as Lisette's husband Christian Nees von Esenbeck (a botanist and "philosopher of nature"), the jurist Carl Friedrich Savigny, and members of the famous literary Brentano family. Günderrode corresponded with many of these individuals until her death.

After Günderrode's father died, the family moved to Hanau, where Günderrode's mother worked as a companion to Auguste von Hessen-Kassel, the sister of the King of Prussia. Despite this position and a widow's pension, the family struggled financially. In part, this was due to Günderrode's mother's failure to manage money, and in 1803 Günderrode and her surviving sister, Wilhelmine, tried unsuccessfully to gain control of their finances.[12] After this, the sisters' relationship with their mother, which had always been strained, broke down.

In 1797, at the age of 17, Günderrode was sent to live in the Cronstett-Hynspergische Damenstift, a convent in Frankfurt. This was a respectable

---

[8] Dagmar von Gersdorff, *"Die Erde ist mir Heimat nicht geworden." Das Leben der Karoline von Günderrode* (Insel: Frankfurt, 2006), 19.

[9] *Was ist der Übergang von Leben zum Tode? Wer löst die großen Räzel?* (Gersdorff, *Heimat*), 16, 63.

[10] Günderrode, Letter to Karoline von Barkhaus, April 18, 1800, in *Ich sende Dir ein zärtliches Pfand. Die Briefe der Karoline von Günderrode*, ed. Birgit Weißenborn (Frankfurt: Insel, 1992), 65.

[11] Gersdorff, *Heimat*, 30, 39.

[12] Gersdorff, *Heimat*, 17, 124, 126.

living arrangement for unmarried and widowed aristocratic women without much money, enabling them to live in the city where they could socialize and perhaps find husbands. The convent regulated dress, dining, excursions, and visitors, but Günderrode was able to receive female visitors and travel to stay with friends and family. She made excursions to Butzbach to see her grandparents and to Hanau, where she nursed two of her sisters through their fatal illnesses. The young women staying at the convent were called by their last names, and it was there that Günderrode was first given the appellation "die Günderrode" (literally: "the Günderrode").[13]

While at the convent, Günderrode continued to read science, philosophy, and works of literature. Her study books include notes on the writings of philosophers, poets, novelists, theologians, and other intellectuals of her time. These include, among others, the philosopher and literary critic Johann Gottfried von Herder (1744–1803), the Dutch philosopher François Hemsterhuis, the pastor and theologian Friedrich Schleiermacher (1768–1834), the early German Romantic poet, novelist, and philosopher Novalis, Novalis' friend, the influential philosopher, philologist, and literary critic Friedrich Schlegel (1772–1829), and the poet Friedrich Hölderlin (1770–1843). With the help of friends who sent her reading materials, Günderrode also studied Indian and Egyptian mythology, ancient history, history of religion, chemistry, and physiognomy, and taught herself Latin and Greek. Contributors to Günderrode's continued self-education included Georg Friedrich Creuzer (1771–1858), an influential philologist and mythologist, who encouraged Günderrode to learn Greek and sent her study materials on (among other things) the ancient Greek philosophers Pythagoras and Heraclitus and religions and mythologies from Asia and Egypt. Other friends including von Mettingh, von Barkhaus, Nees, and Savigny sent writings by Fichte, Schelling, Johann Gottfried Kiesewetter (a well-known popularizer of the ideas of Immanuel Kant), and other philosophers.

By this time, Günderrode suffered from health problems, including headaches and painful eyes, which continued for the rest of her life. To protect her eyes, she often used green paper to write or dictated to friends. It is possible that these symptoms were due to tuberculosis, which she could have contracted while caring for her sisters Charlotte and Amalie as they died. Günderrode's letters from this period reflect the misery and claustrophobia of sitting beside her sisters' beds as they slowly succumbed to their illness.

---

[13] Gersdorff, *Heimat*, 21–26.

It is important to remember this context, as some of her statements at this time can give the impression that she was by nature depressive, prone to escapism, or had a longstanding death wish. It would be difficult to draw these conclusions based on writings from such a period of grief and loss.

Günderrode's work during this time was supported by several well-known intellectual figures in her social circle. Her mother was friends with the famous novelist Sophie von La Roche (1730–1807), who published two pieces by Günderrode in the journals she edited. Günderrode also became acquainted with La Roche's grandchildren Kunigunde (Gunda) Brentano, Bettina Brentano (later von Arnim), and Clemens Brentano, the latter two of whom also became well-known writers. Brentano-von Arnim, whom Günderrode met in 1801, was a close friend for some years and later wrote the epistolary novel *Günderrode* based on their correspondence, as well as a *Report on Günderrode's Suicide* for Goethe's mother Catharina Elisabeth Goethe. Clemens Brentano, a famous novelist and poet, was fascinated with Günderrode. He wrote letters to her about her work that were sometimes admiring and sometimes jealous, and once attempted to kiss her. Günderrode's letters back to Clemens show her repeated efforts to keep him at arm's length, and after he tried to kiss her, she avoided him completely.[14]

As well as the Brentano family, Günderrode's friends included other prominent individuals such as the botanist Christian Nees von Esenbeck (1776–1858). In addition to his work on botany, in 1841, Nees published a philosophical text titled *Philosophy of Nature* (*Die Naturphilosophie*) and, in 1852, a text on *The General Doctrine of Forms of Nature* (*Die Formenlehre der Natur*). Nees often read and commented on Günderrode's writing and also negotiated with publishers on her behalf, until he was replaced in this role by Creuzer. It is very likely that his ideas on philosophy of nature were influenced by Günderrode, since he developed them after reading her work. Another friend, the doctor Karl Christian Wolfart (1778–1832), was also a well-known writer on philosophy of nature, a proponent of mesmerism and animal magnetism, and an amateur poet. Wolfart left an original poem in Günderrode's notebooks titled "To the Genius of the Departing Century."[15]

[14] Clemens Brentano, Letter to Günderrode, 2 June 1804, in *Der Schatten eines Traumes. Gedichte, Prosa, Briefe, Zeugnisse von Zeitgenossen*, ed. Christa Wolf (Munich: Deutscher Taschenbuch, 1997 [1979]), 217; Gersdorff, *Heimat*, 122.

[15] Doris Hopp and Max Preitz, "Karoline von Günderrode in ihrer Umwelt. III. Karoline von Günderrodes 'Studienbuch,'" *Jahrbuch des Freien Deutschen Hochstifts* (1975): 269–273.

In 1799, Günderrode met the future jurist and historian of law Friedrich Carl von Savigny (1779–1861). She was immediately attracted to him, and they began a tentative courtship.[16] However, possibly due to concerns about Günderrode's health, family, finances, and/or supposed unsuitability, as an intellectual woman, for a domestic role, and possibly put off by backbiting from Clemens,[17] in April 1804, Savigny instead married Günderrode's close friend Gunda Brentano. In February of that year, while planning to marry Gunda, Savigny wrote a clearly erotic letter to Günderrode, declaring "I am wholly as ever yours."[18] Günderrode sent him her poem "The Kiss in the Dream" around the time of the wedding.[19]

Later that year, Günderrode met and began an affair with Creuzer. Creuzer was married, but at times promised to divorce his wife, Sophie, to marry Günderrode. However, while his letters often included plans for how to spend time with Günderrode, many were filled with self-pity and talk of "destiny": Creuzer believed it was impossible for him to leave Sophie. For example, he wrote: "when certain steps have once been taken all remaining actions in life now wholly *cease* to be free. They are words of destiny. [...] Love without measure—hope without measure—despair without measure is the tone of my life."[20]

Despite all this turmoil, Günderrode continued to study and write. Her first collection of poetry, short stories, and philosophical dialogues, *Poems and Fantasies*, was published in 1804, to the reception described above. The next year, Creuzer published Günderrode's plays *Udohla* and *Magic and Destiny* in *Studien*, the journal he edited, and La Roche published "Story of a Brahmin" in her journal *Herbsttage*. Also in 1805, Günderrode published her second collection of dramas and poetry, *Poetic Fragments*.

After this point, Creuzer began to play a more active role in Günderrode's writing and approaches to publishers, persuading her to adopt the title *Melete* and the pen name Ion for her next collection[21] and contributing work to this volume. At the time of Günderrode's death, Creuzer was involved in negotiations for the publication of *Melete*. However, following Günderrode's

---

[16] Günderrode, Letter to Karoline von Barkhaus, 4 July 1804, in Wolf, *Schatten eines Traumes*, 153.

[17] Gersdorff, *Heimat*, 102–103.

[18] Savigny, Letter to Günderrode, 8 February 1804, in Wolf, *Schatten eines Traumes*, 190–191.

[19] Günderrode, Letter to Savigny, April 1804, in Wolf, *Schatten eines Traumes*, 193.

[20] Creuzer, Letter to Leonhard Creuzer, 2 May 1805, in Karl Preisendanz, *Die Liebe der Günderode. Friedrich Creuzers Briefe an Günderode* (Munich: R. Piper & Co., 1912), 85. See also Creuzer, Letter to Günderrode, 27 January 1805, in Preisendanz, *Liebe der Günderode*, 57.

[21] Gersdorff, *Heimat*, 189, 195f., 226–228.

suicide, he and his friends were concerned that its contents might reveal too much of their affair,[22] and he canceled the publication. As a result, Günderrode's last publication in her lifetime was the play *Nikator*, which La Roche included in her 1806 *Taschenbuch*.

Melete was first published in 1906, one hundred years after Günderrode's death. In the intervening time, the last pages of the manuscript were lost, and so we do not know the ending to the final piece in the collection, the short story "Valorich." Tantalizingly, Creuzer, writing of himself in the third person, claimed that "The conclusion of this story (which is very dear to him, through and through) made him melancholy, but in the way that he likes to be melancholy."[23] We can only speculate about how Günderrode might have ended this fairy tale-like romance.

In 1806, after a serious illness through which he was nursed by his wife, Creuzer ended the relationship with Günderrode, writing to her where she was staying with friends in Winkel on the Rhine. In response, Günderrode walked to the river, weighted her skirt with rocks, and stabbed herself in the heart. According to Brentano-von Arnim, Günderrode had been carrying a dagger for some time with this purpose in mind and had been instructed by a doctor regarding exactly where to insert the blade.[24] She left a handkerchief stained with drops of her blood and a note for Creuzer, claiming the blood-stained handkerchief was a "pledge" of their union after death.

There was immediate fascination with Günderrode following her suicide, the dramatic nature of which continues to impress people today. In 1814, Goethe visited the site of her death and wrote: "They showed me the place on the Rhine, in a willow thicket, where Miss Günderrode took her life. The narration of this catastrophe on the very site, by people who were nearby and had taken part in it, gave me that unpleasant feeling that a tragic loca-tion always arouses."[25] As mentioned earlier, an unfortunate effect of this fascination has been the tendency to focus on biographical interpretations of Günderrode's writings, with particular weight placed on her suicide and affair with Creuzer. This is often accompanied by an oversimplification of her work that emphasizes its attention to the topics of death and love. Günderrode's suicide has often been presented as a direct result of the failed

---

[22] Creuzer, Letter to Leonhard Creuzer, 20 October 1806, in Weißenborn, *Ich sende Dir*, 361.
[23] Creuzer, Letter to Günderrode, 8 May 1806, cited in SW 3:207.
[24] Bettina Brentano-von Arnim, "Report on Günderrode's Suicide [1808]," in *Bitter Healing: German Women Writers. From 1700 to 1830. An Anthology*, ed. Jeannine Blackwell and Susanne Zantop (Lincoln: University of Nebraska Press, 1990), 462–463.
[25] Cited in Wolf, *Schatten eines Traumes*, 53–54; my translation.

affair with Creuzer, combined with a morbid interest in the reunion of lovers in death that appears in her writing.[26]

This oversimplified view of Günderrode's life and work does not really do justice to either. Creuzer's letter terminating the relationship was evidently the trigger for Günderrode's suicide, but to view it as the cause neglects other factors that likely contributed. These might have included Günderrode's poor health, the recent loss of two of her sisters and earlier loss of her father and another sister, her poor relationship with her mother, her financial difficulties, her isolation in a convent, her frustration with the roles and activities she was allowed by the social conventions of the time, and the harsh reviews of *Poetic Fragments*.

This oversimplification also does an injustice to Günderrode's work. Günderrode's writings do more than express their author's frustrations and longings: they contain a rich and nuanced philosophy and engage with major existential questions of her time, as well as with literary trends and the nascent reception of Asian, Middle Eastern, and North African thought in Europe. As with any philosopher, Günderrode's thought was influenced by the events of her life and the conditions in which she lived, but efforts to understand her writings should also explore their contributions to the philosophical and literary context in which they emerged.

Günderrode as a Philosopher

Günderrode was an original thinker, immersed in the philosophy of her time, with a ready grasp of nuance and complexity and a gift for using literary forms to engage readers in working through philosophical ideas. Her work provides novel responses to the same problems that concerned her male contemporaries, especially those in the German idealist and early German Romantic traditions: What is the nature of the universe? What forces and processes shape the objects around us and drive the events we experience? How are we related to these processes? Do we have free will, or are our actions determined by operations beyond our control? What happens to us after we die? How should we behave while we are alive? What forms of social and political life should we foster and develop? The discussion below outlines Günderrode's approach to these questions and suggests how some

---

[26] E.g., Burwick, "Liebe und Tod."

of her philosophical claims might be placed in dialogue with those of other writers and thinkers of her day.

Metaphysics

As the foundation of her response to the above questions, Günderrode developed a unique metaphysics that adapts and synthesizes concepts from contemporary and ancient European philosophy as well as ideas from Asia. Günderrode's clearest statements on metaphysics are found in her unpublished essay "Idea of the Earth," but many points outlined in this text are developed in more detail in her published writings, especially "Letters of Two Friends," "The Manes," and "Story of a Brahmin." Other pieces, such as "An Apocalyptic Fragment," "A Dream," and "The Wanderer's Descent," depict strange kinds of experience that reflect the unusual metaphysics developed in these texts. Günderrode's fragmentary writings on ethics, aesthetics, and music also fit within the worldview encapsulated by her metaphysical writings and are best understood within the framework of this worldview. In short, Günderrode's metaphysics form an excellent starting point for approaching her philosophy.

This section highlights four related points that are central to Günderrode's metaphysics and important to other areas of her thought. First, Günderrode's claim that the universe is comprised of changeable clusters of indestructible "elements." Second, her claim that the force that causes these elements to combine and recombine into different objects over time is a "law of attraction." Third, the claim that successive combinations of individual elements (ideally) move the universe toward becoming a single, perfect, harmonious organism. And fourth, Günderrode's version of the idea (shared with many of her contemporaries) that the universe is constituted by a single, infinite essence that differentiates itself into the individual beings of the world.

Let us begin with the first of these points. In "Idea of the Earth" and "Letters of Two Friends," Günderrode states that every individual entity in the universe, whether a living being or an inanimate object, is constructed from many indestructible "elements." These elements combine, disperse, and recombine to form plants, animals, and other objects. Some of the elements join together to constitute each new being when it is born or otherwise formed; they are then scattered when the entity dies and decomposes (or, if it is an inanimate object, breaks down). The elements themselves are never destroyed, but simply recombined into new entities. As Günderrode phrases it: "life is immortal and surges up and down in the elements, for they are life itself. But determinate and individual life is only a life-form given through this determinate connection, attraction and contact, which can last no longer than the connection." In other words, individual beings live and die, but the living universe itself, and the elements of which it is constituted, continue forever.

Günderrode claims that the mechanism by which the elements combine into individual beings is "attraction" or the "law of attraction." She also describes this as a "harmony" between elements and as "laws of affinity" according to which they "seek what is similar to them."[27] That is, those elements that have an affinity, i.e., that harmonize with each other, are attracted to each other and, if nothing prevents them, will naturally join together. This mechanism accounts for basic processes such as chemical reactions and the absorption of nutrients by plants and animals. But Günderrode also uses this metaphysical picture to describe phenomena such as friendship and love. For example, her poem "The Malabarian Widows" describes lovers uniting after death as their "separate elements" are "unified." Similarly, in "Letters of Two Friends," one correspondent writes to the other of their fear that after death "your I and mine should be dissolved in the ancient primordial matter of the world," but consoles themselves that "our befriended elements, obeying the laws of attraction, would find each other even in infinite space and join with each other." A similar principle underlies the reflections in Günderrode's philosophical dialogue "The Manes." In this piece, a teacher explains that his student's feeling of connection to certain other people is due to an attraction or harmony between aspects of their personalities: "As surely as all harmonious things are connected in a certain way [. . . ,] we, too, are connected with *that part* of the spiritual world that harmonizes with us."

The third central aspect of Günderrode's metaphysics concerns the relationship of individual beings to the earth or universe as a whole. Although the elements are indestructible, Günderrode claims that, over time, they change: they become more animated and vigorous. This change is caused by the interaction of elements with each other during their time as parts of individual beings. In "Letters of Two Friends," Günderrode explains that this is because "The elements are [. . .] alive, and every living thing is strengthened

---

[27] Günderrode may have derived some of these ideas from her studies of chemistry (see the introduction to Günderrode's notes on chemistry later in this volume).

by exercise." She expands on this claim using an analogy, arguing that the increase in liveliness and strength of the elements occurs on the same basis as when "two [individuals] who have trained in long struggle are stronger when the struggle has ended than they were before." In other words, struggle, interaction, movement, friction, and use make the elements more energetic, lively, and animated.

Since, on Günderrode's model, the universe is comprised exclusively of the elements, the gains in strength and animation that these obtain also apply to the whole. These gains are retained even after individual beings die or are destroyed: after all, the elements themselves are never destroyed; they last forever. Thus, Günderrode claims, "each mortal gives back to the earth a raised, more developed elemental life, which it cultivates further in ascending forms." The result is that, through the successive emergence, activity, interaction, and eventual destruction of individual entities, the world as a whole gradually becomes more animated. Through this process, inert matter slowly evolves into living creatures. These then progressively develop into more advanced forms of life. Our own life and death contribute to this process: "however my elements may be dispersed, when they join to what is already living they will elevate it; when they join to those things whose life resembles death [i.e., inanimate objects], they will animate them." In other words, the progressive emergence and destruction of individual entities gradually increases the liveliness and complexity of the earth as a whole, tending over time toward sentience, consciousness, and higher forms of awareness.

In "Idea of the Earth" and "Letters of Two Friends," Günderrode posits a potential endpoint or goal for the process described above. She claims that this process reveals the earth's repeated attempts to integrate all its elements into one living, perfectly balanced, harmonious entity, which she calls an "organism." Through the repeated production and destruction of finite beings, the earth gradually combines the elements—which become more and more lively and sentient—into a balanced whole. Thus, "the organism, by assimilating ever more developed elements, must become ever more perfect and universal." The end point of this process, if it were ever completed, would be a single, perfectly harmonious entity that would endure forever.

However, Günderrode states that the above picture of the development of the earth into an organism is only an ideal: "I do not assert whether the earth will be altogether successful in organizing itself immortally like this." That is, it is possible that the cycle of emergence and destruction of finite beings—of life and death—will continue forever, never arriving at this perfect final state.

The last major feature of Günderrode's metaphysical thought to which I want to draw attention is her idea of something infinite that lies behind or within the finite beings of the world—something that forms them and drives their emergence and subsequent destruction. In Günderrode's writings, the concept of the "infinite" refers not just to everything that is (the universe) but to a single being or principle that divides itself into the individual beings that make up the universe. In "Idea of the Earth" and "Letters of Two Friends," Günderrode calls this the "whole," the "earth," the "life-principle," and the "All [*Allheit*]"—it is the flux of elements in ever-changing combinations that we call the universe, and the driving force that produces and organizes these combinations. In "Story of a Brahmin," she describes this principle more broadly as "an infinite force, an eternal life, that is everything that is, that was and will become, that engenders itself in mysterious ways, that remains eternal during all change and dying."

The concept of an infinite "All," "Absolute," or "universal principle" that manifests itself in the finite things of the world was widespread at the time Günderrode was writing, although different individuals understood this concept in different ways.[28] This idea sometimes took the form of pantheism, in which the Absolute was seen as a divine being (God) that was co-extensive with the universe and present in all its parts. There were also secularized versions of this idea, which downplayed or discarded the idea of the divine and focused instead on nature and natural processes, viewing these as one infinite, dynamic whole. At the time Günderrode was writing, many people believed that not only the secular version of this idea, but also the pantheistic version, entailed atheism, because both reject the idea of a God who exists independently of his creations.

Although Günderrode's writings tend to focus on natural, physical processes, her idea of a productive Absolute or "All" does include a concept of the divine. In "Idea of the Earth," the only hint that the productive principle of the universe should be conceived as divine is in the last sentence, which mentions "the god of the earth." However, in "Letters of Two Friends" and "Story of a Brahmin," Günderrode refers to the world as a whole not only as "nature," "spirit," and "infinite spirit" but also as "the divine" and declares

---

[28] There are similarities between Günderrode's descriptions of an infinitely productive nature and a popular 1794 piece called "Nature" (*Die Natur*) published in the *Tiefurter Journal*. At one point, this was thought to be by Goethe, but was in fact most likely written by the minister Georg Christoph Tobler (1757–1812).

that a relationship to this infinite "ground of all things" is the true content of all religions.

On the basis of the four central metaphysical claims described above, Günderrode develops her thought in several unusual directions. These include her ideas about virtue, beauty, political organization, the human vocation, religion, knowledge, personal identity, and life after death. The next section explains how Günderrode uses her metaphysics to derive an account of human identity that rethinks the role of consciousness in how we understand ourselves, with implications for what happens to us after we die. Subsequent sections look at Günderrode's epistemology, her social and political thought, her ethics and aesthetics, and her views on gender.

Identity, Consciousness, and Death

Günderrode was especially interested in the implications of her metaphysics for human experience, including what it means to be or have a self. Her writings ask: What constitutes us, as individuals? To what extent are we identical with our conscious minds? Do we continue to exist in some form after we die? What possibilities are there for us to relate to other individuals and the universe as a whole? Are we the same person today as we were yesterday? Many of Günderrode's works describe or evoke the kinds of experience she claims we will have after we die, i.e., after we stop existing as individual human beings and (as she believes) take on other forms. Works that take this approach include "An Apocalyptic Fragment," "A Dream," "The Manes," "The Malabarian Widows," "The Aeronaut," and "Once I Lived Sweet Life." Günderrode's letters also consider issues of identity and the nature of selfhood.

According to Günderrode's metaphysics (see previous section), after we die, our constituent elements are recycled into new beings. Put like that, this simply sounds like a description of the chemical and biological processes of decomposition, including the recycling of decomposed material to fertilize plants, feed animals, or compose new substances such as soil, oil, gases, and other materials. However, Günderrode claims that in some way we survive the decomposition of the elements out of which we are made, although we will be different from how we are now. In both "Idea of the Earth" and "Letters of Two Friends," Günderrode states that "The Indian idea of the transmigration of souls corresponds to this opinion." Similarly, in "Story of a

Brahmin," the Brahmin explains how "the forces[29] wander through all forms until they develop consciousness and thought in human beings; how from human beings on an infinite series of migrations leading to ever higher perfection awaits souls." In other words, the "elements" Günderrode describes are not just physical elements (like molecules or atoms), to which consciousness somehow attaches only when they are combined into certain kinds of being (such as human beings). Rather, they carry consciousness with them as they dissolve and are combined into new entities, in a process that Günderrode claims is a kind of reincarnation.

This claim places human consciousness on a continuum with other sentient creatures, living beings in general (e.g., plants), and apparently inert matter, suggesting that consciousness is just a particular form of "elemental life" that can develop when the elements become more active and animated. While Günderrode was not the only writer of her time to see continuity between unconscious and conscious things, or between matter and mind (Schelling, notably, also did so), her version of this idea is unusual. Günderrode seems not only to ascribe a kind of sentience to animals, plants, and even inanimate objects but also to suggest that this sentience can be broken up and combined with the sentience of other beings. This is quite different from how we usually think of awareness or sentience, including (perhaps especially) human consciousness. Generally, we view a person's consciousness as a single thing: a unity. We tend to think that existing as a single, unified being is essential to being a self. But Günderrode claims that sentience can be divided up and, even more strangely, joined with (parts of) other minds after death to form new beings that are, nonetheless, somehow continuous with the old. Her model of reincarnation is therefore quite different from most other versions of this idea. In most accounts of reincarnation, for example in Hindu and Buddhist traditions, individual beings are reborn in different forms; however, their rebirth does not involve mingling their minds or selves with the minds and selves of others, as it does for Günderrode.

The difficulty of conceptualizing this strange kind of reincarnation is perhaps one of the motivations for Günderrode's use of poetry to present her ideas on this topic. Evocative poetic language helps Günderrode convey

---

[29] In "Story of a Brahmin," Günderrode refers to the basic constituents of the universe as "forces" rather than "elements." The relationship between these two terms in Günderrode's work has not yet been explored.

what she thinks our experiences might be like after we die. For example, her prose poem "An Apocalyptic Fragment" and the fragment "A Dream" invite readers to use their imagination to grasp forms of experience beyond consciousness and even beyond individual existence. Both pieces describe ways of being that are more than, or different from, human life, suggesting new forms of awareness that accompany these ways of being. Thus, the two texts give concrete form to the metaphysical claims in "Idea of the Earth" and "Letters of Two Friends," focusing on the implications of these claims for our experience.

For example, in "An Apocalyptic Fragment," Günderrode describes the process of repeated dissolution and reconstitution of individual entities that lies at the basis of her metaphysics. The narrator has a vision in which they witness individual beings emerging from an ocean, to which they then return before reemerging as new entities: "the creatures that had climbed from the ocean returned to it, and generated themselves again in changing forms." This is a poetic depiction of the type of metempsychosis described in theoretical terms in "Idea of the Earth" and "Letters of Two Friends." These later pieces include details such as the existence of indestructible elements, the inseparability of mind and matter, and the organic nature of the relationship of individuals to the whole of the earth. "An Apocalyptic Fragment" presents only the broad strokes of this model, describing a repeated process of individuation, dissolution, and re-individuation from the perspective of someone undergoing this process.

What "An Apocalyptic Fragment" does that "Idea of the Earth" and "Letters of Two Friends" do not is present this process in a concrete, visceral way that helps the reader imagine what it would be like to actually experience these changes of state. The narrator describes themselves losing consciousness and entering a state of deathlike sleep (or sleeplike death), before emerging again from "the womb of [the] ocean." While in this state, the narrator "encountered nothing that reminded me of time" and had only "muffled and tangled dreams." Without the categories of time and space that are essential to human perception and consciousness, the narrator's experiences during this period cannot be organized conceptually and therefore appear as confused and murky.

It is very likely that this poetic description is meant as a response to Kant. On the Kantian model, human experience is inescapably mediated by our perceptual and conceptual faculties. Günderrode studied Kant and, in her letters, suggests that the perceptual apparatus that enables us to organize our experiences will drop away after death, allowing us to perceive things as they really are (i.e., the Kantian thing-in-itself). She claims: "we have no consciousness other than perception of effects, never of causes. [. . .] if we really ever enter the borders of a second life, then one of our first inner phenomena would have to be that our consciousness would grow larger and clearer."[30]

"An Apocalyptic Fragment" portrays a form of awareness that is "larger and clearer," expanding beyond the (Kantian) constraints of human consciousness. The narrator describes their mind being dissolved by "numbing mists," which dissipate to reveal that their self has expanded beyond individual existence: "I could no longer find my borders, my consciousness had overstepped them; it was bigger, other, and yet I felt myself in it." In this form, the narrator is "released from the narrow bounds of my being" and exists as diffused throughout the natural world, part of everything that previously appeared separate from the self. This union with others, and with the whole of nature, allows the narrator to escape the "longing . . . that did not know its object," which characterized individual existence. Instead, the self is "given again to everything, and everything belonged to me." This description suggests a form of awareness that Günderrode thinks we might have after death, once we are dispersed or dissolved in the whole of nature.

Günderrode's writings provide rich materials for novel ways of conceiving of selfhood, consciousness, the relationship between human beings and the rest of the world, and what happens after death. The idea of forms of awareness that differ from ordinary consciousness is important to Günderrode's conception of the self as continuing beyond the dissolution of the individual in death. It is also crucial for her claim that human beings—including their conscious minds—are continuous with and the same in kind as the rest of nature. The evocative portrayals of this kind of non-conscious awareness in poetic works such as "An Apocalyptic Fragment" and "A Dream," which attempt to convey to the reader what it would be like to experience these states, are therefore integral to Günderrode's philosophy.

Epistemology

One of the issues Günderrode was most interested in was the question of knowledge: how we can come to know things about the world, and whether

---

[30] Letter to Gunda Brentano, 11 August 1801, translated in the Letters section of this volume.

we can know things that are not available to discursive thought or ordinary perception. This was partly motivated by Günderrode's interest in the nature and limitations of consciousness and its relationship to personal identity. As mentioned in the last section, she was dismayed by Kant's claim that we can know nothing beyond the impressions brought to us through our perceptual and intellectual apparatus. Resisting Kant's position, Günderrode explored possibilities for encountering the world beyond these limitations. In this respect, she was working in the tradition of philosophers such as Hemsterhuis, Schleiermacher, and Friedrich Heinrich Jacobi (1743–1819), who maintained the importance of feelings, intuitions, and introspection for our knowledge of the world. Günderrode was also responding to work by Novalis, by turns working with and against his claim that the subject–object distinction is necessary for all knowledge.

Günderrode's interest in epistemology is clearest in her first book, *Poems and Fantasies*, and features prominently in many texts from this collection. These include "The Wanderer's Descent," "The Adept," "The Frank in Egypt," "The Manes," *Immortalita*, and "Muhammad's Dream in the Desert."[31] Günderrode's later pieces, "Story of a Brahmin" and "Letters of Two Friends," also consider this topic. Together, these texts show Günderrode taking a nuanced approach to the question of whether knowledge beyond normal human experience is possible.

In some pieces, Günderrode indicates that human conceptual and perceptual limits cannot be transcended, can be transcended only in part, or can be transcended only at great cost. For instance, in "The Wanderer's Descent," Günderrode's protagonist learns that, as an individual being, he cannot truly encounter the one infinite force or being that manifests itself in individual entities. His individuality itself separates him from this universal source of all things. However, he is consoled that, as part of the universe, he is also a reflection of it: he is "the cosmos' seeing mirror." As a result, he can gain limited knowledge of the world by studying his own soul, and *vice versa*. In "The Adept," the protagonist does succeed in peering beyond the veil of appearances but is paralyzed by the overwhelming nature of what he sees there: as a finite being, he is not equipped to comprehend the infinite. Taking a slightly different approach, "The Frank in Egypt" and *Immortalita* suggest that the search for knowledge is a mistaken attempt to find union with others

---

[31] For an English translation of the latter, see "Karoline von Günderrode, 'Muhammad's Dream in the Desert,'" trans. Anna Ezekiel, *Trail of Crumbs* (October 2021), https://acezekiel.com/2021/10/18/karoline-von-gunderrode-muhammads-dream-in-the-desert/.

and the world outside us; this attempt is better satisfied by feelings, particularly in the experience of love.

In many other texts, however, Günderrode indicates that we *can* become aware of the real nature of the universe, that is, the universe as it exists outside the limitations of human perceptual and intellectual capacities. In direct opposition to "The Adept," "Muhammad's Dream in the Desert" shows a character emerging from a terrifying vision of the world beyond human categories of comprehension with usable knowledge of this reality. In "The Manes," it is a secret "inner sense" that allows human beings to perceive the infinite that permeates us and all other things. In "An Apocalyptic Fragment," "Story of a Brahmin," and "Letters of Two Friends," the narrators learn truths about the nature of the world through visions.

Rather than providing a single positive epistemology, Günderrode considers several possible views of the nature and limits of knowledge. Spreading her thinking across multiple texts, she invites us to consider that extending ourselves beyond our perceptual and cognitive limits is impossible (even if we can stretch these limits a little); or that it leads to madness; or that it is possible and results in brief glimpses of the true nature of things (and even that these are useful); or that we should abandon the attempt and instead seek a connection with people and the world outside us through love. Günderrode's thinking on epistemology shows a preference for exploring many sides of the issue over providing answers and for finding ways to engage and motivate readers to explore these questions with her. This polyvalence and ambiguity also appear in relation to some of the other philosophical issues she considers, for instance in her work on power and agency.[32]

Social and Political Thought

As discussed in the previous sections, Günderrode's metaphysics are central to her thinking on individuality, selfhood, consciousness, death, and knowledge. Her metaphysics also have implications for her social and political thought. Günderrode is interested in how human beings should live, given the nature of the world and their relationship to it, as she sees them. How should we lead our lives, as individuals? How should we come together

---

[32] Anna Ezekiel, "Introduction to *Muhammad, the Prophet of Mecca*," in Karoline von Günderrode, *Poetic Fragments by Tian*, ed. and trans. Anna Ezekiel (Albany: SUNY Press, 2016), 121–151.

in friendship and community? What form or forms should ideal societies take? What drives political change? What is the essence and role of religion in human communities? Günderrode explored these questions throughout her works, and they are major themes in the short story "Story of a Brahmin," her dramas *Udohla* and *Muhammad, the Prophet of Mecca*, and her letters.

In Günderrode's time, many philosophers saw human history as a continuation of natural history, both proceeding on the same principles. Those who did so often claimed that both human civilization and the natural world were necessarily progressing to become more perfect and rational.[33] Günderrode, by contrast, indicates that while improvement and even perfection are possible, it will not *necessarily* occur.[34] Instead, what is essential in Günderrode's model is the repeated formation and dissolution of individual forms, through which progress may or may not take place. This applies to her accounts of both the natural and political realms.

Thus, like many other thinkers of her time, Günderrode presents political and social institutions as subject to the same processes as the natural world. In Günderrode's case, this idea is based on an analogy between, on the one hand, elements and their relationship to individual beings[35] and, on the other, human individuals and their relationship to corporate bodies such as nation states, religious institutions, and other forms of community. Just as (she claims) individual entities are formed from temporary groupings of elements which subsequently break apart and can then be reused, so too are social and political institutions formed as groups of individuals which endure for a time and then fall apart. Subsequently, new institutions can be formed from the scattered individuals. In the political realm, Günderrode claims, this process is characterized by often violent revolutions.[36] This topic is a major theme in Günderrode's plays *Udohla* and *Muhammad, the Prophet of Mecca*, which consider the nature of and justifications for political

---

[33] E.g., J. G. Fichte, *The Vocation of Man*, trans. Peter Preuss (Indianapolis: Hackett, 1987 [1800]), 83; J. G. Herder, *Ideen zur Philosophie der Geschichte der Menschheit* (Riga: Hartknoch, 1784f.), vol. 1, 20–21, 27; vol. 4, 239, 246; Friedrich Schlegel, "Rede über die Mythologie" [1800], in *Friedrich Schlegel: Kritische Ausgabe seiner Werke*, ed. Ernst Behler, 35 vols. (Munich: F. Schöningh, 1958–2002) [hereafter "KFSA"], 2:322.

[34] In "Idea of the Earth," Günderrode applies this ambiguity to the metaphysical realm, writing "I do not assert whether the earth will be altogether successful in organizing itself immortally." On the political level, an example is the open-ended conclusion to *Udohla*: the characters await a revolution that may or may not come.

[35] See the above section on Günderrode's metaphysics.

[36] See Anna Ezekiel, "Revolution and Revitalisation: Karoline von Günderrode's Political Philosophy and Its Metaphysical Foundations," *British Journal of the History of Philosophy* (2022; online 2020).

revolution, connecting revolutionary impulses to loss of cohesion and vitality in the nation state as well as to experiences of discrimination.

In addition to considering revolution an inevitable aspect of both nature and political life, Günderrode was sympathetic to the idea of political revolution as a means of self-determination and liberation for oppressed peoples. This is clearest in *Udohla*, in which a subjugated Hindu population simmers on the edge of revolt against their Mughal rulers. Günderrode here constructs a novel model of agency, incorporating characteristics that, at the time, were often assigned to women and Asians and considered antithetical to political subjecthood.[37] Whereas the traditional European view of a political subject is a rational, active, masculine individual who imposes his will on events, in *Udohla* Günderrode suggests that political activity is best embodied through care for others, gentleness, acknowledging emotions, and negotiation with other agents. These characteristics fit stereotypes of women and of a feminized "east," allowing Günderrode to argue for the right to self-determination of all peoples, whether or not they conform to traditional European ideals of political maturity.[38] In the context of European colonialism, this claim supports a demand for the withdrawal of colonial interests in Asia or, if this is not forthcoming, overthrow of colonial powers by colonized peoples.

Considering Günderrode's clear interest in revolution and tyranny, it is curious that until recently she was considered an apolitical thinker, more concerned with spiritual and internal individual development than with politics. In several texts, including "The Manes," "Story of a Brahmin," *Muhammad, the Prophet of Mecca*, and the unpublished fragment "Excellence is a whole …," Günderrode claims that human beings are faced with a choice between two ways of living: an "earthly" and a "heavenly" way. The first is focused outward, on living as a productive member of society, and would be consistent with an interest in politics. The second is focused inward, on introspection, self-development, and contemplation of the divine.[39] Some scholars argue that Günderrode advocates the latter path: a life of contemplation and a "turn inward," away from considering ideals for

---

[37] On Günderrode's account of agency, see the section on gender, below, and the introduction to *Mora*.

[38] For details, see the introduction to *Udohla* later in this volume.

[39] Cf. Schleiermacher's idea of a contrast between an outward and an inward life (Friedrich Schleiermacher, *Monologen. Eine Neujahrsgabe* [Berlin: Christian Sigismund Spener, 1800], 12, 20, 22). Günderrode excerpted this text in her notes.

community toward a focus on the inner life of the individual.[40] The latter point is often associated with the claim that Günderrode's turn inward was also a form of self-negation and longing for death, conceived as an escape from the world.[41]

However, Günderrode's account is more complex than this. Rather than a turn away from others, she suggests that the inward, "heavenly" path is, at its best, a step on the way to participating in a new kind of a community: a community united in spirit. For example, the narrator of "Story of a Brahmin" claims that "a community exists between human beings in whom the inner sense has arisen and the world-spirit."[42] In this way, the outward and inward paths can be reconciled. In "Excellence is a whole . . . ," Günderrode says explicitly that "Many people hover between the two [ways of life]" and in "Story of a Brahmin" the character Almor remarks that "A twofold life seemed to dwell in" his teacher, the Brahmin. In *Muhammad, the Prophet of Mecca*, Günderrode presents Muhammad as walking both paths simultaneously, hearing God's voice but also acting politically to share his message and found a new community.[43] In other words, a "turn inward" is not necessarily a turn away from others, but rather an important stage in developing deeper relationships. Ideal communities, Günderrode claims, are formed by individuals who have first worked on themselves and can then develop relationships based on real self-awareness, including awareness that they share the same underlying nature as all beings.

In her letters, Günderrode approaches the question of how individuals should relate to each other from a more personal angle. Here, she shows a concern with the nature of friendship—both successful, fulfilling friendships and friendships that fail and cause harm. For Günderrode, the most crucial aspect of a fulfilling friendship is the sincere, open sharing of one's internal experiences. "I want to share everything with you," she tells her sister Charlotte,[44] but complains to her friend Gunda that they have grown apart to the point that she hesitates to "usher you into the most essential parts of

---

[40] Ruth Christmann, *Zwischen Identitätsgewinn und Bewußtseinsverlust. Das philosophisch-literarische Werk der Karoline von Günderrode (1780–1806)* (Frankfurt: Lang, 2005), 235.

[41] Dieter von Burdorf, "'Diese Sehnsucht ist ein Gedanke, der ins Unendliche starrt.' Über Karoline von Günderrode—aus Anlaß neuer Ausgaben ihrer Werke und Briefe," *Wirkendes Wort* 43.1 (1993): 57.

[42] Cf. Schleiermacher, *Monologen*, 17.

[43] Günderrode, *Poetic Fragments, by Tian*, ed. and trans. Anna Ezekiel (Albany: SUNY Press, 2016), 154.

[44] Günderrode, Letter to Charlotte von Günderrode, 27 August 1800 (translated in the Letters section below).

my inner world."[45] True friends, according to Günderrode, are mirrors to each other, revealing each other in a charitable but honest light.[46] While Günderrode's comments to her friends are often harsh, it is clear that they are motivated by a desire for closer and more authentic friendships: relationships in which the participants build each other up, help each other improve themselves, and develop their inner lives together.

While Günderrode's status as a social and political thinker has tended to be neglected, she was extremely interested in real and ideal relationships between human beings. She explored these relationships with regard to both political arrangements and more personal connections with others, especially the relationships between friends.

Ethics

Günderrode did not develop a full-blown ethics in her work, but her writings include intriguing comments regarding morality, ideals for personal conduct, and the nature of virtue. This section highlights three aspects of Günderrode's work on ethics, morals, and virtue. These are her critique of Kantian morality, her Platonic view of virtues as universal things that can be embodied in individuals, and her claim that virtuous behaviors are those that contribute to harmony and unity, and thereby to realizing the "idea of the earth."

Günderrode's "Story of a Brahmin" gives the clearest indication of her moral thought, which she presents through a critique of Kantian morality. Her critique is threefold. First, she objects to Kant's subordination of the passions to reason which, she argues, demands the suppression of one's emotional life and individual needs. This, she maintains, leads to a denial of one's authentic self and alienation from genuine connections to the rest of the world and other people, which Kant replaces with an abstract citizenship in "the moral realm." Second, Günderrode claims that the supposed conflict between individual desires and the good of society is illusory. Using the character Almor's life journey to illustrate her point, she argues that insight into

---

[45] Günderrode, Letter to Gunda Brentano, 20, 21 October 1801 (translated in the Letters section below).

[46] Günderrode, Letter to Gunda Brentano, 11 August 1801; Letter to Carl Friedrich von Savigny, 27 December 1803 (translated in the Letters section below). See Anna Ezekiel, "Narrative and Fragment: The Social Self in Karoline von Günderrode," *Symphilosophie: International Journal of Philosophical Romanticism* 2 (2020).

the true nature of the universe and our relationship to it reveals that the benefit of society is ultimately based on the flourishing of the individuals who comprise it. This position fits with the metaphysics of "Idea of the Earth" and "Letters of Two Friends," according to which the development and increased "liveliness" that individual beings accumulate during their lifetimes contribute to the development and increasing liveliness of the world as a whole, of which they are a part. Ideally, Günderrode claims, this development would eventually result in a harmonious community of all beings, which she calls "the idea of the earth."[47] In her work on ethics, Günderrode extends these metaphysical claims into the realm of social and moral thought.

Günderrode's third criticism of Kant is that he subsumes human spiritual and religious needs into the realm of morality instead of recognizing these as an important area in their own right. According to "Story of a Brahmin," a fully developed human being lives in three ways: as an animal (oriented to physical needs), as human (oriented to society and morality), and spiritually (oriented to authentic connections with the divine and with other people who share this orientation). Günderrode thinks Kant only recognizes the first two of these needs, subordinating religion to morality in order to create his ideal of a society based on universalizable maxims supported by a rational faith. For Günderrode, by contrast, morality and religion are separate and unrelated areas of human flourishing.

A second interesting aspect of Günderrode's moral thought is her view, clearly influenced by Plato, that virtues or excellences are universal attributes that are embodied in individuals. In other words, what we commonly view as virtuous or excellent individual traits (such as truthfulness, justice, or benevolence) are in fact manifestations of eternal ideas of the virtues (Truth, Justice, and Benevolence). Günderrode expresses this view at the start of her collection of fragments on "excellence" (*Vortrefflichkeit*), where she writes: "Excellence is a whole. We do not have it: it is like the blue of the sky above us, and our excellence is only a striving towards it, a view of it; therefore there is no personal love, only love of the excellent."[48] In a similar vein, she writes to her friend Gunda that "I want to love you, even if I don't love the person directly, but only the excellence."[49]

Lastly, Günderrode's understanding of virtue is based on ideals of harmony and unity and underpinned by her metaphysics. Günderrode claims

---

[47] See the section on metaphysics earlier in this introduction.
[48] See the introduction to the fragments on ethics and aesthetics later in this volume.
[49] Letter to Gunda Brentano, June 1802, translated in the Letters section of this volume.

in "Idea of the Earth" and "Letters of Two Friends" that harmony is the state that will characterize the ultimate end of the earth, which is to exist as a single, interconnected organism. For Günderrode, virtuous actions are virtuous because they contribute to the increasing harmony and integration of the whole.[50] Thus, she writes in "Idea of the Earth" that "Truth is the expression of what *is always the same* as itself; [. . .] love, benevolence, compassion are the longing of the particular [. . .] to become aware of the All in the particular, and, renouncing personhood, to surrender itself to the All." By acting in ways that are consistent with this realization, we can help manifest the connections between finite beings and, thereby, the emergence of the ultimate organism. As Dalia Nassar explains, for Günderrode, "human moral activity [. . .] is essential for the realization of the idea of the earth. [. . .] I must come to identify with the earth's 'communal organism' and, in so doing, help realize the earth's vocation."[51]

Günderrode left only sketches of her thinking on virtue and ethics, but from her remarks on this topic, it is clear that her moral thought is rooted in her ideals for building communities based on shared and deeply felt experiences, grounded in real connections. She rejects legalistic or narrowly prescriptive norms for social behavior, instead focusing on the ways that individual actions can satisfy our needs and desires while at the same time creating profound connections with others and contributing to the greater good of the world.

Aesthetics

Günderrode left only fragmentary comments on aesthetics, mostly relating to music and the nature of beauty. These fragments are translated in this volume in the sections titled "Fragments on Ethics and Aesthetics" and "Fragments on Music."

The pieces in the first of these sections present Günderrode's view of beautiful things as manifestations of a universal, eternal ideal of beauty. In this respect, beauty functions in the same way as the other virtues (see previous section). We can see the influence of Plato on this aspect of Günderrode's

---

[50] Dalia Nassar, "The Human Vocation and the Question of the Earth: Karoline von Günderrode's Philosophy of Nature," *Archiv für Geschichte der Philosophie* 104 (2021).
[51] Nassar, "Human Vocation."

thought, especially in the way she links beauty and love. For example, in "Change and Constancy," the character Narcissus argues that, although he might seem unfaithful because he continually changes the objects of his affections, he is in fact faithful to the ideal of beauty that he seeks in each of these objects. Günderrode makes the same claim in "Love and Beauty," describing love of individuals as really love of the virtues, especially beauty, that they embody. As discussed in more detail in the introduction to Günderrode's fragments on ethics and aesthetics, this reflects Plato's distinction between "vulgar" love of individuals and "divine" love of the virtues, especially beauty, that these individuals embody.

According to Günderrode, like the other virtues, beauty draws on an ideal of harmony: beautiful objects are beautiful because they unite and balance disparate elements into a harmonious whole. This reflects the ideal of a perfectly balanced, harmonious organism toward which, according to Günderrode's metaphysics, the universe is working. Indeed, in "Idea of the Earth," Günderrode claims that the creation of beautiful objects contributes to realizing this ideal. This is a good example of Günderrode's interest in systematizing her philosophical thought. Rather than constituting a separate area of her philosophy, Günderrode integrates her aesthetics with her metaphysics, along with her ethics, political thought, and views of personal identity.

Günderrode's fragmentary writings on music are exciting because they suggest she may have been attempting to create a central role for music in her metaphysics. Owing to the relative dearth of material, interpreting Günderrode's work in this area must remain speculative. Nonetheless, Günderrode's scant writings on the topic suggest that she saw music as an animating or regenerative force, which could connect human beings and nature, stimulate the emergence of life and eventually sentience from originally inanimate matter, and join the living and the dead. This aspect of Günderrode's thought is discussed in the introduction to the fragments on music later in this volume.

Lastly, scholars have noted the significance of Günderrode's work on the sublime—an important concept in German idealist aesthetics. Christine Battersby initiated work in this area of Günderrode's thought in the 1990s, arguing that the Günderrodean sublime is an alternative to Kant's model of the sublime.[52] Günderrode's version of this concept avoids the

---

[52] Christine Battersby, "Stages on Kant's Way: Aesthetics, Morality, and the Gendered Sublime," in *Feminism and Tradition in Aesthetics*, ed. Peggy Zeglin Brand and Carolyn Korsmeyer (University Park: Pennsylvania State UP, 1995), 88–114.

gender-coded Kantian opposition between human reason (male) and the physical world (female), because Günderrode's sublime is firmly embedded in her nongendered, nondualistic metaphysics. This aspect of Günderrode's thought is discussed in the introduction to her poem "Once I Lived Sweet Life."

Gender

Günderrode's views on gender were among the first aspects of her thought to receive attention. Soon after her death, her friend Lisette von Nees described a "scission in [Günderrode's] soul," which she claimed was partly the soul of a woman and partly that of a man.[53] Günderrode herself articulated a similar view:

> Why was I not a man! I have no sense for feminine virtues, for feminine happiness. [. . .] There is a deplorable but incorrigible misrelation in my soul; and it will and must remain so, for I am a woman, and have desires like a man, without male strength. For that reason I am so changeable, and so at odds with myself.[54]

For many years, this supposed conflict between "male" and "female" aspects of Günderrode's personality was said to have contributed to her suicide. The conflict was also seen as emerging in her work—something initially considered unfortunate. Critics claimed that her efforts to write on "masculine" topics such as philosophy or great historical figures worked against her feminine nature, which better suited her to lyrical, mystical writing.[55] More recently, however, scholars have been interested in the ways that Günderrode's writing troubles categories of gender, especially the strict division of gender roles.

The above claims about Günderrode's "masculine" and "feminine" traits reflect gender stereotypes that date back many centuries. In Günderrode's time, even more so than today, views on gender shaped ideas about appropriate

---

[53] Lisette von Nees, Letter to Susanne von Heyden, August 1806, in Weißenborn, *Ich sende Dir*, 350.

[54] Günderrode, Letter to Gunda Brentano, 29 August 1801, in Wolf, *Schatten eines Traumes*, 160.

[55] Clemens Brentano, Letter to Günderrode, 2 June 1804, in Weißenborn, *Ich sende Dir*, 144; Friedrich Creuzer, Letter to Günderrode, 20 February 1806, SW 3:144.

behaviors and roles for both women and men. But many of Günderrode's characters, especially female characters, resist these categorizations and take on roles that would normally have been reserved for the opposite gender. For instance, Günderrode's reworking of Ossian's epic poem "Darthula" focuses on Darthula's taking up of weapons to avenge the deaths of her family. In her play *Hildgund*, the titular character must defend her homeland against the threat of Attila the Hun. And in *Mora*, Günderrode's heroine takes the place of her lover to protect him and fight for her right to choose whom she marries.

Partly due to Günderrode's own words on the topic, the presence of warrior women in her work has sometimes been interpreted as a form of wish fulfillment. It is claimed that she created imaginary possibilities for women to live in ways that in reality would have been impossible for them and to express aspects of their personalities that would normally have had to be suppressed as too "masculine."[56] There is support for this interpretation in Günderrode's letters. For example, at one point, she suggests dressing as a boy in order to travel with Creuzer,[57] and elsewhere she writes:

> Yesterday I read Ossian's Darthula, and it had such a pleasant effect upon me; the old wish to die a heroic death grasped me with great intensity; it seemed intolerable to me to still be alive; even more intolerable to die a peaceful and common death. I had already often had the unfeminine wish to throw myself into, to die in, the wild thick of a battle.[58]

Given the limitations faced by women in Günderrode's time, it would not be surprising if she used her work to create imaginary escapes for herself and other women. However, there are also more interesting interpretations of her gender-transgressing characters. Günderrode's warlike women can be read in the context of a European literary tradition of warrior women and female killers of tyrants,[59] in some cases inspired by real people, for example, Joan

---

[56] Liesl Allingham, "Countermemory in Karoline von Günderrode's 'Darthula nach Ossian': A Female Warrior, Her Unruly Breast, and the Construction of Her Myth," *Goethe Yearbook* 21 (July 2014): 39–40; Elizabeth Krimmer, *In the Company of Men: Cross-Dressed Women around 1800* (Detroit: Wayne State UP, 2004), 134.

[57] Günderrode, Letter to Creuzer, 15 September 1805, Weißenborn, *Ich sende Dir*, 240.

[58] Günderrode, Letter to Gunda Brentano, 29 August 1801, in Wolf, *Schatten eines Traumes*, 160.

[59] Dagmar von Hoff, "Dramatisch Weiblichkeitsmuster zur Zeit der Französischen Revolution. Dramen von deutschsprachgen Autorinnen um 1800," in *Die Marseillaise der Weiber. Frauen, die Französische Revolution und ihre Rezeption*, ed. Inge Stephan and Sigrid Weigel (Hamburg: Argument, 1989), 74–88; Krimmer, *Company of Men*; Simpson, *Erotics of War*, 104–127.

of Arc and Marie-Anne Charlotte Corday d'Armont (1768–1793).[60] These figures were used to motivate discussions around possible justifications for violence, especially violence by women, which was held to different and stricter standards than violence by men. Helen Watanabe-O'Kelly notes that broad rules for legitimate violence by women emerged in literature of this time: to be seen as justified, violent women "must have male authority for their actions; they must transcend, and be seen to transcend, their female nature; they must be virgins; and they must die."[61]

Günderrode's warrior and warlike women tend to meet these criteria. Her heroines Mora and Darthula die in battle, and Darthula and Hildgund are granted authority to act in the field of war by their fathers. All three heroines are unmarried and, by implication, virgins. However, Günderrode also modifies this tradition in subtle ways. For instance, in "Darthula," Günderrode challenges the traditional construction of heroism around masculine traits and male figures. Rather than simply transcending gender boundaries to act in the "male" sphere of warfare, Darthula retains female-coded characteristics such as beauty, empathy, and connection to family while also embodying "male" virtues such as courage.[62] Furthermore, Günderrode's depictions of both male and female characters often blur or reverse, rather than reinscribe, the categories of "masculine" and "feminine." For example, in *Hildgund*, it is the heroine who leaves to defend her homeland against Attila while her fiancé Walther remains at home to care for her aging father. In general, scholars note, Günderrode creates "effeminate men and heroic women," highlighting the arbitrary nature of traditional gender roles and of the supposed dichotomy between the personality traits of people of different genders.[63]

Günderrode also uses her female characters, including female warriors, to explore possibilities for female agency in a world dominated by male power. Several of her texts feature powerful men whose behavior removes or constrains the freedom of female characters, for example Attila's blackmailing of Hildgund and, in the play *Muhammad, the Prophet of Mecca*, Muhammad's autocratic decision regarding who Halima will marry.

---

[60] Corday assassinated the French revolutionary leader Jean-Paul Marat in 1793.

[61] Helen Watanabe-O'Kelly, *Beauty or Beast? The Woman Warrior in the German Imagination from the Renaissance to the Present* (Oxford: Oxford UP, 2010), 145.

[62] Allingham, "Countermemory," 53; Licher, *Mein Leben*, 132.

[63] Krimmer, *Company of Men*, 137; Karin Obermeier, "'Ach diese Rolle wird mir allzu schwer': Gender and Cultural Identity in Karoline von Günderrode's Drama 'Udohla,'" in *Thalia's Daughters: German Women Dramatists from the Eighteenth Century to the Present*, ed. Susan Cocalis and Ferrel Rose, with Karin Obermeier (Tübingen: Francke, 1996), 99–114.

By contrast, in *Udohla*, the Sultan's decision to let Nerissa choose whether she will marry him or leave with her brother is the condition of possibility for Nerissa to realize her agency. Similarly, in both *Hildgund* and "Darthula," Günderrode's heroines are able to enter the political sphere when they are granted authority by their fathers. In this way, Günderrode provides a commentary on the ways that social conditions, especially the actions of men who hold power, can promote or obstruct women's ability to act freely and determine their own destiny.

Another interesting feature of Günderrode's work on gender results from her metaphysics, which undermine the importance of gender dichotomies. At the time Günderrode was writing, some philosophers claimed that dualities such as spirit and body, mind and matter, consciousness and the unconscious, and activity and passivity, applied not only to human men and women but also to the world as a whole. They viewed the world as fundamentally split by a division that was analogous to and represented in the division between male and female human beings. A major problem facing this kind of dualistic worldview is how the two aspects of this world—spirit and matter, or mind and body—can connect to each other or function together.

This problem led some philosophers, including the early German Romantics, to grant enormous significance to the idea of romantic love—that is, specifically heterosexual love. For Novalis and Friedrich Schlegel, the union of a man and a woman did not simply connect two individuals, but embodied the merging of the male- and female-coded characteristics of the universe as a whole. As Sarah Friedrichsmeyer puts it, "the early Romantics apotheosized the physical union of the sexes as the means for overcoming the dualism accepted by so many of their precursors."[64] In heterosexual relationships, according to Schlegel and Novalis, men could take on characteristics of women and *vice versa*, overcoming the rigid dichotomy of masculine men and feminine women as well as the separation between "male" and "female" aspects of the world.[65] Since men were thought to embody the rational, active, conscious aspect of the universe while women were seen as connected to the emotions, the body, and nature, the adoption of feminine features by men and of masculine features by women would begin to heal the rift between these two sides of the world.

---

[64] Sara Friedrichsmeyer, *The Androgyne in Early German Romanticism: Friedrich Schlegel, Novalis, and the Metaphysics of Love* (Bern: Lange, 1983), 53.
[65] KFSA 8:45.

Günderrode's view of love and its function within her philosophy are completely different. In the first place, her metaphysics are monistic, viewing spirit and matter as two sides of the same coin and present in varying degrees throughout every part of the universe.[66] There is no fundamental split between two halves of the world that need to be unified. Love, for Günderrode, is the attraction of certain "elements" (the basic building blocks of every entity, including human beings) to each other. When some of the elements from which we are made are drawn to elements within someone else, we feel love or attraction for that person. According to Günderrode, this attraction occurs, not on the basis of opposition or complementarity as it does for Novalis and Schlegel, but due to similarity, specifically a similarity in the level of animation or liveliness of the elements that are attracted to each other.

One result of this model is that there is no special significance for heterosexual relationships in Günderrode's work. This is because, on her account, what attracts people to each other is completely unrelated to gender; instead, it is due to the level of activity, animation, or "liveliness" of the elements out of which they are made. In keeping with this position, Günderrode's work includes examples of both same-sex attraction (e.g., "Piedro," "The Manes," "Story of a Brahmin") and attraction between people of different sexes (e.g., "The Frank in Egypt," "The Malabarian Widows").

Due to this enormous difference between Günderrode's account of love and that of the early German Romantics, some of Günderrode's texts that seem derivative of early German Romanticism actually present radically different ideas. In fact, her work often subtly critiques Romantic models, especially the gender dualism that this movement adopted. In addition to its heteronormativity, the early German Romantic view of gender is problematic because it essentializes the nature of men and women, even while claiming to advocate greater flexibility in gender expression. Furthermore, it seems to leave no space for the possibility of *Bildung*, or self-development, for women. It is easy to see how, on this model, men—supposedly rational, active, and characterized by the life of the mind—can go out into the world and cultivate themselves by adopting "feminine" characteristics. However, it is much harder to create a narrative around the *Bildung* of women, who are viewed by the early German Romantics as passive, emotional, and bound to the body. For a passive, physical being, any change or development would have to be

---

[66] For details, see the section on Günderrode's metaphysics, above.

done to them rather than actively sought out. Indeed, many critics point out that Novalis and Schlegel depict only the *Bildung* of male characters, leaving their female characters unchanged by the end of their stories, or alternatively dead or pregnant. The only "development" these thinkers seem to imagine for women is to conceive a child and become a mother.[67]

An example of Günderrode engaging subtly with the lack of female *Bildung* in early German Romanticism occurs in her poem "The Frank in Egypt." This poem shares many features with Romantic stories of *Bildung*: a young man's journey to the east, his motivation by a vague sense of longing, and the eventual satisfaction of this longing through falling in love with an Egyptian woman, Lastrata. However, unlike Novalis and Schlegel, Günderrode carefully maintains the symmetry between .the male protagonist and the woman he meets. Just like the Frank, Lastrata has been longing for something distant and unnamable, and this longing is satisfied by meeting him. There is no need for a separate account of female development as there is in early German Romanticism; for Günderrode, men and women experience the same feelings of love, attraction, friendship, and longing, and these are satisfied in the same way for each. This is consistent with Günderrode's metaphysical picture, as described above, according to which love, longing, and attraction in general are based on similarity, not difference or opposition.

In addition, Günderrode undermines the claim that it is specifically romantic love that can satisfy the longing her characters feel. In "The Frank in Egypt," Lastrata specifies that her father also longs for his distant birthplace in Europe, and invites the Frank to join them at their home. The inclusion of a third member in the group also fits with the metaphysics underlying Günderrode's work: for Günderrode, there is no particular reason why an attraction between similar elements needs to involve elements within just two individuals; this model is perfectly amenable to imagining loving communities of several or many people. Consequently, Günderrode deprioritizes the significance of romantic and sexual attraction as well as the idea of a gender dichotomy. In contrast to the early German Romantics, for Günderrode, the best way of healing the gaps in the world and bringing the universe into harmony is not romantic love or sexual attraction, but the creation of communities of like-minded people.

---

[67] Friedrichsmeyer, *Androgyne*, 104–105; Schrage-Früh, "Subversive Weiblichkeit?" 377–378.

Günderrode and Genre

Günderrode did not develop her metaphysics, epistemology, political views, critique of gender, or conception of the self as dry, academic exercises; instead, she used literary forms to enliven her philosophical claims and make them seem plausible and concrete. Poems and narratives also allowed her to emphasize the role of feelings and intuition, as opposed to only the mind, in knowledge and learning. This section of the introduction considers these literary forms and some of the challenges of deciphering a philosophical position from writings that do not take the shape we tend to expect of philosophical texts.

The pieces translated in this volume represent a variety of genres, including a draft essay, a fictional exchange of letters, dramas, dialogues, poems, a short story, unfinished scraps and fragments of writing, notes from Günderrode's studies, and excerpts from her correspondence. The introductions to the notebooks and Günderrode's letters later in this volume explain the importance of these two formats as ways of accessing Günderrode's philosophical thought. This section therefore focuses on the other types of writing in the collection, considering Günderrode's choices of genre in the context of the social conditions of her time as well as European traditions of using literature, poetry, dialogues, and fragments as formats for doing philosophy.

At the time Günderrode was writing, women faced social and institutional barriers to doing philosophy, including exclusion from higher institutions of learning, prejudices about their intellectual abilities, and social sanctions for attempting to write in fields considered unsuitable to their "feminine nature" or their roles as wives, mothers, and housekeepers.[68] However, many women found ways to circumvent these difficulties, and one such strategy was to mask philosophical ideas in literary forms. Unlike scholarly essays or academic books, these were considered acceptable formats for women. This helped avoid accusations of writing "like a badly-disguised man"[69]—i.e., as if one had pretensions to independent and highly intellectual thought, which were considered exclusively male characteristics. Even when writing literature, women were urged to avoid the wrong kind of subject matter (great

---

[68] B. Becker-Cantarino and Jeanette Clausen, "Gender Censorship: On Literary Production in German Romanticism," *Women in German Yearbook: Feminist Studies and German Culture* 11 (1995): 81–97; Anna Ezekiel, Introduction to *Poetic Fragments by Tian* (Albany: SUNY Press, 2016), 1–38.

[69] Fichte, cited in Becker-Cantarino and Clausen, "Gender Censorship," 82.

historical figures and events) or the wrong kind of writing (anything too intellectual). Günderrode largely ignored the first of these strictures, but her
writing style conformed in some respects to expectations of women's writing
as lyrical, mysterious, and "mystical."

Undoubtedly, Günderrode's choice of genre and writing style were
influenced by social expectations. However, Günderrode, like other
philosophers, did not adopt literary genres only because of external pressures.
There are good reasons for using novels, dramas, poems, short stories,
dialogues, and other such formats for doing philosophy. These include
making one's work more accessible and engaging, making one's points more
persuasive, and working through or "testing" the implications of philosophical claims in situations that approximate the real world.[70] For example, in
"An Apocalyptic Fragment," Günderrode gives a visceral description of how it
would feel to experience the kinds of non-human existence that, in her metaphysical work, she claims will occur after we die.[71] This is important both
for helping explain what exactly she means by her unique (and quite strange)
model of reincarnation and for convincing readers that this model is plausible.
Another example is "Story of a Brahmin," in which Günderrode explores the
implications for her protagonist and society at large of the various worldviews
and associated moral attitudes that he adopts throughout the narrative.

Recently, there has been increased scholarly interest in the use of alternative textual and verbal forms for doing philosophy and the importance of
literary genres not just for communicating philosophical claims but also as
ways of thinking philosophically. This scholarship has highlighted the extent to which the focus on specific forms of writing—journal articles, essays,
books—as exclusively appropriate to philosophy is a recent development.[72]
Since the earliest records, European philosophy has been written not just
in these formats but also in dialogues, poems, dramas, novels, short stories,
letters, sermons, disquisitions, commentaries, biographies, aphorisms,
parables, allegories, folk tales, and travel narratives.[73] If we look outside

---

[70] Astrid Weigert, "Gender and Genre in the Works of German Romantic Women Writers," in *The Oxford Handbook of European Romanticism*, ed. Paul Hamilton (Oxford: OUP, 2016), 248–249.

[71] For details, see the section on Günderrode's metaphysics earlier in this introduction.

[72] E.g., Berel Lang, "The Ethics of Style in Philosophical Discourse," in *Literary Form, Philosophical Content: Historical Studies of Philosophical Genres*, ed. Jonathan Lavery and Louis Groarke (Madison: Fairleigh Dickinson UP, 2010), 220.

[73] E.g., poems were used by Greek and Roman philosophers such as Heraclitus, Hesiod, and Lucretius, while novels often used in academic philosophy include Thomas Moore's *Utopia* (1516), Rousseau's *Émile* (1762), Voltaire's *Candide* (1759), and works by existentialist philosophers Simone de Beauvoir, Albert Camus, and Jean-Paul Sartre.

western philosophy, we find a similar profusion of genres. These days, we can add blog entries and podcasts to the list.

In addition to this longstanding tradition of literary philosophy, at the time Günderrode was writing, there were specific theories that favored literary genres as ways of doing philosophy. In particular, this position was central to the movement known as early German Romanticism (also Jena Romanticism or, in German, *Frühromantik*). Early German Romanticism developed in the last years of the eighteenth century among a group of intellectuals living in the university town of Jena, including Friedrich Schlegel, his friend Novalis, and the talented but often uncredited writers, editors, and translators Caroline Schlegel-Schelling (1763–1809) and Dorothea Veit-Schlegel (1764–1839). Other figures formed part of the broader circle of the Jena Romantics and are also often referred to as early German Romantics; these include Hölderlin and Schelling as well as Friedrich Schlegel's brother August Wilhelm Schlegel (1767–1845), the poet and editor Ludwig Tieck (1773–1853), and the physicist and philosopher Johann Wilhelm Ritter (1776–1810).

The early German Romantics argued that philosophy, which could seem dry and divorced from the world it attempted to describe, should merge with "poetry" or "poesie" to arouse the imagination and become "alive." Poetry, they claimed, was also helpful for communicating about aspects of experience that eluded concepts and discursive language.[74] Both Novalis and Friedrich Schlegel also emphasized the contingency of narrative and the possibility of multiple interpretations of events, which they opposed to the single, conclusive, true account that they claim science and philosophy aspire to present.[75] They suggest that presenting different perspectives—and using various formats to do—so both enlivens philosophical reflection and allows it to move beyond the limitations of one-sided, monolithic academic discourse.

Günderrode used many different genres and often presented several competing positions on a single issue, suggesting that she shared the Romantic appreciation for multiple perspectives and forms of presentation,

[74] Novalis, *Schriften. Zweite, nach den Handschriften ergänzte, erweiterte und verbesserte Auflage in vier Bänden*, ed. Paul Kluckhohn and Richard Samuel (Stuttgart: W. Kohlhammer, 1960f.), 3:520. Novalis wrote extensively on the value of different forms of literary genre for philosophy: see also 2:424–425 #27, 2:436–439 #66, 2:524–555 #13, 2:533–546 #31–51, 2:568 #207, 2:573–574 #226, 2:580 #242.

[75] Peter Firchow, Introduction, in *Friedrich Schlegel's* Lucinde and the Fragments (Minneapolis: University of Minnesota Press, 1971), 28.

especially those that are not purely discursive or univocal. This, combined with her focus on questions that are typically considered within the purview of philosophy—such as the nature of the universe, the relationship between the mind and the body, the role of consciousness in personal identity, the question of how we can know things, and the foundation and purpose of morality—places her writings in a tradition of literary philosophy that includes the early German Romantics and many others.

One of the literary forms that Günderrode used most frequently is the dialogue. This collection includes one prose dialogue, "The Manes," and three poems in dialogue form: "The Wanderer's Descent," "The Frank in Egypt," and "Change and Constancy." Two other pieces translated here share some characteristics with the dialogue: "Letters of Two Friends" is an epistolary exchange, or a dialogue in letters, and "Story of a Brahmin," which at first seems to be a short story narrated in the first person, turns out to be a dialogue: about halfway through a second speaker interjects and converses with the narrator. Dramas, including Günderrode's *Udohla*, *Immortalita*, and the short sketch *Mora*, share some characteristics with dialogues, such as the use of multiple characters to present two or more positions on an issue in interaction with each other.

The written dialogue has a long history as a philosophical genre. In Europe, it dates back at least to Plato and has been in continual use until today. Famous examples include Augustine's dialogues on the immortality of the soul and freedom of will, Peter Abelard's *Dialogue between a Philosopher, a Jew, and a Christian* (1136–1139), George Berkeley's *Three Dialogues between Hylas and Philonous* (1713), Hemsterhuis' *Sophyle* (1778) and *Simon* (1787), and Schelling's *Bruno* (1802). Dialogue was also used in texts from Asia that were becoming available around the time Günderrode was writing. For example, the *Bhagavad Gita* is a dialogue that considers (among other topics) the nature of virtue, duty, the self, and the relationship between human beings and the divine; this text was published in German translation by 1801.

Among other advantages, the dialogue is a natural way of representing the give-and-take of an argument, which in other kinds of philosophical writing can be indicated by stating and responding to objections. The use of more than one speaker makes it easy to articulate different perspectives on an issue. The writer of a dialogue can present strengths and weaknesses of each perspective without taking a position on which view is correct, or they can show one or more speakers persuaded by another, encouraging the reader to be similarly persuaded.[76]

At the time Günderrode was writing, the philosophical dialogue was popular not just for these reasons, but also due to theories that attributed special significance to conversation, including as a medium for doing philosophy. This was the age of salons, where people from different social backgrounds came together to converse on the widest possible range of topics, including ethics, politics, aesthetics, literature, and philosophy. The early German Romantics developed an ideal of *Symphilosophie*, or doing philosophy together, which valued the same kind of quick-thinking wit and interaction of perspectives that (ideally) characterized salon conversation.[77] In opposition to what was sometimes considered the dead letter of academic writing, conversation and dialogue were seen as ways of doing living philosophy.

Günderrode's dialogues embody many characteristics of the philosophical dialogue. "The Manes" depicts a teacher instructing and persuading a less experienced student, who asks questions and raises objections to which the teacher responds. In "Change and Constancy," Günderrode uses the dialogue form to present a debate between two opposing views of love. The characters raise and respond to objections: in particular, Violetta objects to Narcissus' description of his fleeting performances of love, asking, "What, then, is love, has it no subsistence?" Narcissus responds: "Love only wants to change, not wither [...] It will hunt down what is excellent." By the end of the poem, Günderrode has defended the position articulated by Narcissus, but she has also, through Violetta, exposed some weaknesses of his position. In this way, she provides readers with material to consider and make up their own minds about the nature of love and faithfulness.

There are challenges when reading literary texts as works of philosophy. Literary forms are often deliberately ambiguous and open to multiple interpretations. Even where this is not the case, they may suggest, rather than explicitly state, what they mean. This is particularly so in the case of poems, which function by metaphor, imagery, emotion, and the effects of

---

[76] This is typical in Plato's dialogues, e.g., *Meno*, where Meno repeatedly confirms Socrates' statements, encouraging the reader to agree with each step of the argument: "Certainly ... Exactly ... True ... Yes ... That, Socrates, appears to me to be an admirable answer ... Quite true ... Yes ..." (Plato, *Meno*, trans. Benjamin Jowett [Upper Saddle River, NJ: Prentice Hall, 1949 (1871)], 30–31).

[77] Sabina Becker, "Gelebte 'Universalpoesie.' Rahel Varnhagen und die frühromantische Gesprächs- und Geselligskeitskultur," in *Rahel Levin Varnhagen. Studien zu ihrem Werk im zeitgenössischen Kontext*, ed. Becker (St. Ingbert: Röhrig, 2001), 22–30.

formal considerations such as meter, rhyme, alliteration, and assonance. For example, several scholars have noted the importance of vertical movement in Günderrode's poem "Once I Lived Sweet Life," arguing that this contributes to establishing her philosophical claims.[78] In some works of literature, it can be hard to determine the author's stance on the issues raised in the text. This is especially the case where multiple characters embody different perspectives and perhaps disagree, or where characters appear in an ambiguous light, making it unclear to what extent we should sympathize with or reject their worldview. This ambiguity is often deliberate and can be considered a strength if the author wants to highlight more than one side of an issue, deny their own authorial authority (a technique used by Kierkegaard and Nietzsche, for instance), or encourage readers to think for themselves.

As with many philosophers, Günderrode also wrote non-literary texts that articulate her philosophical claims more clearly. These can help in interpreting her literary works. We can also relate her stories and poems to work by other thinkers, determining their place in a discussion the terms of which may already have been articulated. For example, Günderrode's play *Muhammad, the Prophet of Mecca* can be read in the context of a literary tradition that used Muhammad as a stand-in for Napoleon and Luther in order to criticize contemporary European culture.[79] Similarly, we can ask how Günderrode's poem "The Aeronaut" responds to the widespread use at the time of the metaphor of hot air balloons to critique European society and politics, German idealism, human hubris, and other phenomena.[80] In this way, we can add to an understanding of Günderrode's philosophical thought and identify her contributions to the intellectual context in which she wrote.

Let us consider one more literary form with a philosophical history that may be significant for reading Günderrode: the fragment. The term "fragment" appears repeatedly in relation to Günderrode's work: scholars sometimes refer to her writing as "fragmentary" or to specific pieces as "fragments,"[81] and Günderrode's unique model of personal identity has

---

[78] Battersby, "Stages on Kant's Way"; Sabine Eickenrodt, *Augenspiel. Jean Pauls optische Metaphorik der Unsterblichkeit* (Wallstein, nd), 263–264; Gabriel Trop, "Arts of Unconditioning: On Romantic Science and Poetry," in *The Palgrave Handbook of German Romantic Philosophy*, ed. Elizabeth Millán Brusslan (Palgrave Macmillan, 2020), 441–442.

[79] Ezekiel, "Introduction to *Muhammad*."

[80] For details, see the introduction to "The Aeronaut" later in this volume.

[81] E.g., Helga Dormann, "Die Karoline von Günderrode-Forschung 1945–1995. Ein Bericht," *Athenaeum* 6 (1996): 197; Schärf, "Artistische Ironie," 454.

been described as presenting a "fragmentary" self.[82] The description of Günderrode's work as fragmentary often refers simply to the fact that she left so many short pieces, unfinished texts, and partly articulated ideas that she had not yet explored in detail or integrated into a larger picture. In that respect, her work resembles "accidental" fragments of texts by other authors that have been retained or rediscovered in incomplete form. As with other such fragmentary texts, for example, those of the pre-Socratic philosophers, interpretation of Günderrode's philosophical claims often involves piecing together information from the scraps that are left and trying to understand them in relation to their cultural context. Helpfully, some of her works are detailed enough to provide a framework for this kind of interpretation.

A number of factors make it important to query whether some of Günderrode's work might also be regarded as "deliberate" fragments—that is, as texts that were always intended to be short, disconnected, and apparently incomplete. At the time Günderrode was writing, deliberate fragments were very much in vogue, both in general and in the particular way they were understood by the early German Romantics. Günderrode's philosophical proximity to early German Romanticism, as well as the discovery of a "fragmentary" model of identity in her writings, makes this an exciting question. Did Günderrode engage with early German Romantic ideas about fragments? What role, if any, did the fragment play in her thought?

Günderrode would have been familiar with early German Romantic writings on the fragment and the conceptual commitments behind them. To Novalis and Friedrich Schlegel, all knowledge and all attempts to convey knowledge using language are necessarily incomplete and imperfect. Fragments have an advantage over texts (or speech) that pretend to be complete or fully adequate to their subject because they remind the reader of this incompleteness.[83] In addition to being honest, this overt acknowledgment of a text's own limitations is valuable because it stimulates the reader to further thought.[84]

Günderrode herself uses the term "fragment" infrequently—I have found only six instances in which she does so, all in titles for her work. These pieces seem to have little in common: they include her second published collection, *Poetic Fragments*, the prose poem "An Apocalyptic Fragment," a dialogue

---

[82] Bohrer, "Identität als Selbstverlust"; Ezekiel, "Narrative and Fragment."
[83] See, e.g., KFSA 2:159 #103, 2:200 #200; Novalis, *Schriften*, 2:672–673.
[84] KFSA 2:183 #116.

("The Manes") and an elegy ("The Cathedral in Cologne"), both subtitled "A Fragment," part of a letter ("Fragments from Eusebio's Answer" in "Letters of Two Friends"), and a play, *Muhammad, the Prophet of Mecca*. The latter, ironically, is Günderrode's longest work; in this case, we know Günderrode added the subtitle "A Dramatic Fragment" in response to a complaint by her friend Nees von Esenbeck.[85]

Furthermore, Günderrode left no writings about the term "fragment" to indicate whether her use of the word is underpinned by a philosophical account of fragmentariness such as the one articulated by Novalis and Schlegel. This is representative of a broader challenge in reading fragmentary work such as Günderrode's. Much of what Günderrode left behind is incomplete, undeveloped, or simply brief. As a result, we must establish many of her ideas on the basis of limited remarks, short explanations, or literary presentations of ideas. In other cases, we can carefully draw out the implications of her claims on topics that she considers in detail in order to illuminate her thought on topics she wrote on more succinctly. We can also look to the work of other thinkers of the time to identify the conceptual parameters within which Günderrode's thought developed and to which it responded.

In the rest of this volume, Günderrode's writings are translated next to introductions that describe relevant features of this intellectual context, suggest ways of using her texts to elucidate each other, and point to plausible interpretations of the philosophical claims that permeate her writings. Through careful use of the above techniques, we can develop a philosophical reading of Günderrode's fragmentary texts and, in so doing, unearth original responses to questions within German idealism, Romanticism, philosophy of nature, and the history of European thought.

Overview of This Volume

The translations in this volume are collected in three parts: selections from Günderrode's published and unpublished works, notes from her philosophical studies, and letters. The texts are preceded by introductions that orient

---

[85] In a letter to Savigny, Günderrode writes that Nees criticized *Muhammad* as incomplete and full of failings, but that she does not want to take his advice and include a prologue apologizing for these. Instead, "As a consolation I must tell him [. . .] that the whole thing will appear under the title of a fragment" (SW 3:134).

readers to philosophical themes in each piece and situate them within the intellectual context in which they were written.

The first part of the volume is organized loosely to begin with pieces that focus on metaphysics before moving to those considering epistemology, social and political theory, ethics, aesthetics, and, finally, gender. In the second section, notes from Günderrode's study books have been selected for their relevance to the works translated in the earlier part of this volume. Günderrode's notes are not passively copied from her study materials but show her engagement with the texts she was reading, minimally in her selection of text, but also often including commentary and modifications. They include notes on philosophy of nature, chemistry, philosophers from Günderrode's own time, such as Novalis, Friedrich Schlegel, Schleiermacher, and Hemsterhuis, and other philosophical topics and thinkers. The introduction to the notebooks and the individual introductions to each set of notes explain what we can learn from studying Günderrode's notes on these topics.

The letters translated in the final part of this volume have been chosen for their contributions to understanding Günderrode's philosophical commitments. In particular, Günderrode's ideas about selfhood or identity, which are a key feature of her work in both her published and unpublished writings, can be supplemented by attention to her letters. Günderrode's letters are also important for the account of friendship she develops there. The introduction to this section of the volume argues for reading Günderrode's correspondence as integral to her philosophical thought.

PART 1
WORKS

1

Idea of the Earth

Introduction

The short essay "Idea of the Earth" provides one of Günderrode's most focused reflections on the nature of the universe. Here, Günderrode makes claims about the essential features of ordinary objects, the processes that drive change and development among these objects, and our experiences of these. She applies these claims to living beings as well, including human beings. Toward the end of the piece, she also sketches some of her ideas about virtue and beauty. Her remarks on these topics are brief, but offer an intriguing glimpse of Günderrode's application of her metaphysical principles to the realms of ethics and aesthetics.

"Idea of the Earth" was probably written in late 1805, but was not meant to be published in the form in which we find it here. Instead, Günderrode rewrote parts of the text and incorporated these in "Letters of Two Friends" (the next piece in this volume) for inclusion in her third collection, *Melete*. "Letters" is beautifully written and presents its claims about the nature of the universe as the content of a revelation, embedding these claims in a longer discussion about life, death, art, and religion. "Idea of the Earth," on the other hand, is quite short and written in assertoric form using dense philosophical language.

In "Idea of the Earth," Günderrode advances her central metaphysical claims, which underlie the rest of her philosophical thought. According to Günderrode, the universe is made up of ever-changing groupings of indestructible "elements." All individual objects, plants, and animals are assembled from these elements, and when they die or break down, the elements are simply combined into new groupings (i.e., new objects, plants, and animals). Günderrode claims it is possible that all the elements in the universe will eventually be brought into harmonious, perfectly balanced relationship with each other in what she calls "a collective organism" or the "idea of the earth." Importantly, however, she expresses uncertainty about

Karoline von Günderrode. Anna Ezekiel, Oxford University Press. © Oxford University Press 2026.
DOI: 10.1093/9780190089177.003.0003

whether or not this final form will ever emerge: "I do not assert whether the earth will be altogether successful in organizing itself immortally like this."

Günderrode views human beings as part of this ongoing emergence and destruction of individual entities. On her account, humans are not essentially different from the rest of the natural world. Just like every other entity, human beings are formed of indestructible living elements that are recycled again and again. The only difference is that in humans, the elements have achieved a particular level of animation. Günderrode claims that each time the elements are incorporated in a being, they become stronger and more animated: "once these elements have been driven to life in the organism, they become different from what they were before they entered into this organic connection. They have become livelier." Eventually, they become lively enough to form sentient and then conscious beings, such as human beings. After we die, the elements retain this extra liveliness, going on to form new beings at even higher levels of animation and, at the same time, increasing the overall liveliness of the universe as a whole: "each mortal gives back to the earth a raised, more developed elemental life, which it cultivates further in ascending forms." This process continues until the "idea of the earth" is realized.

Günderrode links the above account to an idea of reincarnation, which she calls "The Indian idea of the transmigration of souls." However, Günderrode's kind of reincarnation is quite different from other versions, including those from India. "Idea of the Earth" does not present consciousness as something that attaches to particular beings, such as a certain animal or a certain human, and then reappears in other particular beings after the first one has died. For Günderrode, consciousness belongs to the elements themselves. She explains: "[just] as the whole of the earth only exists through this unification of soul and body, so, too, the individual and smallest things only exist through it and cannot be conceived as split in two, for an outer without an inner, an essence without form, a force without some sort of effect, is not comprehensible." In other words, the elements themselves have both body and soul. Since the elements can be grouped and regrouped in many different combinations, this undermines the usual picture we have of one consciousness corresponding to one being. It seems we must radically rethink our view of consciousness if we are to accept Günderrode's metaphysics and their implications.

In the last paragraph of "Idea of the Earth," Günderrode briefly addresses some of the moral and aesthetic ramifications of her metaphysical claims.

Günderrode states that virtuous actions, as well as beautiful things, are those that contribute to the progressive unification and harmony of the whole— i.e., to the realization of the "idea of the earth." She explains that this is because all forms of virtue and beauty involve various ways of unifying diverse factors: "Truth is the expression of what *is always the same* as itself; justice is the striving of the All in the particular to be the same as itself; beauty is being the same as oneself and harmonious; love, benevolence, compassion are the longing of the particular to enjoy itself in the All, i.e., to become aware of the All in the particular."[1] As a result, any virtuous action increases the harmony of the world and thereby contributes to the emergence of the ultimate organism that, Günderrode claims, would be the ideal final state of the earth.

Scholars have long noted the influence of Friedrich Wilhelm Joseph Schelling's (1775–1854) philosophy on "Idea of the Earth."[2] Schelling was an important figure in the development of German idealism, a student of Johann Gottlieb Fichte (1762–1814) and a friend (and later rival) of Hegel. He was one of the foremost thinkers in the movement known as *Naturphilosophie*, or "philosophy of nature," which aimed to understand the characteristics and development of the natural world as a whole. From 1801, Schelling's writings and teaching shifted focus to the question of the relationship between body and soul, or between nature and spirit; his work during this period is known as *Identitätsphilosophie*, or "philosophy of identity."[3] Günderrode's notes indicate that she read texts from both these periods of Schelling's work, and the central questions of both philosophy of nature and philosophy of identity are strong themes in her writings.

The opening paragraphs of "Idea of the Earth" use Schelling's terminology, describing the universe as comprised of opposing forces that interact with each other to create all the phenomena of the everyday world. These paragraphs present experience as divided into two aspects, inner and outer (also described as "soul" and "body," "essence" and "form," "force" and "extension"), which should be seen as two "poles" of a single thing, rather than two separate things. This is similar to Schelling's work in *Ideas for a Philosophy of Nature* (1797), *First Outline of a System of the Philosophy of Nature* (1799), and *Bruno, or On the Divine and Natural Principle of Things* (1802), which Günderrode excerpted in her notebooks. Schelling likely also influenced

---

[1] Nassar, "Human Vocation."
[2] Christmann, *Identitätsgewinn*, 95–118.
[3] Further developments in Schelling's thought took place after 1806, but these are not relevant to our discussion of Günderrode here as they occurred after her death.

the titular concept of the "idea of the earth" which, on Günderrode's model, realizes itself in the world we experience. This concept appears in Schelling's discussion of Platonist ideas in *Bruno*.[4]

Although Schelling's influence is evident in this piece, Günderrode had already developed many of the central claims of her metaphysics before her encounter with Schelling's writings. Earlier texts including "The Manes," "An Apocalyptic Fragment," and "Story of a Brahmin" also present the universe as unfolding through the successive creation and destruction of individual entities. Arguably, Günderrode adapted Schelling's concepts and terminology to fit, and perhaps fill out the details of, a position she had already developed before reading his work.[5]

Another likely influence on "Idea of the Earth" is the author Christoph Martin Wieland (1733–1813), whose works often considered philosophical themes. In Wieland's novel *Agathodämon*, the characters discuss the pre-Socratic philosopher Heraclitus' conception of metempsychosis, or reincarnation. Günderrode also studied Heraclitus from primary sources, but the terminology and framing in "Idea of the Earth" is similar to that in *Agathodämon*. As in Günderrode's text, in *Agathodämon*, Wieland describes a world in which elements are the basic building blocks of the universe, and these elements strive and struggle to develop through increasing levels of sentience.[6]

Although the metaphysics in "Idea of the Earth" are similar in some ways to the work of Schelling, Heraclitus, Wieland, and others, Günderrode's position forms a distinct alternative to these. Several scholars have explored differences between Günderrode's "Idea of the Earth" and the work of Schelling, Fichte, Hegel, and other philosophers, arguing for the uniqueness of Günderrode's metaphysics and in particular her view of the relationship between humans and nature.[7] Günderrode's work is also distinctive for its attention to the implications of her metaphysics for lived experience and

---

[4] F. W. J. Schelling, *Bruno, oder über das göttliche und natürliche Princip der Dinge. Ein Gespräch* (Berlin: Johann Friedrich Unger, 1802), 16.

[5] See Anna Ezekiel, "Earth, Spirit, Humanity: Community and the Nonhuman in Karoline von Günderrode's 'Idea of the Earth,'" in *Romanticism and Political Ecology*, ed. Kir Kuiken (Romantic Praxis Circle, 2024).

[6] Christoph Martin Wieland, "*Agathodämon* [1796–1797]," in *C. M. Wielands sämmtliche Werke*, vol. 32 (Leipzig: Georg Joachim Göschen, 1799), 226.

[7] Nassar, "Human Vocation"; Karen Ng, "The Idea of the Earth in Günderrode, Schelling and Hegel," in *The Oxford Handbook of Nineteenth-Century Women Philosophers in the German Tradition*, ed. Kristin Gjesdal and Dalia Nassar (New York: OUP, 2024), 527–538; Benjamin Norris, "Necro-ecology in Günderrode's 'Idea of the Earth': Life, Death and *Naturphilosophie* Beyond Schelling," *Idealistic Studies* (2024): 283–303.

how we conceive of personal identity, social relations, and moral obligations. These aspects of her thought are not emphasized in "Idea of the Earth" but appear in other texts translated in this volume, including "The Manes," "An Apocalyptic Fragment," "A Dream," and "Story of a Brahmin." In order to interpret these and other texts by Günderrode in the sense in which she intended them, it is important to understand the metaphysics that underlie her philosophy. This makes "Idea of the Earth" a key text for approaching Günderrode's thought.

Idea of the Earth

The earth is a realized idea, one that is simultaneously effective (force) and effected (appearance). It is thus a unity of soul and body. We call the pole of its activity that it turns outward extension, form, body; the one it turns inwards *intension*, essence, force, soul. Now, as the whole of the earth only exists through this unification of soul and body, so, too, the individual and smallest things only exist through it and cannot be conceived as split in two, for an outer without an inner, an essence without form, a force without some sort of effect, is not comprehensible. Thus the elements are the poles of this identical earth-essence, and each individual is in itself body and soul, yet in various proportions of both, so that either the spiritual pole or the bodily pole can predominate. The most intimate mingling of different elements with the highest degree of contact and attraction we call life; to whatever perfection it may have developed it is still only the product of the synthesis of the elements that gestate life. With the dissolution of this synthesis the product also ends, but the life-principle in the elements is immortal; it requires only contact and connection again like before and new life blossoms with all the blooms that we call thought and sensation, and organism and body and soul.

Thus life is immortal and surges up and down in the elements, for they are life itself. But determinate and individual life is only a life-form given through this determinate connection, attraction and contact, which can last no longer than the connection.

Now, when a person is dead, their mixture returns to the substance of the earth, but that within them that we called force, activity, or rather that of its materials in which the more active pole predominated, reverts to that which is related to it in the earth; the coarser elements likewise seek what is similar to them according to laws of affinity. But once these elements have been driven to life in the organism, they become different from what they were before they entered into this organic connection. They have become livelier and increase the earth's life in returning to the earth, like two who have increased their strength in long struggle are stronger when the struggle has ended than they were before. The elements are like this, for they are alive, and the living force is strengthened in every exercise.

But each form that they produce is only a development of their life-principle. The earth bears the life-material given back to it again in ever new appearances, until through ever new transformations everything capable of life in it has come to life. This would be when all mass would become organic; only then would the idea of the earth be realized.

So each mortal gives back to the earth a raised, more developed elemental life, which it cultivates further in ascending forms, and the organism, by assimilating ever more developed elements, must become ever more perfect and universal. Thus the All comes to life through the downfall of the particular, and the particular survives immortally in the All whose life it developed while alive, and elevates and increases even after death, and so by living and dying helps to realize the idea of the earth. Thus, however my elements may be dispersed, when they join to what is already living they will elevate it; when they join to those things whose life resembles death, they will animate them. The Indian idea of the transmigration of souls corresponds to this opinion, and the life-elements may wander and search no longer only when the earth has thoroughly attained its proper existence, the organic. But all forms of the organism that have been produced until now must not suffice the earth-spirit, for it always breaks them up again and seeks new ones; whereas a form that was totally identical to the essence could not be broken apart from it, for it would be entirely the same as it and inseparable from it.

This perfect unity of essence and form cannot be achieved in *separation* and multiplicity, for through precisely *these* the form is different from the essence, because the essence can only be one but the forms are various. The earth can therefore only attain its proper being when its organic and inorganic appearances dissolve in a collective organism, when both factors— being (body) and thinking (spirit)—penetrate each other to the point of indistinguishability, where all body would also at the same time be thought, all thinking at the same time body, and a truly transfigured body, without lack or illness and immortal, and thus wholly different from what we call body or material and to which we attribute transience, inertia, illness and deficiency, for this kind of body is, as it were, only a failed attempt by nature to produce that immortal ideal body. I do not assert whether the earth will be altogether successful in organizing itself immortally like this; there may be a disproportion of essence and form in its primal elements that always hinders it from this; and perhaps the totality of our whole solar system is needed to resolve the task, and perhaps even this does not suffice for it and it is a task for the entire universe.

Truth is the expression of what *is always the same* as itself; justice is the striving of the All in the particular to be the same as itself; beauty is being the same as oneself and harmonious; love, benevolence, compassion are the longing of the particular to enjoy itself in the All, i.e., to become aware of the All in the particular, and, renouncing personhood, to surrender itself to the All. But what is always the same as itself, harmonious with itself, not torn asunder into the particular, that is immortal, without change and illness; in short, it is that which I have called the realized idea of the earth (or of the universe). All single virtues and excellences are therefore mere attempts by the earth-spirit to bring itself nearer to this state (as much as can occur in the particular). Through any kind of truth, justice, beauty and virtue it becomes more like itself, more harmonious, and freer of the bonds of personhood; through every act of injustice, untruth and selfishness this state is made more distant and the god of the earth, who expresses his longing for a better life in every mind through receptivity to what is admirable, is bound in chains.

2

Letters of Two Friends

Introduction

"Letters of Two Friends" consists of three letters or parts of letters between a character called Eusebio and his unnamed friend, with a dedicatory poem at the start. The piece is written as an epistolary dialogue, or conversation in letters, which is a form that readily lends itself to philosophical discussion. Günderrode uses the back-and-forth between the correspondents to consider different perspectives on modern and ancient art, the ills of her contemporary society, European and Indian religions, death, friendship, and the nature of the universe. The end of the last letter comprises the final version, intended for publication, of the metaphysical claims and remarks on virtue and beauty that Günderrode worked out in draft form in "Idea of the Earth."

"Letters" was written in late 1805 and early 1806 and intended for Günderrode's third collection, *Melete*. However, Günderrode's lover, Georg Friedrich Creuzer, who was dealing with the publisher on her behalf, canceled its publication when she died. He was afraid of a scandal: the unnamed correspondent ("the Friend") expresses a hope to be united with Eusebio in death, which could be seen as a motivation for suicide. The two correspondents are easily read as foils for Creuzer and Günderrode, especially because in their real-life correspondence, the pair sometimes referred to themselves as "Eusebio" and "the friend."[1] On the other hand, parts of "Letters" resemble Günderrode's correspondence, not with Creuzer, but with her friend Gunda Brentano and Gunda's brother Clemens.[2] One should therefore be cautious

---

[1] Creuzer's letters show that he saw himself as the teacher-figure Eusebio in this piece (SW 3:203–204). The Greek word *eusebeia* (εὐσέβεια) refers to a type of pious virtue; Günderrode and Creuzer also sometimes referred to Creuzer as "the pious one" (*der Fromme*). Creuzer and Günderrode used the masculine form (*der Freund*) to describe Günderrode (e.g., Weißenborn, *Ich sende Dir*, 216, 309, 317).

[2] In the opening line, the "friend" describes their feelings on meeting Eusebio in terms similar to Günderrode's description of meeting Gunda (Letter to Gunda Brentano, 29, 30 August 1801, translated in the Letters section of this volume). The idea of friends as an "echo" for each other, which is referenced in the dedicatory poem, also features in Günderrode's correspondence with Gunda (Letter to Clemens Brentano, 10 June 1804; Letter to Gunda Brentano, 11 August 1801; both translated in the Letters section of this volume).

Karoline von Günderrode. Anna Ezekiel, Oxford University Press. © Oxford University Press 2026.
DOI: 10.1093/9780190089177.003.0004

about reading the correspondents as simply representing Günderrode and Creuzer.

"Letters of Two Friends" covers many central ideas in Günderrode's thought, partly repeating claims from "Idea of the Earth," particularly toward the end. Although this part of "Letters" is very similar to the draft version in "Idea of the Earth," there are interesting differences. Perhaps most significantly, in "Letters," the metaphysical claims are framed as a vision, narrated by a literary character who does not necessarily represent Günderrode herself. By contrast, in "Idea of the Earth," the claims are introduced directly as Günderrode's own, in a densely philosophical account of "forces" and "poles." This creates an enormous difference in the status of the information. Instead of purporting to be a quasi-scientific, objective account of the nature of the universe, the claims in "Letters" are presented as (a) personal (grasped and communicated by a specific individual) and (b) the result of revelation. To Günderrode, this kind of knowledge has higher status than the results of philosophical or scientific inquiry.[3]

"Letters" is also longer than "Idea of the Earth" and therefore includes more information. Günderrode develops some metaphysical claims in more detail, presents them in more concrete terms, or imagines their implications for human experience. For example, "Letters" repeats the claim from "Idea of the Earth" that all individual entities, including human beings, are comprised of immortal "elements" that will mix together after our death and then emerge in new combinations to form new entities. However, in "Letters," this is given a personal and emotional interpretation as the Friend reassures themselves that they will be reunited with Eusebio after death. Against the fear "that your I and mine should be dissolved in the ancient primordial matter of the world," the Friend writes, "I consoled myself that our befriended elements, obeying the laws of attraction, would find each other even in infinite space and join with each other."

The general introduction to this volume outlines some of the implications Günderrode draws from her metaphysics for what happens to us when we die and what this might feel like. In "Letters," Günderrode explores the idea of a form of altered awareness after death from the perspective of individual human experience. Eusebio explains that the deterioration of the body that occurs due to aging is actually the early stages of losing one's individual or particular existence as one dies. Loss of eyesight, hearing, and memory is,

---

[3] See the section on epistemology in the general introduction to this volume.

on this account, the start of losing one's individual perspective and returning to a unified existence merged with the rest of the world: "in age we die away from this particularity. That is why the senses dwindle, memory becomes fainter." Eusebio is claiming that memory and information from sensory organs are required to experience oneself as an individual, separate from the rest of the world; as these are lost, so is one's individuality. He writes: "It is the outer senses that reveal to us the manifold degrees of our opposition with the alien world, but when the partition of personhood crumbles, they may be extinguished." This loss, he adds, is compensated by an increasing focus on an "inner sense"[4] that joins individuals to the infinite: "For eyes are not needed to see what is within us and what is one with it; even without ears we can hear the melody of eternal spirit; and memory is for the past, it is the organ of knowledge of ourselves in the fluctuation of time."

In addition to expanding on many of the ideas drafted in "Idea of the Earth," in the earlier part of "Letters," Günderrode discusses the ills of modernity and the best ways to foster art, religion, and self-cultivation. In the first letter, the Friend bemoans what they see as the impoverishment of the modern age, which they associate with Protestantism. The Friend blames this spiritual impoverishment for a lack of contemporary artistic accomplishment, complaining about a lack of "intuitions that inspire an artist of any kind." They compare this situation unfavorably with artistic production in ancient and medieval periods: "Let us gaze back to more beautiful days," they write, and suggest that they should study "the poets of the past."

To an extent, this admiration of the artistic accomplishments of ancient Greece and Rome (and, more occasionally, medieval Europe) simply echoes typical enlightenment and Romantic attitudes toward certain past cultures.[5] We see something similar, for example, in Friedrich Schlegel's "Speech on Mythology," a seminal early German Romantic text which Günderrode quoted in her notebooks. In this piece, Schlegel argues that modern literature is not as creative, powerful, or original as ancient poetry, and attributes this to a lack of cohesive culture in modern times: "our poetry," he writes, "lacks a central point, as mythology was for the Ancients."[6] This claim motivates Schlegel's call for a "new mythology" to unite and revitalize modern literature.

---

[4] See "The Manes" and "Story of a Brahmin."
[5] Novalis, "Christenheit oder Europa," in *Schriften* 3:507–524.
[6] KFSA 2:312.

In "Letters," Günderrode takes up Schlegel's demand for a new mythology. Like Schlegel,[7] Eusebio and the Friend conclude that one's creative powers can develop through engagement with great cultures—not just from the past but also from outside Europe, especially India. In other words, we can expand and renew our creative and spiritual life by absorbing and assimilating ideas from outside our own milieu.

However, at first, Eusebio and the Friend disagree on what is needed to promote artistic and creative greatness. When the Friend suggests they should revive the glory days of poetic production in the ancient world, Eusebio rejects this idea: "The great masters of the ancient world are certainly there to be read and understood, but [. . .] those masters *were there* [at that specific time and place], and that is why they shall not be born again; infinite nature will always reveal itself anew in infinite time." Rather than trying to recreate the accomplishments of one's predecessors, everyone must develop their own capacities in their own way.

Eusebio also suggests that the Friend may be mistaken about the spiritual and creative poverty of their own culture. Their individual perspective is too narrow to permit a meaningful evaluation of the contributions of their own time: "we see only a few features of the immeasurable carpet into which the earth-spirit weaves the times." He rebukes the Friend for complaining about the state of the world and recommends instead trying to achieve a broader perspective and remember their humble place in the infinite universe.

Eusebio sends the Friend "some books about the religion of the Hindus," which he thinks will inspire this shift in orientation. After reading these, he says, "There will be moments in which you feel yourself stripped of this personal particularity and poverty and again surrendered to the great whole." The books, Eusebio claims, will help the Friend see that everything that exists ("sun and moon, and flower and gemstone, and ether and ocean"), including themselves, is in fact a single, divine unity, which Eusebio describes as "one thing, a holy thing."

This view—that the whole universe and everything in it is one single, infinite spirit or nature that produces itself in all forms—expresses what Günderrode believes is the shared insight of all religions. It is also a foundational tenet of her metaphysics, as she explains in "Idea of the Earth" and the later part of "Letters of Two Friends." This claim is also highlighted in the dedicatory poem at the start of "Letters," titled "To Eusebio," where

---

[7] KFSA 2:319–320.

Günderrode writes: "nature in its holy fulness / Reveals itself fully in each act." That is, divine, infinite nature is embodied in every part of the world. This claim echoes the Christian doctrine that God is fully present in all parts of creation, but Günderrode wants it to be understood as the essential core of *all* religions. In "Letters of Two Friends," she is most concerned to apply this teaching to Hinduism.

"Letters" includes further attempts to syncretize ideas from Christianity and Hinduism. Referring to the vision of the one nature-spirit, which he claims is communicated by the "religion of the Hindus," Eusebio asks:

> Is this not nature beckoning us to turn back from particularity to the common All, to leave the divided life in which the creature wants to be something for itself and yet cannot be? I see rightful damnation in the selfish pride that could not rest in the womb of the eternal but, abandoning it, wanted to cover its poverty and nakedness with the manifold of forms, and became tree and stone and metal and animal and covetous human beings.

This passage—describing "creatures," "damnation," "selfish pride," and covering one's nakedness—clearly references the Christian narrative of the Fall, and fallen humanity's subsequent and ongoing quest for reconciliation with God. As a summary of supposedly Hindu ideas, the passage certainly does not attend to the cultural or historical specificity, let alone diversity, of Indian religions.[8] But that is largely the point of a syncretistic approach such as Günderrode's: the specifics of any religion are largely irrelevant to her; what matters is the shared fundamental insight into the divine unity of nature that she thinks is at the heart of all religions.

Günderrode's knowledge of cultures outside Europe was relatively sophisticated for her time. She had access to cutting-edge research by Creuzer, one of the leading scholars of his day in European, Asian, and North African mythologies. Nonetheless, both Creuzer's and Günderrode's understanding of religions other than Christianity was inevitably less detailed than that of their own Christian culture and, furthermore, filtered through a lens of enlightenment-era attitudes that were themselves shaped by Europe's Christian heritage. Nonetheless, "Letters" remains a key text for

---

[8] On Günderrode and Indian religions, see David Takamura, "Illusion and Individuation in the Orientalisms of Arthur Schopenhauer and Karoline von Günderrode," *The German Quarterly* 96.3 (2023): 308–325.

understanding Günderrode's metaphysics and her views on personal identity, aging, self-development, creativity, culture, and religion.

Letters of Two Friends

To Eusebio.

Forgive, oh friend! that I with childish speech,
Dare to, babbling, softly echo chords,
From your heart's deep sanctuary,
But like a schoolchild hush before the highest.

And still I want to speak, yes, to your glory,
Forgive my boldness, that I do not quail.
For I mean the summer with one flower,
And I stole only one beam from the day.

But nature in its holy fulness
Reveals itself fully in each act,
The highest life in the deepest silence.

I glimpsed a trait from your image,
However richly thoughts transform in you,
It is you, wholly, in your pious mildness.

To Eusebio.

I often think back with joy to the day when we first found each other, when
I faced you with reverent shyness, like a layperson eager for knowledge faces
the high priest. I had set myself to please you, if possible, and my sense of
my own worth would have been shaken to its foundations if you had turned
away from me indifferently. But I still do not grasp how I managed to win
you over to such a degree; in that conversation a double portion of my own
spirit must have been upon me.[9] With that conversation, a new life began

---

[9] Cf. 2 Kings 2:9: "Elisha said, I pray thee, let a double portion of thy spirit be upon me" (King
James Bible online). In this story, Elisha is inheriting Elijah's power of prophecy and asks for a double
portion.

for me, for only in you have I found, as a prevailing condition, that true el-
evation to the highest intuitions in which everything worldly disappears as
an insubstantial dream: in you, the highest ideas gain earthly reality for me.
We other mortals must first fast and prepare ourselves bodily and spiritually when we want to take communion; you receive God daily without these
institutions.

Oh friend, the heavenly powers are not so favorable to me, and I am often
morose, and do not know what I should be most morose about: whether
about myself, or about this time, for it too is poor in intuitions that inspire an
artist of any kind. Everything great and mighty has been shared out among
an infinite mass, in which it almost disappears.[10] Ill-fated fairness of destiny!
So that none feast and none hunger, we must all make do with meager scant-
iness. Is it a wonder, then, that economy, in every sense and in all things,
has grown into such a considerable virtue? This wretchedness of life, let us
admit, emerged with Protestantism. Everyone is allowed access to the communion cup, laypersons as well as the consecrated, so that no-one can drink
enough to become full of God, and the drops are enough for no-one. Then
they do not know what is missing, and dispute and protest about it.

—But why am I telling you this! You have often beheld these evils of
our time in others, but they cannot touch you, for you can only see them
as opposed to your innermost nature, and they do not arouse oppositions
within you.

So enough of this bloated century, the folly of which will sicken even distant times. Let us gaze back to more beautiful days, to what has been. Perhaps
now we have achieved a level of cultivation where our highest and worthiest
aspiration should aim at understanding the great masters of the ancient
world, fertilizing our meager life with the wealth and fullness of their ideas,
so rich in poetry. For we are isolated from nature by restricted circumstances,
from true enjoyment of life by even more restricted concepts, from all large-
scale activity by our forms of government. Thus, firmly surrounded on all
sides, all that is left to us is to turn our gaze to heaven, or to turn it broodingly
within ourselves. Are not nearly all kinds of modern poetry determined by

---

[10] Günderrode is referring to the emphasis on individual piety in Protestantism, particularly in
the Lutheran and pietistic forms that were prevalent in Germany at the time. These movements
prioritized the inner relationship of each person with God over the mediation of a priest between
God and the congregation (as in Catholicism). Elsewhere (e.g., "Story of a Brahmin"), Günderrode
claims that the most essential aspects of religion are found through individual introspection, but here
she criticizes this idea, or at least suggests that something important might be lost through excessive
focus on individualized religion.

this, our condition? They are either line-drawings, which strive up incorporeally to dissolve in infinite space, or pale, light-shy spirits of earth that we conjure speculatively from the depths of our being; nowhere are they powerful, fleshy figures. We may boast of the heights and the depths, but we are completely unable to spread out comfortably. Like Shakespeare's Julius Caesar I want to cry: "Bring fat people to me, and those who sleep peacefully, I fear this haggard Cassius."[11]

—Because I cannot reach beyond the bounds of my time, does it not seem better to you if I abandon the path of my own poetic production and begin a serious study of the poets of the past and especially of the middle ages? Indeed, I know that it will cost me effort. I will have to cut off a branch of my nature, as it were, for I behold myself most happily in something my spirit has produced, and I only have true consciousness through this begotten thing. But to gain something more surely one must always give up something else; that is a universal destiny, and it should not frighten me.

But one thing has always painfully assailed my deepest soul, and it is this: that behind every peak there hides a downward slope. This thought makes joy fade for me even when it is fresh and young, and adds an unnamable sorrow to all my life. That is why every beginning delights me more than anything that has been completed, and nothing touches me so deeply as the sunset: I would like to sink with it each evening into the same night, so as not to survive its going out. Happy are those to whom it is granted to die in the bloom of joy, who may rise from the Eucharist of life before the candles have faded and the wine is poured more sparingly. Eusebio! If one day the friendly light of your life should be extinguished for me, oh! then kindly take me with you, like the divine Pollux took his mortal brother,[12] and let me go together with you to Orcus[13] and to the immortal gods, for I do not want to live without you, you who are the dearest content of my thoughts and feelings, around whom all the forms and blossoms of my being wind, like the labyrinthine veins around my heart, which fills them all and sets them aglow.

---

[11] Paraphrasing William Shakespeare, *The Life and Death of Julius Caesar*, Act 1, Scene 2.

[12] In Greek and Roman mythology, Castor and Pollux were twins born to Leda, a married woman who was seduced by Zeus. Pollux was Zeus' son, and immortal, whereas Castor was the mortal son of Leda's husband. After Castor died, Zeus allowed Pollux to share his immortality with Castor and the twins became the constellation Gemini.

[13] The Roman underworld and also the name of its king.

Fragments from Eusebio's Answer

—The only things that have form for us are those we can survey, but we are surrounded by this time like embryos by the body of their mother, so what can we meaningfully say about it? We see single symptoms, hear one heartbeat of the century, and want to conclude from this that it is diseased. Perhaps even those indications that seem alarming to us are part of the individual health of this time. But each individuality is an abyss of deviations, a night that is illuminated only sparingly by the light of universal concepts.[14] Therefore, friend, because we see only a few features of the immeasurable carpet into which the earth-spirit weaves the times, let us be humble. There is a surrender in which alone lies bliss and perfection and peace, a kind of contemplation, which I might call dissolution in the divine; let us strive to reach this, and not complain about the destinies of the universe.

But so that you see more clearly what I mean by this, I am sending you some books about the religion of the Hindus. The wonders of ancient wisdom, set down in mysterious symbols, will touch your soul; there will be moments in which you feel yourself stripped of this personal particularity and poverty and again surrendered to the great whole; where you more than just think that everything that is now sun and moon, and flower and gemstone, and ether and ocean, is one thing, a holy thing, which rests unceasingly in its depths, blessed in itself, eternally embracing itself, without desire for the action and suffering of the duality that stirs its surface. In such moments, when we can no longer think reflectively, because that which awakens our individual, earthly consciousness has disappeared to our outer senses under the dominance of inner contemplation[15]—in such moments I understand death, the mystery of religion, the sacrifice of the son,[16] and love's unending longing. Is this not nature beckoning us to turn back from

---

[14] At its most basic, the idea of "universal concepts" is simply that general concepts, such as the concept "horse," apply to many particular objects (e.g., all individual horses). However, Günderrode's reference to "deviations" suggests that she may be referring to a philosophical tradition that saw universal concepts as more than this: as ideal forms, which actual objects imperfectly embody or realize. This tradition goes back to Plato's doctrine of the forms (or "ideas"); Plato's model was adapted by many philosophers including Kant (in the Third Critique) and Schelling (e.g., in *Bruno*), as well as by Goethe in his *Metamorphosis of Plants* (1790). On Goethe's model, for example, the leaves of every kind of plant are variations on the same ideal underlying structure—the ideal leaf—but deviate from this ideal in various ways. We never encounter the ideal leaf in reality, but have to extrapolate its characteristics from studying real leaves.

[15] Cf. "The Manes," where the Master explains the contrast between the outer senses (sight, touch, hearing, etc.) and "inner sense" or the "eye of spirit."

[16] I.e., the sacrifice on the cross of Jesus Christ.

particularity to the common All, to leave the divided life in which the creature wants to be something for itself and yet cannot be? I see rightful damnation in the selfish pride that could not rest in the womb of the eternal but, abandoning it, wanted to cover its poverty and nakedness with the manifold of forms, and became tree and stone and metal and animal and covetous human beings.

Yes, oh friend, even that which no-one wants to contemplate without grumbling and doubt: dull age—I understand its higher sense now. A person's life shall develop over the course of the years, delight in *being for itself*, celebrate its triumph in the bloom of youth; but in age we die away from this particularity. That is why the senses dwindle, memory becomes fainter, desire weaker, and being's joyful courage is dulled in intimations of approaching dissolution.—It is the outer senses that reveal to us the manifold degrees of our opposition with the alien world, but when the partition of personhood crumbles, they may be extinguished anyway. For eyes are not needed to see what is within us and what is one with it; even without ears we can hear the melody of eternal spirit; and memory is for the past, it is the organ of knowledge of ourselves in the fluctuation of time. But where there is no time, no past nor future, but eternal present, memory is not needed. Thus what dies off from us in age is the entirety of our relationship to the external world; and someone in old age who did not know anything except this relationship might well be called *dead*.—Thus I do not fear the later years, and death is welcome to me; and may the goal of our efforts be to achieve this peace of contemplation in all things.

Your course lies clear before me, most beloved! For I have known you from the first moment we drew near to each other, which—the awareness of this will remain with me forever—was ordained by God. Never have I beheld a person's face for the first time like that, never have I had such a feeling at a human voice; and this divinity and necessity has always remained with me when I think of you. And so I also know what is necessary in you and for you, and how you should live fully in nature, poetry, and divine wisdom. I know that it does not befit *you* to prescribe such timid studies for yourself. The great masters of the ancient world are certainly there to be read and understood, but, if it is a question of art *schools*, then I say that those masters *were there* [at that specific time and place], and that is why they shall not be born again; infinite nature will always reveal itself anew in infinite time. In the wealth of the centuries Brahma appeared often, but always in new transformations; he never chose the same form again. Thus everyone does and poeticizes[17] that to which they are called, to which spirit drives them, and does not deny themselves any songs except discordant ones. But I am not seriously apprehensive for you: the striving force will not let someone it inhabits rest; their heart will be sore and anxious until the newborn idea has stilled birth's pain and longing.

Yesterday I lived a pair of blessed hours far above the earth. I had climbed a mountain, around which any trace of human cultivation for purpose and use disappeared: I felt serene and well. Two magnificent herons hovering over me bathed their carefree breasts in the blue air of heaven. Ah! To belong to heaven like that, I thought, and everything earthly seemed small to me. In such moments only the eternal holds value, the creating genius and the holy mind. Then I thought of you, as always when nature moves me. I often gave thoughts of you to the river, when the sun's last beams illuminated it, as if its waves would carry them to you and play around your head. Farewell! In my best hours I am always with you.—

To Eusebio.

One of the greatest epochs of my little life has passed by, Eusebio! I stood on the dividing line between life and death. Why do human beings baulk at dying, I said to myself in that moment? I look forward to each night when I choose unconsciousness and dark dreams over brighter life; why do I dread the long night and deep slumber? What deeds still await me, or what better knowledge on earth, that I should have to live longer?—A necessity births us all into personhood; a common night devours us all. Years will give me no better wisdom, and if learning, doing, and suffering are still needed there below,[18] a god will give me what I need. So I comforted myself, but the thoughts that I love came to me, and the heroes I have worshipped from youth called out to me: "Why are you longing for the night at high noon? Why plunge into the ancient ocean and melt away in it with all that is dear to you?" So the ideas [Vorstellungen] changed within me, and I thought of you, and always of you, and almost everything else only in relation to you, and if

---

[17] The German word *dichten* can mean simply "to write poetry," but in early German Romanticism conveys the idea of "raising," "romanticization," or "poeticization," i.e., the working of human creativity upon natural events to make them more spiritual (Novalis, *Schriften* 2:545 #105; see also 2:568 #207, 2:533 #31–51).

[18] I.e., the underworld or realm of the dead.

it were indeed granted to mortals to save one of their goods from the ship-
wreck of earthly life then I would certainly have taken your memory with me
down to the shadows. But [the thought] that you could be lost to me was the
most painful of thoughts. I said[19] that your I and mine should be dissolved in
the ancient primordial matter of the world; then I consoled myself that our
befriended elements, obeying the laws of attraction, would find each other
even in infinite space and join with each other. So hope and doubt surged up
and down in my soul, and courage and faintheartedness.

But destiny willed it—I still live.—But what is it, then, life? This possession, already relinquished and acquired again?[20] I often ask myself this. What
does it mean, that from the All of nature a being cuts itself loose with such
consciousness, and feels torn off from it? Why do human beings cling with
such strength to thoughts and opinions, as if they were what is eternal? Why
can they die for them, when precisely these thoughts are lost to them with
their death? And why, if these thoughts and concepts die with individuals
anyway, why are they always brought forth from these individuals all over
again, to forge ahead, through the ranks of the generations that follow each
other, to immortality in time?

For a long time I did not know an answer to these questions, and they
bewildered me. Then suddenly, in a revelation, everything was clear to
me, and will remain so forever. I know that life is only the product of the
deepest contact and attraction of the elements;[21] I know that all its blossoms
and leaves, which we call thoughts and sensations, must wither when that
contact is dissolved, and that individual life is given up to the law of mortality. But as certain as this is to me, just as much is something else beyond all
doubt for me: the immortality of life in the whole. For this whole is just life, it
surges up and down in its parts—the elements—and whatever has returned
to it through dissolution (which we sometimes call death) mingles with it
according to laws of affinity, i.e., the similar mingles with what is similar to
it. But once these elements have been driven to life in the organism, they
become different; they have become livelier, like two who have trained in
long struggle are stronger when it has ended than before they struggled. The

---

[19] Morgenthaler's edition has "hesitated" or "was apprehensive" (*zagte*) instead of "said" (*sagte*)
(SW 1:358).
[20] This sentence has connotations of the Christian idea of resurrection. It is also consistent with
Günderrode's claim that the world is comprised of living beings which, after they die, decompose so
that the materials that formed them can become parts of new living beings.
[21] From this sentence until the end of the letter, cf. "Idea of the Earth."

elements are like this, for they are alive, and every living force is strengthened by exercise. Thus when they return to the earth, they increase the earth's life. The earth bears the life-material given back to it again in other appearances, until through ever new transformations everything capable of life in it has come to life. This would be when all mass had become organic.—

So each mortal gives back to the earth a raised, more developed elemental life, which it cultivates further in ascending forms; and the organism, by assimilating ever more developed elements, must become ever more perfect and universal. Thus the All comes to life through the downfall of the particular, and the particular survives immortally in the All whose life it developed while alive, and elevates and increases even after death, and so by living and dying helps to realize the idea of the earth.

Thus, however my elements may be dispersed, when they join to what is already living they will elevate it; when they join to those things whose life resembles death, they will animate them. And it seems to me, Eusebio, that the idea of the Indians of the transmigration of souls corresponds to this opinion; and the elements may wander and search no longer only when the earth has thoroughly attained its proper existence: the organic. But all forms of the organism that have been produced until now must not suffice the earth-spirit, for it always breaks them up again and seeks new ones; whereas it would not be able to destroy things that were wholly the same as it, for they would be the same as it and inseparable from it.

This perfect sameness of inner essence and form cannot, it seems to me, be achieved in a multiplicity of forms. The essence of the earth is only one, therefore its form may also only be one, not various, and the earth would only attain its actual true being when it dissolved all its appearances in a collective organism, when spirit and body penetrated each other so that all body, all form would also at the same time be thought and soul, and all thought at the same time form and body, and a truly transfigured body, without lack or illness and immortal, and thus wholly different from what we call body or material, when we attribute to it transience, illness, inertia, and deficiency, for this kind of body is, as it were, only a failed attempt to produce that immortal divine body.—I do not know whether the earth will be successful in organizing itself immortally like this. There may be a disproportion of essence and form in its primal elements that always hinders it from this; and perhaps the totality of our solar system is needed to bring about this equilibrium; perhaps even this does not suffice for it and it is a task for the entire universe.

From this perspective, Eusebio, it also became clear to me what the great thoughts of truth, justice, virtue, love, and beauty claim, which germinate in the soil of personhood and, soon overgrowing it, stretch up to the free heavens, an immortal growth that does not perish with the soil in which it developed, but always generates itself anew in new individuals. For it is the enduring, the eternal; but the individual is the fragile vessel for the drink of immortality.—For let us consider more precisely, Eusebio: are not all virtues and excellences approximations to that highest perfect condition, to the extent that particularity can approach it? Truth is only the expression of what is altogether the same as itself, and therefore only the eternal, which is subjected to no changes of times and conditions, is perfectly true. Justice is striving, in isolation from each other, to be the same. Beauty is the outer expression of equilibrium achieved with itself. Love is the reconciliation of personhood with the All, and virtue of all kinds is only one thing, i.e., a forgetting of personhood and particularity for the All.

Thus the condition of the dissolution of multiplicity in unity is already prepared here[22] in a spiritual way by love and virtue, for where love is, there is only one mind [*Sinn*], and where virtue is, there is the same striving for acts of justice, goodness, and concord. But whatever is the same as itself, and externally and internally bears the expression of this harmonious being in itself, and itself is this expression; whatever is one and not torn asunder in multiplicity, that is precisely that perfect, immortal, and unchangeable thing, that organism, that I consider the goal of nature, history, and the times—in short, of the universe. Through every act of untruth, injustice, and selfishness this blessed state is made more distant, and the god of the earth, who expresses his longing for a better life in every mind through receptivity to what is excellent, is bound in new chains, but in violated conscience laments that his blessed, divine life is still far off.

---

[22] I.e., in this world, as opposed to the afterlife.

3

The Manes

Introduction

Günderrode's dialogue "The Manes" was published in 1804 in Günderrode's first collection, *Poems and Fantasies*.[1] The "Manes" of the title refers to a kind of spirit in ancient Roman mythology, which occupied an intermediate place between deities and ghosts. They were sometimes considered the souls of dead relatives or loved ones and are associated with the practice of ancestor veneration, in which dead ancestors are thought to protect and intercede for their living descendants. At the time Günderrode was writing, Manes featured relatively frequently in works of literature;[2] Günderrode may also have known details about them through her study of ancient history and mythology.

The idea of spirits of the dead that could be contacted by the living and intercede on their behalf is one that was readily integrated with Günderrode's other claims. In particular, it fits well with her focus on exploring possibilities for experiences after death and her position that all things in the universe are ultimately connected as part of the same underlying, infinite unity.[3]

In "The Manes," a teacher explains to his student the nature and significance of the student's strange sense of longing for a long-dead king. The teacher makes three claims that are integral to Günderrode's thought. First, that the dead "live on" in the living. Second, that our feelings of longing for the dead are due to an "affinity," "harmony," or "connection" with them that is not destroyed by death. And third, that we can be aware of this connection and other aspects of the world that are hidden to our normal perceptual apparatus through an "inner sense."

---

[1] A different version of "The Manes" appeared in Brentano-von Arnim's book *Günderode* ("Selections from *Günderode*," in *Women Philosophers in the Long Nineteenth Century: The German Tradition*, ed. Dalia Nassar and Kristin Gjesdal [New York: OUP, 2021], 92–121).

[2] E.g., Karl Ludwig von Knebel's 1796 poem "Cynthia's Shade," which Günderrode excerpted in her notebooks.

[3] For details on these aspects of Günderrode's thought, see the section on metaphysics in the general introduction to this volume.

Karoline von Günderrode. Anna Ezekiel, Oxford University Press. © Oxford University Press 2026.
DOI: 10.1093/9780190089177.003.0005

First, the teacher explains that the student's strange feelings about the dead king are due to the fact that the dead continue to live and have an effect on the living. The student summarizes his teacher's explanation: "Thus a great man lives on and continues to work in me [...] according to the way that I absorb him, according to how and whether I want to remember him." Here, Günderrode is building on ideas about the relationship between the living and the dead that were in circulation at the time. For example, the early German Romantic writer Novalis claims: "The human being continues to live, to be effective, only in the idea, through the memory of his being. For the time being there is no other means for spirits to be effective in this world. For this reason it is a duty to think of the dead. It is the only way to remain in community with them."[4] "Novalis" was the pen name of the poet, novelist, and philosopher Friedrich von Hardenberg (1772–1801), one of the most influential figures in the development of Romanticism. Similar claims appear in work by other prominent thinkers of the time, including in the theologian Friedrich Schleiermacher's *Soliloquies*, which Günderrode excerpted in her notebooks,[5] in writings by the philosopher, theologian, and mystic Emanuel Swedenborg (1688–1772), and in Kant's response to Swedenborg in his early essay "Dreams of a Spirit-Seer."[6]

In her later work, Günderrode developed an idea of the continued life of one individual in another (or in several others) after death: she will claim that the elements that comprise one individual are reused to form new beings and therefore literally live on.[7] In "Idea of the Earth" and "Letters of Two Friends," she explains that they do so according to "laws of affinity" or "harmony," which is also the explanation given by the teacher in "The Manes" for why aspects of one (dead) individual reemerge in another. He explains that the dead king "only lives on in you to the extent that you have a sense for him, to the extent that your disposition makes you capable of receiving him inwardly, to the extent that you have something homogeneous with him." On Günderrode's model, remembrance of the dead is explained as the literal continued life and activity of the dead through the incorporation of aspects of their personality in living individuals. In her later version of this idea, she

---

[4] Novalis, *Schriften* 2:426–427 #34.

[5] Schleiermacher, *Monologen*, 125–226. See the chapter on Günderrode's notes on Schleiermacher, later in this volume.

[6] Immanuel Kant, *Träume eines Geistersehers, erläutert durch Träume der Metaphysik* (Königsberg: Johann Jacob Kanter, 1766), AA II, 317–373.

[7] For more detail on this feature of Günderrode's thought, see the section on metaphysics in the general introduction to this volume.

adds a more detailed account of what these "homogeneous" factors are: the "elements" of "Idea of the Earth" and "Letters of Two Friends."

When she wrote "The Manes," Günderrode had not yet added these metaphysical details to her model. In fact, the metaphysical implications of her account are not her main concern in this text; instead, she focuses on how this idea of "living on" can explain experiences of friendship and love. She claims that these experiences can be understood as the feeling of part of you being drawn to a corresponding thing within someone else. For Günderrode, the same process occurs whether that person is living or dead. In "The Manes," the teacher claims, "Death [. . .] does not tear the bond between me and similar souls. But the progress of one soul while another remains behind can cancel out this fellowship, like someone who has advanced in all virtues will not harmonize with a friend of their youth who remains ignorant and crude." Friends, on the other hand (or any individuals who share ideas and outlooks), do harmonize with each other.

"The Manes" continues with an account of what makes it possible for us to be aware of and understand this attraction to others: our "inner sense." The teacher discloses that the student's experience of longing for the dead king indicates that he is ready to develop his capacities further. He explains that "Someone whose spiritual eye has opened sees things that are invisible to others, which are connected with that person." This, he adds, is the essence of religion and religious revelation. The teacher claims that we can become aware of the connections between "all harmonious things" through the development of an "inner sense," which he also calls an "inner eye," a "spiritual eye" (or "mind's eye"), and "the deepest and finest organ of the soul."

At the time Günderrode was writing, the idea of an "inner sense" was a popular one that carried diverse meanings. Helga Dormann, in her book on the inner sense in Günderrode's work, notes that inner sense was construed "on the one hand as an organ of aesthetic feeling that experiences sensations when 'viewing the beautiful' (Hutcheson, Winckelmann, Herder), on the other hand as a sense that serves an individual's self-perception (Locke, Kant). In addition, it is defined as an organ through which the individual is able to communicate with the spiritual world (Swedenborg, Mesmer)."[8]

As well as the thinkers just mentioned, Günderrode's idea of the "inner sense" can be linked to the Dutch philosopher François Hemsterhuis'

---

[8] Helga Dormann, *Die Kunst des inneren Sinns. Mythisierung der inneren und äusseren Natur im Werk Karoline von Günderrodes* (Würzburg: Königshausen und Neumann, 2004), 99.

conception of the "moral organ"[9] and Schleiermacher's focus on introspection as the source and location of genuine religious experience, which he also calls "inner sense."[10] Both these thinkers present this inner sense or organ as a natural capacity that must be developed in order for human nature to be fully realized. Similarly, in "The Manes," the teacher claims that the inner sense "is totally undeveloped in almost all people and only there in seed form." Most people, he explains, are distracted from the development of their inner sense by the business of everyday life and are therefore cut off from understanding the real nature of the universe, deeper connections with other people, and religious experience.

Toward the end of the dialogue, the teacher heads off a potential objection by "doubters and vilifiers" of the inner sense, claiming, "I do not need to explain everything miraculous as fraudulent or as a deception of the senses." This statement may be a response to Kant's dismissive view of certain accounts of inner sense, especially that of Swedenborg. In his 1766 piece "Dreams of a Spirit-Seer," Kant addresses Swedenborg's conception of the "inner sense" as a means of communicating with spirits. His description of Swedenborg's claims in this piece includes numerous points that correspond with "The Manes," including the possibility of an "immediate inner connection" with the spirit world; the idea that everyone has the capacity to connect with the spirit world but only those whose inward "spiritual sense" has awakened can do so; the claim that individuals connect with the spirits of those with whom they have something in common; the claim that this connection endures through death; and the possibility of an effect by spirits, including spirits of the dead, on the living. The number of correspondences suggests that Günderrode may have read "Dreams of a Spirit-Seer" and intended to refute Kant's objections.[11]

Günderrode mobilizes multiple meanings that have been ascribed to inner sense, according to which, in Dormann's words, it can "serve the knowledge of hidden connections, perceive an immaterial force, synthesize multifarious sensory impressions, open what is secret and forgotten, and be aroused by beautiful nature."[12] Despite their diversity, these meanings all see the inner

---

[9] See the introduction to Günderrode's notes on Hemsterhuis later in this volume.

[10] Dormann, *Kunst des inneren Sinns*, 104, 117–119; Christmann, *Identitätsgewinn*, 170–171.

[11] There is some debate about the extent to which Kant was criticizing Swedenborg and the extent to which his mockery masked a degree of identification with Swedenborg's ideas (see Michelle Grier, "Swedenborg and Kant on Spiritual Intuition," in *On the True Philosopher and the True Philosophy: Essays on Swedenborg*, ed. Stephen McNeilly [London: The Swedenborg Society, 2002], 1–2).

[12] Dormann, *Kunst des inneren Sinns*, 130.

sense as allowing us to experience aspects of existence that are not available to our normal perceptual apparatus and that elude our conscious grasp. In other pieces translated in this volume,[13] Günderrode suggests what it would be like to have such experiences and develops an epistemology that justifies the attempt to look beyond discursive concepts into the realm of revelation and intuition.

The Manes

A Fragment.

Student. Wise master! Yesterday I was in the catacombs of the kings of Sweden. The day before I had read the story of Gustav Adolph,[14] and I approached his casket with the most peculiar and painful feeling. His life and his deeds passed before my spirit: I saw at the same time his life and his death, his great activity and the deep peace in which he has already slumbered for almost two centuries. I recalled the dark, dreadful time in which he lived, and my mind resembled a crypt out of which climb the shadows of the past, pale and faltering. I wept for his death with hot tears, as if he had only fallen today. Gone! Lost! Past! I said to myself; are these all the fruits of a great life? These thoughts, these feelings overpowered me, and I had to leave the crypt.

I sought distraction, I sought other kinds of pain, but the gloomy underground spirit follows me everywhere. I cannot be rid of this melancholy; it lies like a mourning band over my present. This age seems insipid and empty to me; a painful longing draws me violently to the past. "Gone! Past!" calls my spirit. Oh, if only I were gone too and had never seen this poor time, in which the earlier world vanishes, in which its greatness is lost.—

Teacher. Lost, young man? It is not lost, in no respect; only our eyes cannot survey the long, infinite chain from a cause to all its effects.[15] But even if you do not want to think about that, still you cannot call something lost and gone that moves you so strongly, that works so powerfully upon you. I have known

---

[13] Esp. "The Wanderer's Descent," "The Adept," "The Frank in Egypt," *Immortalita,* and "Story of a Brahmin."

[14] Gustav II Adolf (or Adolph) "the Great," king of Sweden from 1617 to 1632.

[15] Günderrode is referring to the idea of a causal chain, i.e., the idea that one event causes a subsequent one, which causes another, and so on. At the time, there was considerable philosophical and theological attention to the question whether free will could exist in a material universe in which events are determined causally. Here, Günderrode does not directly address this question, but only suggests that whatever causal effects a person may have in the world continue after death.

you a long time, and it seems to me that your own destiny and the present have hardly moved you so intensely as the memory of this great king. Does he not live in you now? Or do you only call life that which lives on in flesh and in what is visible? And is that gone and lost to you which still works in your mind and is there?

Student. If that is a life, then it is no more than a pale shadow-life, for the memory of what has been, of what is real, is more than the pale shadow of this reality!

Teacher. The positive present is the smallest and most fleeting point; as you become aware of the present, it is already over. The consciousness of enjoyment always lies in the memory. In this sense, the past can only be observed, whether it passed long ago or just now.

Student. It is true. Thus a great man lives on and continues to work in me not according to his way, but according to mine, according to the way that I absorb him, according to how and whether I want to remember him.

Teacher. Indeed, he only lives on in you to the extent that you have a sense for him, to the extent that your disposition makes you capable of receiving him inwardly, to the extent that you have something homogeneous with him. Anything in you that is unlike him cannot become connected with him, and he cannot work upon it. All things work only with this limitation. That for which you have no sense is lost to you, like the world of colors is lost to the blind.

Student. From this it follows that nothing is wholly lost, that causes continue to work (or, as you express it, to *live on*) in their effects, but that they can only work on that which has receptivity or sense for them.

Master.[16] Completely correct.

Student. Good! The world and reason may be satisfied with this *not being lost*, by this kind of living on, but to me it is not enough. A deep longing leads me back into the womb of the past; I want to be immediately connected with the Manes of great antiquity.

---

[16] Here, Günderrode writes "master" instead of "teacher," reflecting the student's first statement to the teacher: "Wise master!" Possibly, this indicates a change between earlier drafts and the final version.

Teacher. Do you think that is possible?

Student. I had thought it impossible before wishing drew me there. Just a short time ago I would have considered any question of this sort to be foolish. Today I wish the connection with the spiritual world might be possible—yes, it seems I am inclined to find it believable.

Teacher. It seems to me that the Manes of Gustav Adolph have helped your inner eye to a happy birth, and you seem to be ripe to hear my opinion about these subjects.

As surely as all harmonious things are connected in a certain way, whether they are visible or invisible, just as surely we, too, are connected with *that part* of the spiritual world that harmonizes with us. A similar or identical thought in different heads, even if they never know of each other, is, in a spiritual sense, a connection. The death of a person connected with me in this way does not cancel out this connection. Death is a chemical process, a separation of forces, but no annihilator: it does not tear the bond between me and similar souls. But the progress of one soul while another remains behind can cancel out this fellowship, like someone who has advanced in all virtues will not harmonize with a friend of their youth who remains ignorant and crude. You will easily be able to apply what I have said in general and to particular cases?

Student. Perfectly! You say harmony between forces is connection, and death does not cancel out this connection, because it only divides and does not annihilate.

Teacher. I added to that: the cancelling out of that which actually makes up this harmony (for example, changes of outlooks and opinions, if the harmony consists in these) must also necessarily cancel out this connection.

Student. That did not escape my attention.

Teacher. Good. A connection with the dead can therefore take place, if they have not stopped harmonizing with us?

Student. Granted.

Teacher. It just comes down to becoming aware of this connection. Forces that are only spiritual cannot be revealed to our outer senses; they do not work upon us through our eyes and ears, but through the only organ by which a connection with them is possible: through the inner sense—on this they work immediately. This inner sense, the deepest and finest organ of the soul, is totally undeveloped in almost all people and only there in seed form.— The noise of the world, the business of trade, the habit of considering only the surface and only what is superficial, do not allow this organ to develop, to become clearly conscious. For this reason, [the existence of this organ] is not generally acknowledged, and what is revealed in it here and there in all ages has always encountered so many doubters and vilifiers, and until now it has only been received and had an effect in the rarest people of the rarest individuality.—I am far from arguing for ridiculous spiritual apparitions and visions, but I can think clearly that the inner sense can be affected to such a degree that inner appearances can come before the bodily eyes, just as, conversely, outer appearances usually come before the spiritual eye. So I do not need to explain everything miraculous as fraudulent or as a deception of the senses. Still, I recall that in everyday speech one calls this development of the inner sense "oversensitive imagination."

Someone whose spiritual eye has opened sees things that are invisible to others, which are connected with that person. Religions emerged from this inner sense, and many apocalypses[17] of ancient and modern times. Out of this capacity of the inner sense to perceive connections which are invisible to other people (whose spiritual eye is closed) emerges prophecy, for this is nothing other than the gift of connecting the present and the past with the future, of seeing the necessary connection of causes and effects: prophecy is the sense for the future. One cannot learn the art of divination; the sense for it is mysterious, and it develops in a mysterious way. It often reveals itself only like a quick flash that is then buried again by dark night. One cannot call spirits through incantations, but they can reveal themselves to the spirit, the sensitive can sense them, they can appear to the inner sense.—

The teacher fell silent and his listener left him. Various thoughts moved his inner being, and his whole soul strove to take possession of what he had heard.

---

[17] In its original meaning, "apocalypse" meant "revelation," although in modern times it is used to refer to the end of the world.

4

The Malabarian Widows

Introduction

This poem from Günderrode's third collection, *Melete*, is philosophically interesting because it shows Günderrode using her ideas about metaphysics
to explain human experiences. According to Günderrode's metaphysics, all
beings in the universe, including human beings, are made of indestructible component parts that she calls "elements."[1] Our "elements" disperse
when we die, after which they can join together with other elements to form
new entities. What draws the elements together to create individual beings
is, Günderrode claims, a force of attraction between similar or homogeneous elements. This force is also, she argues, the mechanism that underlies
feelings of love, friendship, and attraction to others. That is, some of our own
elements and some of the elements that constitute certain other people are
pulled together by a force of attraction, and we experience this pull as love
or friendship. After we die, this attraction will pull the mutually attracted
elements together even more strongly, causing them to join together and
create a new being or entity out of the parts of two (or more) beings that
have died.[2]

In "The Malabarian Widows," Günderrode claims that this process
has been understood by Indian cultures and is reflected in the practice of
sati, in which a widow is burned to death on her husband's funeral pyre. In
Günderrode's idealized view of this practice, the bereaved widow hastens
the joining of her constitutive elements with those of her dead husband by
killing herself: "Custom has understood love's meaning," writes Günderrode;
"Death becomes love's sweet celebration, / The separated elements unified."

Günderrode thinks of sati as a voluntary act by a widow, motivated
by the widow's desire to be united with her beloved husband after death.

---

[1] For details, see the section on metaphysics in the general introduction to this volume.
[2] See, e.g., "The Manes" and "Letters of Two Friends," both translated earlier in this volume.

Karoline von Günderrode. Anna Ezekiel, Oxford University Press. © Oxford University Press 2026.
DOI: 10.1093/9780190089177.003.0006

THE MALABARIAN WIDOWS 75

However, this view is highly problematic when considered in relation to the real-world, historical practice of sati. "The Malabarian Widows" has rightly been criticized for romanticizing sati, ignoring its cultural and historical context, and uncritically adopting colonial framings of the practice. Barbara Becker-Cantarino notes that Günderrode's poem misrepresents the nature of marriage in India, which (as in many parts of the world) was historically an economic rather than romantic arrangement. Becker-Cantarino also points out that the poem obscures the coercion and lack of options for widows that led to many instances of sati, which was often either forced or undertaken as an escape from the life of poverty and scorn that awaited many widows. The practice was also highly sexist: only women, never men, were expected to self-immolate on their spouse's pyre.[3] Stephanie Galasso argues that "The Malabarian Widows" takes up a tradition of European depictions of sati that neglects cultural diversity within India and repeats colonial narratives about the practice.[4] In reality, sati was never a widespread or universally accepted practice; it has long been illegal in India and, even before this, had a patchy and contested history. As Galasso notes, rather than reflecting the complex historical realities of sati, Günderrode's poem adopts European literary depictions that romanticize the practice or present it as an instance of native savagery in contrast to European "civilization."[5]

Despite Günderrode's problematic representation of sati, "The Malabarian Widows" is useful for understanding her philosophical views, in particular the connections between her metaphysics and her views on love and death. The poem also provides an interesting perspective on Günderrode's appropriation of cultural practices in order to express philosophical claims.

---

[3] Barbara Becker-Cantarino, "The 'New Mythology': Myth and Death in Karoline von Günderrode's Literary Work," in *Women and Death 3: Women's Representations of Death in German Culture since 1500*, ed. Clare Bielby and Anna Richards (Rochester, NY: Camden House, 2010), 66.

[4] Stephanie Galasso, "Form and Contention: *Sati* as Custom in Günderrode's 'Die Malabarische Witwen,'" *Goethe Yearbook* 24 (2017): 197–220. Examples include Antoine-Marin Lemierre's tragedy *La Veuve du Malabar* (1780) and Mariana Starke's English adaptation *The Widow of Malabar* (1791), Goethe's poem "The God and the Bayadere" (1797), and Gerhard Anton von Halem's "The Flower Oschaddi" in *Blüthen von Trümmern* (Bremen: Friedrich Wilmans, 1798), 175–176. Günderrode owned a copy of the latter (SW 3:182).

[5] Galasso, "Form and Contention," 214.

The Malabarian Widows

To flaming death on the shores of the Indus[6]
With their husbands, in youth's glory,
Go the women, without hesitation, without sorrow,
Adorned festively, like in bride clothes.

Custom has understood love's meaning,
Freed it from separation's harsh disgrace,
To its priests even death is consecrated,
Its bonds given to immortality.

Separation no longer threatens such a union,
For the previously sundered flames of love
Are struck ardently together into one.

Death becomes love's sweet celebration,
The separated elements unified,
The end of being becomes the peak of life.

[6] Malabar is an old name for the southwest part of India, especially the coast around Kerala. However, the first line of the poem refers to "the shores of the Indus"—a river that originates in Tibet and runs through Kashmir and modern Pakistan.

5

"An Apocalyptic Fragment" and "A Dream"

Introduction

"An Apocalyptic Fragment" appeared in Günderrode's first collection, *Poems and Fantasies*, while the second piece considered here, "A Dream," was left unpublished. Both were written between 1802 and 1804, and Günderrode may have worked on them simultaneously.[1] The pieces consider similar themes, both describing forms of awareness beyond normal human experience. However, they provide contrasting perspectives on these imagined experiences.

"An Apocalyptic Fragment" is notable for several features: its use of biblical language to create a sense of revelation and religious authority; its use of water imagery as a metaphor for the lifecycle of individual beings within the greater whole of nature; and its attempt to work through, in terms of experience, metaphysical claims that are outlined elsewhere in Günderrode's work.

The text is presented as the content of a vision. In the vision, the narrator undergoes a shift in their perception of time and space and witnesses individuals emerging from and returning to a great ocean. They then experience a change in their own consciousness, passing out and awakening to a new form of existence. In this new life, they find themselves joyfully integrated with the natural world: "I thought, and felt, surged in the ocean, gleamed in the sun, circled with the stars; I felt myself in everything, and enjoyed everything in me."

Günderrode uses imagery associated with the ocean and the water cycle to convey the idea of individuals, imagined as drops of water, emerging from and returning to a unified substance or solution, described as an ocean. The narrator sees creatures rising from and submerging in this ocean, which they call "the source of life," and recognizes their own place in this cycle. They experience themselves as a "drop of dew" consorting with other drops, forming water vapor, a rainbow, and a halo around the moon. Their subsequent loss

[1] SW 3:88, 266.

Karoline von Günderrode. Anna Ezekiel, Oxford University Press. © Oxford University Press 2026.
DOI: 10.1093/9780190089177.003.0007

of consciousness is also described in watery terms: they are dissolved by "numbing mists," after which they become more than just a "single drop" and enjoy a unified existence with "everything."

Günderrode uses this imagery to convey an important and original aspect of her philosophy: the imagining of ways of being beyond human and individual experience. According to Günderrode, all beings, including human beings, exist as part of a cycle of life, death, and reincarnation. In this cycle, beings are repeatedly born (or, in the case of inanimate objects, formed) as individual entities before eventually, after their death or destruction, dissolving again in the whole of nature, only to be born again in a different form. Importantly, for Günderrode, we can experience some kind of awareness, though foggy and unclear, even when we exist as part of the whole of nature rather than as individuals.[2] In works like "An Apocalyptic Fragment" and "A Dream," Günderrode attempts to give an impression of what this kind of beyond-human, non-individuated awareness might be like.

The wording of "An Apocalyptic Fragment" deliberately references biblical language, situating the piece in a Christian tradition of creation and revelation. The opening, which describes the wind "resting upon the sea," draws on the description of God's creation of the world in Genesis 1:2: "And the earth was without form, and void; and darkness was upon the face of the deep. And the spirit of God moved upon the face of the waters."[3] The depiction of beings emerging from an originally unformed ocean in the rest of the poem also mirrors this passage and later points in Genesis.[4] In Günderrode's version, however, there is no mention of God; instead, the forces of nature—wind, ocean, time, planets, rain—acquire creative (or re-creative) force.

At the end of the piece, Günderrode quotes from Matthew 11:15: "whoever has ears to hear, let them hear!"[5] In the Bible, this phrase is spoken by Jesus to emphasize his claim to authenticity as the son and messenger of God and, therefore, to assert the authenticity of revelation through Christ. In Günderrode's text, the phrase functions similarly to claim authenticity

---

[2] Anna Ezekiel, "Through Consciousness Parted from Dream: Alternative Knowledge Forms in Karoline von Günderrode," in *The Significance of Negation in Classical German Philosophy*, ed. Gregory Moss (Dordrecht: Springer, 2023), 163–180.

[3] King James Bible online. Genesis 1:2 is also referenced at the start of Günderrode's poem "Piedro" (*Poetic Fragments, by Tian*, trans. Anna Ezekiel [Albany: SUNY Press, 2016], 106).

[4] E.g., Gen 1:20–21. Like "An Apocalyptic Fragment," Genesis 1 notes the passage of days and nights during God's creation of the earth.

[5] Adapted from Lutherbibel, bibel-online.net. I have added gender-neutral language. Variations of this statement also appear in Mark 4:9 and at multiple points in Revelations.

for the revelation described in this piece. The word "apocalypse" in the title refers to this revelation. Although now used to refer to the end of the world, the original meaning of "apocalypse" is "uncovering," "disclosure," or "reve-lation," from the Greek ἀποκάλυψις (*apocalypsis*). Günderrode is using the word partly in this sense, indicating that she intends the poem to be read as communicating genuine religious insight. However, she also retains the second meaning of the term, taking up themes and imagery from the biblical book of Revelation, which describes the end of the world.[6]

Günderrode borrowed some of her concepts and language in this piece from a passage in Christoph Martin Wieland's novel *Agathodämon*. Wieland (1733–1813) was a popular novelist and poet in the late eighteenth and early nineteenth centuries, and one of Günderrode's favorite writers. In *Agathodämon*, one of his characters describes a vision that is very similar to the one in "An Apocalyptic Fragment." However, Günderrode's creative reworking of the vision gives it a meaning that is almost opposite to the one it has in Wieland's text. Wieland's character Apollonius explains that the vi-sion in *Agathodämon* reveals our "inability to soar over the sensory world [. . .] to real intuition of the eternal, necessary, and independent infinite."[7] This realization, Apollonius claims, is a sign that we should limit our actions to the mundane, human realm—the only area in which we can be effective. By contrast, as we saw above, in "An Apocalyptic Fragment," Günderrode suggests that we can and will exist beyond the limits of conscious and indi-vidual human existence, and she uses the narrator's vision to show us what this might be like.

Like "An Apocalyptic Fragment," "A Dream" describes a muffled and con-fused form of awareness experienced by the dead. However, there are major differences between the texts. Whereas "An Apocalyptic Fragment" describes this awareness as a memory, in "A Dream" the narrator does not personally experience this state but is only a witness to the futile efforts of the dead to rise from their numbed and powerless "slumber." Furthermore, while in "An Apocalyptic Fragment" the experience of having these confused dreams is emotionally neutral or even pleasant, in "A Dream" it is presented as dark and claustrophobic.

---

[6] Cf. esp. Rev 20:13f.: "And the sea gave up the dead which were in it . . . "; see also Rev 21.1 (King James Bible online).

[7] Wieland, *Agathodämon*, 232–233.

The "dream" in the title of this shorter work refers not to the experiences of the sleeping "spirits" but to the dream of the narrator. It is likely that in this regard Günderrode was inspired by the Romantic writer Wilhelm Heinrich Wackenroder (1773–1798),[8] and in particular by his poem "The Dream: An Allegory." The language in Wackenroder's poem, like in Günderrode's "A Dream," is dark, claustrophobic, and threatening. Wackenroder writes, for instance, that "Night closed around us, like a dark ligature" and describes memories fleeing in a storm.[9] However, Wackenroder's narrator is consoled by a "friend" who accompanies him until the return of light, which illuminates a beautiful scene from nature. In contrast to both Wackenroder's piece and "An Apocalyptic Fragment," Günderrode's "A Dream" lacks this optimism, ending with the spirits sinking "back into numbed slumber."

"An Apocalyptic Fragment" and "A Dream" both present Günderrode's imaginings of what it would be like to exist as something other than an individual human being. But whereas "An Apocalyptic Fragment" imagines an expanded, if muffled, form of consciousness that is felt as playful, gentle, and enjoyable, "A Dream" describes a claustrophobic state of incapacity and murky awareness of that incapacity. As is often the case, Günderrode presents more than one viewpoint on a single topic, leaving it up to the reader to evaluate the possibilities she describes.

An Apocalyptic Fragment

1. I stood on a high cliff in the Mediterranean, and before me was the east, and behind me the west, and the wind rested upon the sea.
2. Then the sun sank, and hardly was it shrouded by its descent than the dawn rose again, and morning, noon, evening and night chased each other, in dizzying haste, on the arc of the sky.
3. Astonished, I saw them revolve in wild circles; my pulse flew no faster, my thoughts moved no more swiftly, and within me time went its usual course, while outside me it moved according to a new law.

---

[8] Although Wackenroder is often overlooked today, he was popular in Günderrode's time, known for his emotionally charged literature and his theories connecting music, culture, and anthropology.
[9] Wilhelm Heinrich Wackenroder, "Der Traum. Eine Allegorie" [1799], in *Werke und Briefe*, ed. Gerda Heinrich (Berlin: Union; Munich: Hanser, 1984), 357–358.

4. I wanted to plunge down into the dawn, or dive into the shadows of night, to be drawn with them in their haste and not live so slowly; but because I always beheld them I became very tired and passed on.[10]

5. Then I saw a wide ocean before me, surrounded by no shore, not in the east nor the south nor the west, nor the north; no gust of wind moved the waves, but the immeasurable sea still moved within its depths, as if moved by inner agitation.

6. And various figures climbed up, out of the womb of the deep ocean, and mist rose and became clouds, and the clouds sank, and in quivering flashes touched the birthing waves.

7. And ever more diverse figures rose from the depths, but dizziness gripped me and a peculiar disquietude, my thoughts were driven here and there, like a torch by storm wind, until my memory lapsed.

8. But when I awoke again, and began to know myself, I did not know how long I had slept, whether it was centuries or minutes; for although I had had muffled and tangled dreams, I had encountered nothing that reminded me of time.

9. But there was a dark feeling in me, as if I had rested in the womb of this ocean and had risen from it, like the other figures. And I seemed to be a drop of dew, and moved blithely here and there in the air, and was glad that the sun was reflected in me, and the stars contemplated me.

10. I let myself be borne by the breezes in swift drafts, I consorted with the sunset, and with the rainbow's seven-colored drops; I arranged myself with my playmates around the moon when it would have hidden itself, and accompanied its course.

11. The past was lost to me! I belonged only to the present. But a longing was in me that did not know its object. I was always searching, but everything I found was not what I sought, and I drove myself longingly around in the infinite.

12. All at once I became aware that all the creatures that had climbed from the ocean returned to it, and generated themselves again in changing forms. This epiphany alienated me; for I had not known of an end. Then I thought my longing was also to return to the source of life.

13. And as I thought this, and felt almost more alive than all my consciousness, suddenly it was as if my mind was surrounded with numbing

---

[10] The verb used here is *entschlafen*, literally meaning "to fall asleep," used as a euphemism for "to die."

mists. But they soon disappeared; I seemed to myself no longer to be me, and yet more than ever me, I could no longer find my borders, my consciousness had overstepped them; it was bigger, other, and yet I felt myself in it.

14. I was released from the narrow bounds of my being, and no more a single drop; I was given again to everything, and everything belonged to me. I thought, and felt, surged in the ocean, gleamed in the sun, circled with the stars; I felt myself in everything, and enjoyed every-thing in me.

15. So, whoever has ears to hear, let them hear! It is not two, not three, not thousands; it is one and all. It is not body and spirit divided, so that one belongs to time, the other to eternity; it is one, belongs to itself, and is time and eternity together, and visible, and invisible, enduring in change, an unending life.

A Dream

I came to a dark hollow where past times and the great spirits of antiquity slept a deep sleep.

And they could not awaken even if they wanted to, for they were spellbound in this sinister place and surrounded by night and slumber.

And they made all kinds of violent movements, and wanted to rip them-selves out of their slumber; but the spell's power held them imprisoned in heavy stupefaction.

When I went closer I heard a violent roaring like the wild winds when they pound their heads howling against cliffs.

And I became aware that it was the destinies of this time, the events of the present, that rushed so violently over the hollow.

But the confused roaring of their voices pressed only weakly into the ears of the sleepers. They raised their heads, rubbed their heavy lashes, and stretched their arms out longingly to life.

Violently and ever more violently rushed the circling flight of the times outside, mighty was their progress; ever more fearfully the spirits of the past strove to awaken, in vain! The enchantment's power entwined them firmly and more firmly; they sank back into numbed slumber.

6

The Wanderer's Descent

Introduction

"The Wanderer's Descent" was published in Günderrode's 1804 collection *Poems and Fantasies* and addresses Günderrode's interest in epistemology. Günderrode often explores ways of learning about the world that reach beyond and behind the knowledge we can gain through ordinary experience, philosophical reasoning, and scientific inquiry. In some pieces, Günderrode suggests that this kind of learning can occur in visions, dreams, or revelations, or that we will gain this knowledge after death. But in "The Wanderer's Descent," the protagonist hopes to gain this special insight through a journey into the earth.

The poem is a dialogue between the Wanderer and, first, a guide who leads him into a deep cave, and then the "spirits of earth" who dwell there. Günderrode uses the movement into the depths of the earth to represent several things: the passage from life to death; the attempt to expand one's cognitive and perceptual horizons beyond normal human limits (and the obstacles to doing so); and a journey back in time to witness the creation of life from inanimate matter—and, by analogy, the birth of the human being as a conscious individual. The poem therefore contributes to our understanding of Günderrode's views on death and personal identity as well as her epistemology and metaphysics.

Günderrode's interest in boundaries, and especially in crossing them, is clear in the first lines of the poem. We find ourselves at the opening to a cave on the edge of an ocean at sunset. On one level, these boundaries represent the dividing line between life and death, highlighted by imagery associated with the Wanderer's guide. The Wanderer greets this figure as "Herald of the night" and describes him as "born to day and night," identifying the guide as a psychopomp, someone like the Greek deity Hermes, guide to the underworld and patron of travelers, boundaries, and sleep.

Consistent with Günderrode's claim that new forms of awareness await us after death, in this poem, the border to the underworld also represents the

Karoline von Günderrode. Anna Ezekiel, Oxford University Press. © Oxford University Press 2026.
DOI: 10.1093/9780190089177.003.0008

boundaries of perception. The Wanderer's descent into the earth is a metaphor for searching beneath the things of the everyday world for deeper, more authentic knowledge. For example, the Wanderer states that he wants to "raise the unalloyed treasures / That the gleam [*Schein*] of the living world does not disturb." The German word *Schein* can also be translated as "appearance," "semblance," or "pretense"; consistent with these connotations, Günderrode's use of the term indicates deceptiveness or only apparent truth. Günderrode intends the Wanderer's descent to be read as a deliberate turn away from the "phenomenal" world of everyday appearances—the world of experience to which Kant limits human knowledge. Instead, the Wanderer hopes to gain insight into the "noumenal" world of things as they really are, outside human categories of thought and perception.

In some respects, "The Wanderer's Descent" recalls work by the poet, novelist, and philosopher Friedrich von Hardenberg (1772–1801), also known as Novalis, whose work Günderrode excerpted in her notebooks.[1] Of particular relevance is a passage in Novalis' novel *Henry of Ofterdingen*, in which the protagonist enters a cave and finds a book containing images from his life.[2] In other words, Henry's journey into the earth surprisingly results in an encounter with himself. Novalis' claim is that self-knowledge can be obtained through knowledge of the world, and *vice versa*. According to Novalis, the individual is a microcosm or reflection of the whole universe, meaning that each can be learned about by studying the other. He writes: "We dream of journeys through the cosmos; is the cosmos not within us? [...] The mysterious path goes inwards."[3]

"The Wanderer's Descent" includes a similar moment, when the spirits of earth tell the Wanderer "look down, into your soul's grounds; / What you seek here you will find there, / You are just the cosmos' seeing mirror." For Günderrode, like Novalis, the individual is part of the whole of nature and can therefore learn about this whole through insight into herself or himself. In "The Wanderer's Descent," Günderrode goes on to suggest that, although introspection reveals a reflection of the universe, human beings, as conscious individuals, necessarily remain separate from and unable to fully encounter the whole of which they are a part. The spirits of earth tell the Wanderer that he is "already born to the day; Divided from the life element" and "Through your consciousness already parted from dream." The Wanderer's individual

---

[1] See Günderrode's notes on the early German Romantics translated later in this volume.
[2] Novalis, *Schriften* 1:264–265.
[3] Novalis, *Schriften* 2:417–419 #17.

consciousness separates him indelibly from the undivided source of life. The "primal being" or "primal force" that the Wanderer seeks "has no lips to express itself": it is undifferentiated and therefore exceeds language; even more basically, it exceeds divisions such as the subject–object division that are necessary for knowledge.[4]

In addition to traversing the boundaries of life and death and of normal human perception, "The Wanderer's Descent" depicts a passage back in time to witness how (according to Günderrode) individual things emerge from this originally undifferentiated, infinite source of life.[5] This emergence is shown in reverse: the Wanderer sees violently struggling elements which, as he descends, gradually enfold each other until, at the deepest point, they are joined together and at peace. Günderrode provides an archaeology of the emergence of the apparently stable phenomenal world of individual objects from a clash of active forces and, at an even earlier stage, the emergence of these forces from the single primal force that lies at the heart of creation.

Since human beings are individual entities just like all other beings, this picture of objects emerging from a unified source via a clash of forces also applies to the birth of human beings. Günderrode highlights this by using maternal imagery to describe the depths of the earth: the cave is a "womb" where "the unborn rests enveloped"; emerging life is like a child that "nestles against its mother"; and the poem makes numerous references to birth, engenderment, and penetration.[6] Thus, like Novalis' character Henry, Günderrode's Wanderer learns about his own nature and origins through a movement deep into the earth, beyond the boundaries of perception and of life itself.

The Wanderer's Descent

Wanderer.

This, if the master did not deceive me, is

The western ocean, in which the night wind roars.

---

[4] Cf. Novalis, *Schriften* 2:104–105; J. G. Fichte, "[First] Introduction to the *Wissenschaftslehre*," in *Introductions to the Wissenschaftslehre and Other Writings (1797–1800)*, ed. and trans. Daniel Breazeale (Indianapolis: Hackett, 1994), 12–13.

[5] For more information on how Günderrode thinks individual entities emerge from an originally single, infinite whole, see the section on metaphysics in the general introduction to this volume, as well as her texts "Idea of the Earth" and "Letters of Two Friends" and their introductions also included in this volume.

[6] Dormann, *Kunst des inneren Sinns*, 172, 174, 177.

This is the way down surrounded by gold,
And this the grotto where my guide resides.—
Are you not the one, born to day and night,
Crown kissed by the friendly sunset,
In which Helios[7] lost his life,
And whose girdle already flows around the night.

Herald of the night! Is it you who leads to her,
The son she bears the sun-god?

Guide.
Yes, you are at the grotto,
Of the one who grasped the reins
Of the strong sun god.
Who steers the steed westwards
That the wagon sinks behind
At the day's goal.

And the god still sends me
Back glances, lovingly;
Parting, he kisses me;
And I see it, weep tears,
And a sweet silent longing
Colors me paler;

Paler, until she has embraced me,
She, out of whom I half arose,
The veiled night.
Into her depths a desire leads me
My eyes still see the sun's splendor
But deep in the valley she has enfolded me
The twilight already engulfed by midnight.

Wanderer.
Oh guide me! You know well the paths
To the old realm of dark midnight;

---

[7] In Greek mythology, Helios is the god of the sun, often pictured driving a chariot from east to west across the sky.

Down will I go to the gloomy shore
Where never the morning, never the midday smiles.
I will renounce the day's shimmer
That unwillingly weds us to the earth,
That glimmer only blinded me, deceitfully,
Never chose the earth as its homeland.
Vainly I wanted to grasp the fugitive,
But it can never leave constant change.
So guide me to the circle of silent powers,
In whose deep womb chaos slept
Before, from the dark of eternal midnights,
The light-spirit called it up to life.
There, where the earth's womb, still unforced,
Modestly envelops itself in dark veils,
Where, never penetrated by bold light,
It does not yet engender this wavering image
Of things' order, this race of earth!
To whom pain and error remain eternal companions.

Guide.
Will you consult the gods,
Who bear the globe's supports,
Love the earth's race,
Who dwell in holy concord,
Undazzled by earthly suns,
Eternally stern and just;
Then come, before I wholly breathe out my life,
Before the night submerges me in its shadows.

[*Wanderer.*]
Hear! Loud howl the winds,
And the winding of my way
Grows narrow through chasms.
The sealed streams roar,
And I see with cold horror
That I am without guide.
I saw him grow faint, ever fainter,
And the night buried my companion.

In floods of water I hear fire hiss
See how roaring elements mix,
How what order separates unites.
I see how east and west enfold each other here,
The mild south plays around Boreas'[8] cheeks,
Hostile things embrace their enemies
And sweep them along in their strong arms:
What is cold must be warmed in fiery heat.

Deeper still the paths lead
Me down, to the shore
Where quiet dwells,
Where life's colors pale,
Where the elements fall silent
And peace is enthroned.

Spirits of Earth.
Who bade you descend into the depths
And interrupt our eternal silence?

Wanderer.
The stirring drive: to fathom the truth![9]

Spirits of Earth.
So you would find the light in the night?

Wanderer.
Not that light that sojourns on the earth
And only deceptively escapes its seeker;
No, that primal being that rests here below
And glows purely only in the source of life.

---

[8] Boreas is the ancient Greek god of the north wind.
[9] Raisbeck suggests this is an indirect quote from Lessing (*Karoline von Günderrode: Philosophical Romantic* [Cambridge: Legenda, 2022], 148). The passage in question reads: "If God held enclosed in his right hand all truth, and in his left hand the ever-stirring drive for truth, but with the caveat to be always and forever wrong, and said to me: 'Choose!' I would fall humbly upon his left hand and say: 'Father, give [it to me]! The pure truth is only for you alone!'" (Gotthold Ephraim Lessing, "Eine Duplik. Über die Wahrheit" [1778], in *Gotthold Ephraim Lessings sämtliche Schriften*, ed. Karl Lachmann, vol. 13 [Leipzig: Göschen, 1897], 23–24).

I would raise the unalloyed treasures
That the gleam of the living world does not disturb
The primal force that, like a pearl, leads
From life into the depths of being's ocean.
To see life in the womb of life,
As it, childlike, nestles against[10] its mother;
To behold nature in her workshop,
See how creation lies at her bosom.

Spirits of Earth.
Then know! The eternal fullness of life rests
Still bound here in sleep's shroud
And hardly lives or stirs.
It has no lips to express itself,
It cannot yet break silence's seal,
Its being is still dream
And we, we take care that sleep still covers it,
That it does not wake before time awakens it.

Wanderer.
Oh you! who preside in the earth,
Who shaped things' depths,
Unveil, unveil yourselves to me!

Spirits of Earth.
Not offerings nor magic words
Penetrate the earth's gates,
There is no audience here.
Here the unborn rests enveloped,
Mysterious, until its time has come.

Wanderer.
Then gather me up, mysterious powers,
Oh rock me into deep slumber.
Envelop me in your midnights;

---

[10] Morgenthaler has "twines around" (*schlingt an*) instead of "nestles against" (*schmiegt an*) (SW 1:72).

I step gladly from the ranks of the living.
Let me sink again to the mother's womb,
Drink forgetfulness[11] and new being.

Spirits of Earth.
In vain! On you our might is lost,
Too late! You are already born to the day;
Divided from the life element.
We can command becoming, not being
And you are already divided from the mother's womb
Through your consciousness already parted from dream.
But look down, into your soul's grounds;
What you seek here you will find there,
You are just the cosmos' seeing mirror.
There too are midnights that one day will dawn,
There too are powers that awaken from sleep
There too is a workshop of nature.

---

[11] A reference to the river of Lethe in Greek mythology, from which the dead drink before reincarnation in order to forget their past lives.

7

The Adept

Introduction

"The Adept" was published in Günderrode's first collection, *Poems and Fantasies*. Like several other pieces in this 1804 collection, the poem focuses on the possibility of forms of knowledge beyond what we can learn through ordinary experience or scientific inquiry. In this case, special knowledge is gained by being initiated into a mystery religion following a journey to the east.

The protagonist of the poem, Valus, yearns for knowledge and travels to India to deepen his understanding of the world. The poem describes his transition through several levels of initiation into the secrets of the priests he meets there. At the first level, Valus learns that knowledge of the natural world is superficial and misleading. This kind of knowledge only tells us about the "names and appearance" of things and not the reality that lies behind them. Valus learns to distinguish the real nature of things as "one thing," referred to as "the nature-spirit," that underlies all the changing appearances of the world. At this point, he can "listen in" to nature and "see its deepest workings": he "sees through everything." Finally, he "masters nature" and perceives the eternal cycle of the universe, witnessing generations passing before his eyes with dizzying speed.

However, it turns out that this new level of knowledge is useless. Valus is repelled by the changing forms that he sees, paralyzed by the rapid changes, and isolated from the rest of humanity by his perspective; he can only hope for death.

Valus' fate echoes the "revenge of nature" trope associated with the attempt to penetrate nature's secrets, which famously featured in Friedrich Schiller's 1795 poem *The Veiled Image at Saïs*.[1] According to this trope, anyone who attempts to "lift the veil" of nature (embodied by the veiled statue of the goddess Isis) to see beyond individual objects and events to whatever lies behind or within these will die or go mad. This was a popular metaphor for human

---

[1] Dormann, *Kunst des inneren Sinns*, 153.

Karoline von Günderrode. Anna Ezekiel, Oxford University Press. © Oxford University Press 2026.
DOI: 10.1093/9780190089177.003.0009

overreach in Günderrode's time: a lack of appropriate humility in the face of nature's vast and mysterious forces seemed to invite punishment or disaster. Günderrode herself uses the motif relatively frequently. For example, she mentions the Isis trope in "Story of a Brahmin" and *Magic and Destiny*, while references to veils and unveiling in "The Wanderer's Descent" also work with this association in a more subtle way.

In her pieces on the topic of hidden knowledge, Günderrode provides several different responses to the idea that the true nature of the universe is inaccessible to living human beings. She does not always suggest that "lifting the veil" of nature will result in disaster. In "The Wanderer's Descent," the Wanderer is told that, as a living individual, he simply cannot see what lies behind the individual objects and events of everyday life. By contrast, in the poem "Muhammad's Dream in the Desert,"[2] a prophet survives visions of the chaos that lies behind ordinary things and can even use what he learns there to guide his actions in the everyday world. The protagonist of "Story of a Brahmin" enjoys glimpses of the infinite life force that underlies the natural world, which allow him to join a happy community with other individuals who share this insight. Nonetheless, in "The Adept," Günderrode follows the "revenge of nature" trope quite closely: Valus' vision of the infinite drives him to loneliness, paralysis, and despair.

By treating this question so differently in several pieces, Günderrode leaves us with a nuanced set of reflections on epistemology and the freedom to work our own way through the perspectives she provides. "The Adept" shows her considering the cost, for finite and limited creatures such as we are, of a direct encounter with the infinite and infinitely powerful forces of nature.

The Adept

A sage, who had studied much,
But never tired of research,
Once reached the land of India,
After long years of wandering.

The priests of this land boast
Of much secret scholarship,

---

[2] For an English translation, see Günderrode, "Muhammad's Dream."

They can distinguish being and appearance,
And know the force within all things.

Valus was consecrated as a pupil,
Bound himself by an oath,
Mysteriously, to this order,
As the priest bade him.

How vain all his former knowledge;
That Valus soon realized,
He never knew things' souls,
Made do with names and appearance.

Now he sees one thing in each sum,
Sees the nature-spirit ever new
And ever old in eternal change
As it is in all forms.

Now he can listen in to nature,
He can see its deepest workings,
Knows how substances are joined
And how earths are built.

Now they give him the third consecration,
Privilege of only a few sages;
For whoever sees through everything
Now masters nature.

After he was thrice consecrated
He had taken the great step
That parted his life's long journey
From humanity's course.

Many times pass before him,
He sees the generations fly,
And remains alone in all change,
While things come and go.

Having often seen the cycle
That ever nature made,
Shudders seize his soul,
For everything spins like day and night.

Novelty's charm is lost to him,
He knows what the earth bears,
He finds himself alone on earth,
Humanity is not his race.

He has emptied life's cup
And lives ever, ever on,
He cannot rise from the ocean
And yet has landed in port.

Woe to those! he cries: who on the peak
Of being thus stand still.
Human beings cannot bear the eternal,
And it is well for them when they pass away.

8

The Frank in Egypt

Introduction

"The Frank in Egypt," published in *Poems and Fantasies* in 1804, describes
the journey of a European man (the "Frank") to North Africa in search of
knowledge and fulfillment. Having failed to find satisfaction in study, war,
and even exploring the pyramids, he finally meets and falls in love with
Lastrata, an Egyptian woman of European descent. The poem ends with the
Frank learning that the way to satisfy the longing and discontent that have
been driving him is not knowledge, action, or imagination, but love.

The term "Frank" is an old name for inhabitants of a large area in north-
west Europe, including France. One reading of the poem is that the Frank
represents the French Emperor Napoleon Bonaparte,[1] who in 1789–1801
led a campaign in Egypt and Syria. Günderrode wrote several pieces inspired
by Napoleon, including her plays *Hildgund* and *Muhammad, the Prophet of
Mecca*. In these two plays, Attila and Muhammad, respectively, stand in for
Napoleon, providing a critique of tyrannical power and the thirst for conquest. Günderrode's unpublished poems "Brutus," "The Sun Sinks . . . ," and
"Bonaparte in Egypt" present a more positive view of Napoleon as an idealist
and revolutionary hero fighting for freedom.

The references in "The Frank in Egypt" to wars and science reflect the way
the French framed their invasion: as a mission to promote freedom, equality,
and science. However, the friendly meeting between the Frank and Lastrata
and the implication that the Frank will remain in Egypt do not fit well
with Napoleon's actual retreat from defeat by British and Ottoman troops.
Similarly, there is a disconnect between the poem's expression of a desire
for union between Europeans and North Africans and the real outcome of
Napoleon's invasion, which included the official end of the longstanding
Franco-Ottoman alliance.

---

[1] Raisbeck, *Philosophical Romantic*, 82.

Karoline von Günderrode. Anna Ezekiel, Oxford University Press. © Oxford University Press 2026.
DOI: 10.1093/9780190089177.003.0010

Napoleon's retreat was precipitous, and he abandoned troops in North Africa, so another possibility is that Günderrode's Frank is a Napoleonic soldier left behind after the wars. Perhaps Günderrode and her disillusioned Frankish soldier are imagining an alternative and more successful approach of Europeans to people of other countries after the disappointment of Napoleon's campaign—an approach built on connections between individuals rather than the invasion and conquest of nations.

The poem can also be read on other levels.[2] In some respects, Günderrode is using the Frank's journey to the east in a conventional Romantic way: as a metaphor for discovering one's lost origins and reconnecting with oneself, nature, and the divine. This metaphor is used, for example, in Novalis' novel *Henry of Ofterdingen*.[3] However, Günderrode's poem disrupts the model used by Novalis and other early German Romantics, in which encounters with an "other" (a woman, a foreigner, or the natural world) allow the protagonist to experience homecoming, self-knowledge, *Bildung*, and completion. In "The Frank in Egypt," Lastrata, like the Frank, describes a "longing," a "wishing without wish"—in her case (and her father's) focused on the distant coasts of Europe. In early German Romantic texts by men, only the male European protagonists are driven by a nameless longing to seek their lost origins and true selves,[4] but Günderrode portrays Lastrata as driven by the same motivations as the Frank and her father. In other words, Günderrode undermines the early German Romantic reduction of women and the east to the "other" of a European male protagonist; Lastrata, too, has her longings and her need for self-knowledge and personal development, and these are satisfied by her encounter with the Frank in the same way that his are satisfied by meeting her.

---

[2] It would be interesting to explore the influence of Goethe on this text. Goethe's 1772 poem "The Wanderer" ("Der Wandrer") is a dialogue between a traveling poet and a mother concerned with the exigencies of life. Unlike in "The Frank in Egypt," the pair in Goethe's poem talk past each other and eventually go their separate ways; the poet, having rejected the woman's invitation to rest and eat with her family, dreams of an eventual homecoming to just "such a woman." Günderrode wrote other pieces set in Egypt that were also likely inspired by Goethe. Her poems "Egypt" and "The Nile" have parallels with Goethe's poems "Muhammad's Song," "Calm Sea," and "Prosperous Voyage." (See Kevin Hilliard, "Orient und Mythos: Karoline von Günderrode," in *Frauen: MitSprechen. MitSchreiben. Beiträge zur literatur- und sprachwissenschaftlichen Frauenforschung*, ed. Marianne Henn and Britta Hufeisen [Stuttgart: Heinz, 1997], 244–255.)

[3] Novalis is the pen name of the writer and philosopher Friedrich von Hardenberg (1772–1801), whose work Günderrode excerpted in her notebooks (see the chapter on Günderrode's notes on the early German Romantics, later in this volume).

[4] Anna Ezekiel, "Women, Women Writers, and Early German Romanticism," in *The Palgrave Handbook of German Romantic Philosophy*, ed. Elizabeth Millán Brusslan (Palgrave Macmillan, 2020), 483; Friedrichsmeyer, *Androgyne*, 104–105, 158.

Günderrode's metaphysics also lend a different significance to the relationship between Lastrata and the Frank than this relationship would have in a piece by Novalis or his friend and collaborator Friedrich Schlegel. This is because Günderrode discards the gender dualism that pervades early German Romantic thought, including their metaphysics and view of love. Early German Romantics such as Novalis and Schlegel saw romantic love as a union of opposites embodied by a man and a woman. They believed that men were rational, active, conscious, and verbal; women were emotional, mysterious, and connected to the subconscious, the body, nature, and the divine. As a result, relationships between men and women would supposedly not only join two individuals but also begin to mend the split between spirit and nature, mind and matter that they believed afflicted the whole world.

Günderrode, however, creates a completely different metaphysics in which gender is basically irrelevant. Günderrode saw all forms of love, friendship, and attraction as resulting from similarities between the constituent elements that make up individuals.[5] There is no difference in her account between the elements that make up people of different genders. Rather, what is significant is the degree of development—that is, the degree of liveliness and animation—of the elements that constitute us. Where these are similar, we feel a pull toward each other that we may experience as friendship, attraction, or love.

Thus, while love has a unifying function for both Günderrode and the early German Romantics, the way that it unifies is different in each case. For Novalis and Schlegel, love unifies opposites and is best exemplified in romantic relationships between one man and one woman. For Günderrode, love unifies similar things and may occur between people of any gender— and any number. At the end of "The Frank in Egypt," it is implied that the Frank will return to Lastrata's hut to settle with her and her father there, thus satisfying the longing that has called to all three of them across great distances.[6] For Günderrode, the ideal relationship between human beings is not romantic love as it is for the early German Romantics, but a sense of connection based on shared or similar attributes, which may develop between lovers, family members, or friends.

---

[5] For details of Günderrode's metaphysics, including the role of "elements," see the general introduction to this volume.

[6] Cf. the end of "Story of a Brahmin."

The Frank in Egypt

How discontent oppresses my breast,
How happiness flees me, smiling derisively.
Is there nothing, then, that slakes my soul?
Nothing to fill this life's anxious void? –
This longing, I imagined, seeks antiquity,
My sick spirit craves the time of heroes.
This heart will rise to bygone greatness,
And so I hurried to your shore,
To antiquity's holiest ruins,
You fabulous land, Egypt!
Ha! I thought I was unloaded of all burdens
When I had hurried from my homeland's border.
Dreaming, I pilgrimaged with antiquity's shadows,
But soon I felt I was among the dead,
Life stirred in me anew,
The grave could not answer me. –
Into battles' turmoil
I threw myself thirstily,
But fame and battles,
Left me sorrowful:
A laurel wreath[7] upon the brow,
Does not always gratify.
Then science offered me its hand,
And obediently I went to its side,
I descended into the pyramids' night,
I measured Lake Moeris, ancient Memphis' greatness,
And all other grandeur that swelled my heart,
Only knowledge's cup suffices the thirsty.
I only thought, studied, forgot I sensed. –
But ah! The old longing is awakened,
Anew, searching, I feel its might.
What shall I give it? Where shall I throw myself?
What will season life's long wasteland?

---

[7] In ancient Greece, the laurel symbolized victory in war or athletic contests. It may also symbolize poetic prowess.

Ha! Look, a girl! How full of grace,
How sweetly fair she seems to me!
Should I resist her features?
But no! I speak to her boldly.
Is this the way to the pyramids?
Oh, beautiful girl! Tell me!

Girl.

You are not on the way to the pyramids,
Oh stranger! But I will show it to you.

Frank.

Burning scorches the hot midday sun,
Every flower bows its lovely head,
But you, the loveliest of flowers, raise
Young and fresh your brown-locked head.

Girl.

If you would cool yourself in my father's hut
Come, the old man will gladly receive you.

Frank.

What name do you bear, beautiful girl?
And your father; speak, where does he live?

Girl.

Lastrata I am called; and my good father
He lives with me in a small palm valley,
But not the valley's pleasant coolness,
Nor brooks' murmuring, nor the sun's circling
Gladdens my good father any more.

Frank.

What? The stream's springing does not please your father,
Nor the palms' mild springtime sighing?
That I grasp; but how there may be a grief
That might resist your solace,
Only that, Lastrata, I do not grasp.

Girl.

Italy is the old man's fatherland,
And only much misfortune brought him here.
With longing gaze he stares across the Mediterranean
To the much-loved land.
And, sighing, I also long
For those blossom-rich coasts.
Sickened, my spirit rests on that blue distance,
And beautiful dreams bear me there.
Say, does the stream of life not surge more beautifully there?
Do sick breasts there also yearn in vain?

Frank.

Ah, girl! Deceived by the same wish,
I imagined: beauty is only hidden in the distance,
But in vain I sailed through the waves,
This intimation also lied to me
That you, girl, now awaken in me. –

Girl.

Stranger! Can you divine this longing?
Do you feel this indeterminate sorrow?
This wishing without wish?

Frank.

Yes, I feel a longing, feel a sorrow.
But now I can divine these wishes,
And I know what this striving wants.
Not on far shores, not in battles!
Sciences! Not at your hand,
Not in the colorful land of fantasies!
Dwells the thirsty heart's satiation.
Love must beckon the tired pilgrim,
Myrtles[8] sprout in the laurel wreath,
Love must lead to heroes' shadows,
Must speak to us from the spirit world. –

---

[8] In ancient Greece, the myrtle was a symbol of love.

Mighty stream! I felt your waves,
Unknowingly I felt myself drawn on,
Only whither! whither! That I did not know.
It is well! I have found you and me.
Love has wrested itself from chaos.

9

Immortalita

Introduction

Günderrode published *Immortalita* in her 1804 collection *Poems and Fantasies*. This short play features the successful journey of the hero, Erodion, to find the goddess Immortalita, who has appeared to him in dreams and as a vague sense of longing. Erodion is driven to enter the underworld to search for Immortalita; when he finds her, she urges him to tear down the partition between the worlds of the living and the dead, allowing lovers to be reunited beyond the barriers of death and transforming the shadowland that she inhabits into a paradise.

The setting and characters in Günderrode's play are inspired by Greek mythology, with a little Roman mythology thrown in. The setting is Erebus: a place of darkness between the lands of the living and the dead; Immortalita also mentions that the "residents of Orcus" (the realm of the dead) remain animated—though trapped in the underworld—by her "breath." At the end of the play, the setting transforms into the paradisical Elysian gardens.

Secondary characters include Charon, ferryman of the dead, and Hekate, goddess of magic, witchcraft, ghosts, necromancy, and the night. There are also references to Aphrodite, goddess of love; Eros, god of beauty and desire; Hebe, goddess of youth; Helios, god of the sun; and Pluto, ruler of the underworld. The Roman pantheon is represented by Jupiter, god of thunder and king of the gods; Minerva, goddess of wisdom, art, justice, and war; and Vesta, goddess of hearth, home, and family.

The goddess Immortalita is an invention by Günderrode, used to represent the idea of immortality. Günderrode presents Immortalita as banished to the underworld, constrained by a circle formed from a snake biting its tail—an ancient symbol for the eternal cycle of life, death, and rebirth. With the appearance of Erodion, representing love and beauty, Immortalita is able to step out of this circle and the cycle of life and death is transformed into a paradise in which the dead and the living are no longer separated.

Karoline von Günderrode. Anna Ezekiel, Oxford University Press. © Oxford University Press 2026.
DOI: 10.1093/9780190089177.003.0011

Erodion[1] states that he is the offspring of Aphrodite and Aphrodite's son Eros and that this parentage gave him a "double union of love and beauty." It is this heritage that drives him to search for Immortalita, imbuing him with the sense for something wonderful that he cannot locate in the everyday world. He describes this as "a pleasure which I could find nowhere, but which I intuited and searched for everywhere." Erodion's search for the source of this intuition and the need to travel to the land of the dead to find her connect the play to Günderrode's concern with the nature and possible sources of knowledge, especially knowledge of things that are hidden beneath everyday appearances. This is a topic she also explores in other works such as "The Wanderer's Descent" and "The Adept," both translated in this volume.

Günderrode's account of Erodion's search for Immortalita also makes use of Plato's teachings regarding the ideas. According to Plato, these perfect, eternal forms are imperfectly embodied in the things of the world, but can nonetheless be glimpsed in them. In particular, experiences of love and beautiful things can lead us to look beyond the individual people or objects that we love or see as beautiful to encounter the eternal ideas of love and beauty themselves.[2] In keeping with Plato's position, Günderrode tells us that it is Erodion's "double union of love and beauty," inherited from his divine parents, that has given him the urge to see beyond the "shadow goods" of the everyday world to something eternal that lies behind them. This is the urge that leads Erodion to the underworld and Immortalita.

In addition, Günderrode is working with views of love and longing developed by her near-contemporaries, the early German Romantics, drawing especially on the work of Novalis.[3] In "Hymns to the Night," Novalis describes a vision of a dead loved one that communicates a sense of union with the deceased beloved as well as with the divine. Such visions, Novalis writes, are also available in dreams and drunken stupors; however, these are only a foretaste of real union with lost loved ones and the divine, which will have to wait until we die.[4] In *Immortalita*, Erodion similarly notes that he was able to glimpse Immortalita in dreams but had to travel to the land of the dead to really find her. Günderrode collapses Novalis' figures of the dead beloved and the divine into one beloved, eternal, divine figure: Immortalita. Having

---

[1] Günderrode seems to have invented the name Erodion, possibly deriving it from "Eros" and "Dionysus" (Greek god of wine, drunkenness, religious ecstasy, and fertility).

[2] See the fragments on ethics and aesthetics later in this volume.

[3] The pen name of the poet, novelist, and philosopher Friedrich von Hardenberg (1772–1801).

[4] Novalis, *Schriften*, 1:130f.

glimpsed her in dreams and intuitions, Erodion finally finds her in the underworld and overthrows the division between life and death. This ending contrasts strongly with that of Novalis' "Hymns," in which the narrator remains separated from his loved one and the divine, longing for them but separated by the barrier between life and death.

In addition to *Immortalita*'s concern with epistemology, the play can be read at other levels. Dagmar von Hoff argues that the play forms part of Günderrode's critique of the gender roles of her time, contrasting Immortalita's "limited female destiny" with the "masculine activity" of Erodion.[5] Immortalita inhabits a silent shadow-world, constrained within strict borders, until Erodion throws down a partition that, on Hoff's reading, represents not only the boundary between life and death but also that between the male and female spheres.

Immortalita also functions in the context of Günderrode's metaphysics and ideas about human history and development, again drawing on work by Novalis. Günderrode presents Immortalita's banishment to the shadow realm as part of a broader fall of the ancient gods from their thrones. Near the start of the play, Immortalita recollects that, after a "blessed distant past, where I dwelt with gods in eternal clarity," there came "a dark age" in which "the blessed gods were thrust from their thrones" and she "was separated from them."

This recollection takes up the Romantic idea of a golden age, which appears, for instance, in Novalis' "The Apprentices at Saïs." In this text, Novalis similarly describes a past "golden age" from which we have fallen, using imagery from Greek and Roman mythology.[6] However, where Novalis describes the present, fallen state of human beings in terms of scientific advance and alienation from nature, in *Immortalita* the gods have retreated or been banished into the realm of metaphor: "Their life was past, and they went back into the life-elements out of which they had sprung, before my breath had lent them permanence. Jupiter retreated into the forces of the sky, Eros into human hearts, Minerva into the thoughts of the wise, the Muses into the songs of the poets."

Günderrode's reference to "life-elements" in this passage also raises the question of whether she meant to integrate this statement with her metaphysics, according to which the universe is comprised of living "elements."

---

[5] Hoff, "Dramatisch Weiblichkeitsmuster," 100.
[6] Novalis, *Schriften*, 1:82f.

This question is particularly interesting in light of the relatively early date of *Immortalita*, which Günderrode wrote before the texts in which she worked out the details of her metaphysics, including the nature and role of the "elements." These texts, namely "Idea of the Earth" and "Letters of Two Friends," are generally considered part of Günderrode's reception of the work of philosopher Friedrich Wilhelm Joseph Schelling (1775–1854). However, if the reference to "life-elements" in *Immortalita* uses this term in the same sense as her later works, then it shows she had developed this aspect of her metaphysics before her serious study of Schelling's work.[7]

Relatively little has been written about *Immortalita*, but from the brief sketch above, we can see that the play contributes to several areas of Günderrode's thought, including her epistemology, reception of Novalis and Plato, ideas about love, death, beauty, and gender, and perhaps her metaphysics.

Immortalita

A Dramolet

Characters
Immortalita, a goddess
Erodion
Charon
Hekate

First Scene

An open, black cavern at the entrance to the underworld. In the background of the cavern we can see the Styx and Charon's barque, which moves back and forth; in the foreground of the cavern a black altar upon which a fire burns. The trees and plants at the entrance to the cavern are all flame-colored and black, like all the scenery. Hekate *and* Charon *are black and flame-colored, the shadows light grey,* Immortalita *white,*

---

[7] On Günderrode's reception of Schelling, see the chapter "Notes on Philosophy of Nature" later in this volume; Ng, "Idea of the Earth"; Norris, "Necro-ecology"; Nassar, "Human Vocation."

Erodion *clothed like a Roman youth. A great fiery snake, biting itself in the tail, forms a great circle, whose space Immortalita never oversteps.*

Immortalita (as if awakening from a daze): Charon! Charon.

Charon (pausing within his barge): Why are you calling me?

Immortalita: When will the time come?

Charon: Look at the snake at your feet: it is still closed tight. The spell lasts as long as this circle surrounds you. You know that—why ask me?

Immortalita: Ungracious old man, if it would console me to hear once more the promise of a better future, why deny me a kind word?

Charon: We are in the land of silence.

Immortalita: Prophesy to me again.

Charon: Interpret my gestures; I hate speaking.

Immortalita: Speak! Speak!

Charon: Ask Hekate. *(He leaves.)*

Immortalita (strews incense on the altar): Hekate! Goddess of midnight! Unveiler of the future that sleeps in the dark womb of nonbeing! Mysterious Hekate! Hekate, appear!

Hekate: Mighty conjurer! *(She half emerges from behind the altar.)* Why do you call me from the caverns of eternal midnight? This shore is hateful to me, its darkness too bright—yes, it seems that a base glow from the land of the living has strayed here.

Immortalita: Oh, forgive me, Hekate! And hear my plea.

Hekate: Do not plead; you are queen here. You rule here and do not know it.

Immortalita: I do not know it! Why do I not know myself?

Hekate: Because you cannot see yourself.

Immortalita: Who will show me a mirror, that I may behold myself in it?

Hekate: Love.

Immortalita: Why love?

Hekate: Because only its endlessness is a measure for yours.

Immortalita: How far does my realm extend?

Hekate. Over the beyond; one day, over everything.

Immortalita: What? One day this impenetrable partition will crumble, which separates my realm from the world of the living?

Hekate: It will crumble, you will dwell in the light, and everyone will find you.

Immortalita: Oh, when will this happen?

Hekate: When faithful love steals you from the night.

Immortalita: When? In hours? Years?

Hekate: Do not count the hours: for you, there is no time. Look to the earth! The snake writhes fearfully, it bites itself harder; in vain it wants to hold you imprisoned in its narrow circle. Your realm expands, its resistance is in vain: the reign of unbelief, barbarism and the night sinks away.

(She disappears.)

Immortalita: Oh, future, you will be like the past! That blessed distant past, where I dwelt with gods in eternal clarity. I smiled at them all, and on their brows my smile was transfigured into a luster that no nectar could have given them: Hebe owed me her youth, Aphrodite her ever-blooming charms.

But a dark age came: the blessed gods were thrust from their thrones; I was separated from them. Their life was past, and they went back into the life-elements out of which they had sprung, before my breath had lent them permanence. Jupiter retreated into the forces of the sky, Eros into human hearts, Minerva into the thoughts of the wise, the Muses into the songs of the poets. And I, unhappiest of all—I wound no more unwithering laurels for heroes and poets, banished to this realm of night! This land of shadows! This dismal beyond! I must live only for the future.

Charon (passing by with shadows): Bow, you shadows, this is the queen of Erebus! That you still live after your lives are over is her work.

(Chorus of shadows.)
>Silent the barque leads us
>Towards the unknown land,
>Where the sun will never dawn
>On the ever gloomy strand. –
>Anxiously we see it hurry,
>For our gaze would like to tarry
>At life's brightly colored end.

(They leave.)

The Previous Scene

Charon's barque about to land. Erodion *springs from the barque.* Immortalita *is in the background.*

Erodion: Back, Charon, from this shore where no shadow dare tread! Why are you looking at me? I am no shadow like you; a glad hope, a dreamy faith have blown my life's spark to flame.

Charon (to himself): This is surely the young man who bears the golden future within him. *(He departs with his barge.)*

Immortalita (steps forward): Yes, you are the youth whom Hekate prophesied to me. At the sight of you it seems as if a beam of daylight breaks in through these old halls, through this Erebeian night.

Erodion: If I am the man of your prophecies, maiden or goddess—*whatever* I should call you—then believe me, you are the deepest intuition of my heart.

Immortalita: Tell me: Who are you? What are you are called? And where did you find the way to this pathless shore, where neither shadows nor people may wander, but only the gods of the underground?

Erodion: Unwillingly will I speak to you of anything other than my love—but if I relate to you my life, I will speak of my love. Hear me, then: I am the son of Eros and his mother Aphrodite. This double union of love and beauty laid in my being the idea of a pleasure which I could find nowhere, but which I intuited and searched for everywhere. For a long time I was a stranger on earth, and wanted to enjoy nothing of its shadow goods, until, through a dream or inspiration, a dark idea of you entered my soul. This idea, this re-flection of you, led me everywhere, and everywhere I pursued this beloved apparition. Even when it submerged me in the land of dreams I followed it, and so I appeared before the outermost gates of the underworld. But I could never penetrate to you; an ill-fated destiny always called me back to the world above.

Immortalita: What, youth—did you love me so much that you would rather never see Helios and the dawn again than not find me?

Erodion: I loved you that much, and without you the earth could no longer delight me: not the flowery spring, not the sunlit day[8]: beauties that Pluto would gladly have exchanged his somber scepter to possess. But, just as a greater love was combined in the embrace of my parents than all other love, for they were love itself, so the longing that drove me to you was also the most powerful, and my faith that I would find you triumphed over all obstacles. For my parents, who knew that someone who sprung from love and beauty would find nothing higher on earth than himself, gave me this faith, so that my strength would not tire of striving for something higher outside me.

Immortalita: But how did you finally come to me? Charon takes the living unwillingly in his ramshackle vessel, built only for shadows.

---

[8] The critical edition of Günderrode's work adds "not the dewy night" (SW 1:45).

Erodion: My longing to see you became so great that everything humanity had conceived to make you seem uncertain became small and trifling, and an ecstatic courage filled my whole being. I want nothing, nothing but to possess her, I thought, and boldly I threw all the goods of this earth away from me, and steered my vessel to the dangerous cliffs where everything earthly should be wrecked. Once more I thought: what if you lose everything to find nothing? But high confidence suppressed the doubt, and gladly I said my last goodbyes to the world above. The night engulfed me—a ghastly pause! and I found myself with you.—The torch of my life still burns beyond the water of the Styx.

Immortalita: The heroes of antiquity have trod this path; courage dared quarrels in this region; but it was reserved for love alone to found an enduring realm here. The residents of Orcus say my being breathes an immortal life into them; so may you also be immortal, for you have brought about something unnamable in me. I lived a mummy's life, but you have breathed a soul into me. Yes, dear youth! In your love I behold myself transfigured; I know now who I am; I know that a sunny day will illumine these old halls.

Hekate emerges behind the altar.

Hekate: Erodion! Step into the circle of the snake. *(He does so: the snake disappears.)* Too long, Immortalita, through the power of unbelief and barbarism, have you been known by few, doubted by many, banished to this narrow circle. An oracle as old as the world said that faithful love would succeed in finding you in the Erebeian darkness, in pulling you out and founding your throne in eternal clarity, accessible to all. This time has now come. Only for you, Erodion, there remains something more to do.

The scene transforms into part of the Elysian gardens. The scene is faintly lit; one sees shadows straying here and there. To the side is a cliff; in the background the Styx and Charon's barque.

The Previous [Scene]

Hekate: See, Erodion, this cliff threatening collapse: it is the insurmountable partition that separates the realm of mortal life from that of your mistress.

It prevents the sunlight from sending its beams here, and divided love from meeting again. Erodion! Try to bring down this cliff, so that your beloved may climb up on its ruins from the narrow underworld, and so that nothing insurmountable should divide the land of the dead from that of the living.

Erodion strikes the cliff. It collapses. It suddenly becomes bright.

Immortalita: Triumph! The cliff has fallen. From now on may it be granted to the thoughts of love, the dreams of longing, the inspiration of the poets, to descend from the land of the living to the shadow-realm and go back again.

Hekate: Hail! Threefold, immortal life will ensoul this pale shadow-realm. Now your realm is founded.

Immortalita: Come, Erodion, ascend with me in eternal clarity, and all love and every excellence shall partake of my realm. And you, Charon, uncrease your brow—be a friendlier escort to those who want to enter my realm.

Erodion: Good that I remained true to the holy intuition of my heart, like Vesta's fire; good that I had the courage to die to mortality and live for immortality, to sacrifice the visible to the invisible.

10

Story of a Brahmin

Introduction

"Story of a Brahmin" was written in early 1803 and published in Sophie von
La Roche's[1] 1805 collection *Herbsttage*. The story relates the *Bildung* (cultivation, education, or formation) of the narrator, Almor. Günderrode describes
Almor's transition from a life centered on money and pleasure through a
moral awakening, engagement with various religions, and a journey to Asia
in search of his true self. Like many other pieces by Günderrode, "Story of
a Brahmin" explores questions relating to knowledge, especially knowledge
that is inaccessible to scientific investigation or rational thought. In this case,
a variety of methods lead the narrator to grasp the reality behind everyday
experience—these methods include a journey to the east, introspection,
the study of religions, initiation into a secretive religion, and listening to an
"inner voice" and the voices of nature and "spirit." "Story of a Brahmin" also
includes a critique of Kantian morality and outlines an ideal community
which Günderrode presents as an alternative to both European society and
Kant's kingdom of ends.

"Story of a Brahmin" begins by establishing the narrator as someone who
merges east and west. Almor, the son of a French merchant who converted to
Islam, was born in Smyrna, now Izmir, on the west coast of Turkey. Smyrna
was part of the ancient Greek world and subsequently conquered by Persians,
Romans, Byzantines, Crusaders, Turks, and Ottomans; for centuries, it was
an important port on a major trade route between Europe and western
Asia. By beginning her story at a meeting point of east and west, and by
describing Almor's father as a westerner living in the east and a convert from
Christianity to Islam, Günderrode draws on her readers' associations (in
fact, stereotypes) of "east" and "west." She represents Europe, or the west,

---

[1] Sophie von la Roche (1731–1807) was a famous novelist, editor, and *salonnière*, and the grand-
mother of Günderrode's friends Bettina Brentano-von Arnim, Kunigunde "Gunda" Brentano, and
Clemens Brentano.

Karoline von Günderrode. Anna Ezekiel, Oxford University Press. © Oxford University Press 2026.
DOI: 10.1093/9780190089177.003.0012

as modern and developed, with a focus on productivity, usable knowledge, rationality, and the privileging of social needs and roles over the needs of the individual. She presents the east, by contrast, as a place of origins. Almor describes Asia as a land of poetry: it is the site of union with nature, connection with the divine, and the satisfaction of Romantic longings for, on the one hand, the exotic and other and, on the other hand, self-discovery and homecoming.

Almor tells us that his father sent him to Europe to pursue business, but he came to reject the self-centered pursuit of profit and pleasure, which he describes as "earning money in order to spend it again in a pleasant way." Searching for a more meaningful existence, he turns to a moral system that Günderrode intends to represent that of Immanuel Kant. Almor attempts to master "sensuality [and] the passions" and act as "a citizen of the moral realm," oriented to the welfare of all humanity. He describes his new approach as "the free activity of a thinking being that sets its own purpose for its conduct," recalling Kant's ideal of a rational individual who overcomes the heteronomous influence of the passions to become an autonomous subject.

However, Almor eventually rejects Kant's moral system, questioning its prioritization of human rational capacities over emotional needs. He begins to suspect that this has only become necessary because the "nature and harmony of [his] essence" has been corrupted by social conditioning.[2] In order to rediscover his original, authentic nature, Almor abandons Europe and European values and returns to Asia. Günderrode here follows the Romantic stereotype of Asia as a place where people can enjoy a closer connection to the source of life, the divine, and their own inner nature.

Almor states that during this stage in his development, "I wrested myself away from all relations with human beings" to "purify myself from everything alien and become wholly myself again." This description has led scholars to claim that "Story of a Brahmin" shows Günderrode rejecting politics and social concerns[3] or even that it describes a "transition into death" or a "figurative suicide."[4] This seems to be supported by Almor's reflection that "the decision that separates us from [society] is not much smaller than the step from this life into the one beyond," and by the interjection of Almor's

---

[2] This claim recalls the work of Jean-Jacques Rousseau (1712–1778), who claims that civilization has corrupted human beings from their original nature, which is unselfish, non-violent, and good.

[3] Margarete Lazarowicz, *Karoline von Günderrode. Porträt einer Fremden* (Frankfurt: Peter Lang, 1986), 61–74, 95.

[4] Dorothy Figueira, "The Dynamics of Exoticism: Herder's Epigram and Günderrode's Epitaph," in *The Exotic: A Decadent Quest*, ed. Dorothy Figueira (Albany: SUNY Press, 1994), 140.

interlocutor, Lubar, who compares this step to suicide. Ruth Christmann suggests that "Story of a Brahmin" represents a Romantic "turn inward"[5]— that is, a movement away from social and political concerns to focus on subjectivity—and other writers agree that Günderrode advocates a life of contemplation as opposed to a life of action.[6]

However, a life of isolated inward contemplation is not Almor's final resting point. After some time as a hermit, he will travel to India where he will be initiated into Brahminic religion and create a small community with his Brahmin mentor's family. Almor's inward turn is only another developmental stage on his way to establishing a way of life that is consistent with a fully developed human existence.

Nonetheless, Almor's time in solitude is an important part of his development, during which he not only reconnects with his own inner voice and true nature but also experiences his first glimpses of the divine. In fact, Günderrode suggests that Almor's authentic self and the divine are the same thing. Through his "inner sense," Almor "intimates" a connection with a mysterious "something," which he comes to realize is a single, unified force or life that flows through everything, including himself: "a fundamental force in which everything, visible and invisible, was connected." He also realizes that this underlying oneness of everything is the basic fact that all religions try to communicate: "the intuition of their original primal ground, is the deepest soul of religions." In contrast to Almor's childhood attitude to religion, which combined superficial observation of ceremonies with the hope of material advancement within religious institutions, Almor now experiences a profound personal relationship to the infinite.

In addition, Almor learns that his development is a process of coming to embody a "threefold way" of life. At the first, "animal" level, one focuses on physical needs: "health, preservation, propagation." This corresponds to Almor's early life of earning money and seeking pleasure. The second, "human" level is characterized by "morality," in which people take "humankind [as a whole] as their object." This corresponds to the Kantian moral system that formed the first step in Almor's transition to a more meaningful life. The third, "spiritual" level is one's "relation to the infinite, divine." It is this third aspect of the "threefold way" that Almor will pursue from now on.

[5] Christmann, *Identitätsgewinn*, 235.
[6] Helene M. Kastinger Riley, "Zwischen den Welten. Ambivalenz und Existentialproblematik im Werk Caroline von Günderrodes," in *Die weiblich Muse. Sechs Essays über künstlerisch schaffende Frauen der Goethezeit*, ed. Helene M. Kastinger Riley (Columbia: Camden House, 1986), 119.

Lastly, Almor realizes that, although a full human life involves all three ways of living, every individual must develop in a way that fits their unique nature. There is no single course of development that would be appropriate for every person, "for as various as is the outer formation of people, just as various is their inner nature, their life, and their wishes." Almor argues that any philosophical, religious, or moral system that claims there is only one life path for all individuals, or that requires individuals to subordinate their needs to the whole, stunts individual flourishing. This thwarts the purpose for which individual beings exist, which is simply to develop according to their own natures.

This model differs from enlightenment accounts of *Bildung*, in which individuals learn to be productive in order to be useful to society; some writers claim it is closer to a Romantic emphasis on the development of subjectivity for its own sake.[7] However, for Günderrode, these two goals are, in the end, reconcilable, although each must be understood in a new sense that fits with Almor's insight into the true nature of the universe (and with Günderrode's metaphysics).

At this point, driven by Romantic longing, Almor makes his way to India. Here, a "wise Brahmin" teaches him more about the "infinite spirit of nature" that Almor first intuited as a hermit. The Brahmin's description is based on Hindu ideas of reincarnation, but framed in terms (such as "the divinity and universality of the creator") that resonate with a Christian context and (in its talk of "forces") with philosophy of nature and Günderrode's own metaphysics as developed in "Idea of the Earth" and "Letters of Two Friends." The Brahmin teaches Almor:

> how the forces wander through all forms until they develop consciousness and thought in human beings; how from human beings on an infinite series of migrations that lead to ever higher perfection awaits souls; how eventually, through mysterious ways, they will all unite with the primal force from which they emanated and will become one with it, and still at the same time remain themselves, and thus unite the divinity and universality of the creator with the individuality of the creature.

This account presents human beings, not as the highest achievement of existence, but as an intermediate stage in the development of the "primal

---

[7] Dormann, *Kunst des inneren Sinns*, 70.

force" toward perfection. In this respect, Günderrode's model differs from enlightenment and traditional Christian accounts that view human beings as the peak of creation and natural masters or stewards of the rest of the world.[8] For Günderrode, it is not part of human development to cultivate, manage, or develop the rest of the world (whether other human beings or nature); their only task is to develop themselves.

We can now see how Günderrode reconciles the needs of individuals and society, which were framed as conflicting, one necessarily subordinated to the other, in her characterization of European culture and Kantian morality. On Günderrode's model, individual self-development and the development of the whole must necessarily occur together, because each individual is part of the whole and, together, the means by which it develops. The free unfolding of each individual's nature is precisely how the universe cultivates itself.

The self-development of each individual according to their own authentic nature will eventually lead to a state that Almor describes as "a time of perfection [. . .] when each being will be harmonious with itself and with the others, when they flow into each other and become one." That is, if every individual recognizes that they are part of the same underlying life force, their ways of living will naturally align, resulting in a form of social harmony that is independent of moral and legal systems or religious institutions. Almor's time in isolation and his turn inward were necessary so that he could learn to hear his inner voice, which is also the voice of nature or the world-spirit. It is only after doing so that he could turn outward again and become part of an ideal community joined in relationship to the divine.[9]

This form of community is exemplified by the ending of "Story of a Brahmin." After the Brahmin's death, his spirit lives on in Almor and in the Brahmin's daughter, who share a hut in the wilderness.[10] This small group represents the community "between human beings in whom the inner sense has arisen and the world-spirit" that the Brahmin described.

Rather than a rejection of social and political concerns, "Story of a Brahmin" engages with a debate about the "vocation of humankind" that was ongoing at the time Günderrode was writing. There are commonalities,

---

[8] E.g., Fichte, trans. Preuss, *Vocation*, 83; Herder, *Ideen*, vol. 4, 239.
[9] Dormann, *Kunst des inneren Sinns*, 74.
[10] Cf. "The Manes" and "The Frank in Egypt."

as well as significant differences, between Günderrode's thought and in-fluential texts that contributed prominently to this debate. These include Johann Joachim Spalding's popular 1748 book *Reflections on the Vocation of Human Beings*,[11] Johann Gottlieb Fichte's *The Vocation of Humankind*, which was partly a response to Spalding and which Günderrode excerpted in her notes,[12] and Johann Gottfried Herder's *Ideas for a Philosophy of the History of Humankind*.[13] The latter, like "Story of a Brahmin," criticizes Kant's privileging of human reason over the passions and his apparent sub-ordination of the needs of the individual to those of society as a whole. There are also similarities between Günderrode's account of religion and the work of the theologian Friedrich Schleiermacher (1768–1834), whose writings Günderrode excerpted in her notes. In particular, Schleiermacher's rejection of the moral aspect of religion and its replacement by intuition of the infi-nite in nature, his view of the essence of religion as "everything individual as a part of the whole,"[14] and his claim that each individual will have their own religion are echoed in "Story of a Brahmin."[15] However, there are also differences between their accounts. In particular, Schleiermacher views humanity as the paradigmatic place where religion is manifested, while in "Story of a Brahmin," Günderrode explicitly separates the moral sphere of "human" life from the spiritual sphere of religion.

Günderrode's claim that the individual is a unique and essential part of the whole points to her interest in forms of community that reflect this unique-ness and inner essence. Although self-development for Günderrode includes introspection, the final stage of human flourishing involves friendship, love, and connections with other human beings, nature, and the divine. Only in this way does the human being live animally, humanly, and spiritually, and thus close the "gap in their existence" that Almor claims afflicts those who do not live in all three ways.

---

[11] Johann Joachim Spalding, *Betrachtung über die Bestimmung des Menschen* (Leipzig: Weidmanns Erben und Reich, 1768 [1748]).

[12] Fichte, trans. Preuss, *Vocation*, 9.

[13] Herder, *Ideen.*

[14] From Günderrode's summary of Schleiermacher's "On Religion" (see Notebooks section, below).

[15] For details on Schleiermacher's influence on Günderrode, see the introduction to her notes on Schleiermacher later in this volume.

Story of a Brahmin

I was, said Almor, born in Smyrna. My father, a Frenchman and rich merchant who had converted from Christianity to the Muhammedan religion, treated me coldly and unkindly on the rare occasions when I appeared before him, and my mother died before I remember. I felt very abandoned and often deeply embittered by my father. Children, when they begin to contemplate life with the eyes of their spirit, are frightened by the customs, circumstances and demands of human society, and only the gentle hand of good parents can introduce them to the unfamiliar constraints of civic and domestic life without great pain. Nature first speaks to children through their parents. Woe to the poor creatures if this first speech is cold and loveless!

Because I was presented with more unpleasant objects of contemplation than pleasant ones, I soon gave it [contemplation] up completely; even the ceremonies of the Muhammedan service that I had to take part in daily did not arouse my curiosity to understand their meaning. My father often said that religions were useful political institutions, but extremely superfluous for an enlightened individual. In any case, the ceremonial service was onerous for me, so out of convenience I gave this statement my full approval.

I was sixteen years old when my father (who wanted me to become a merchant) sent me to a business associate in one of the greatest cities of Europe. [However, t]he impression that the novelty of so many objects made upon my soul was not significant, because I considered things more with my eyes than with my spirit.

I was forced to occupy most of the hours of the day with business; I applied those that remained to enjoying myself. I visited plays and beautiful women, and went around with frivolous young men; however, I was left with a certain bashfulness and awkwardness in social life that we easterners seldom discard, for our way of life is very unsociable.

Many years went by like this, in which I knew nothing higher than earning money in order to spend it again in a pleasant way. The news of the death of my father first led me to some reflection. I did not mourn his death, but I grieved for my lack of feeling at his loss, and in my heart I reproached myself for that.

A new factor appeared to awaken my spirit from its slumber: the merchant for whom I worked lost almost his entire fortune. He and his wife spent days with me in the greatest distress about it and we drafted hundreds of futile plans to avert this evil. After I seemed to have become almost dullwitted about the means of saving these people, I said to myself: are, then, riches and sensual enjoyment the only desirable goods? This question suddenly opened as yet unknown depths of my own mind to me; I descended into a crowd of thoughts as if into a cave in which springs bubble, ever new and fresh. I had already been on earth a long time; now I began to live, and the wings of my spirit dared their first flight. The moral world, until then invisible to me, was unveiled to me: I saw a community of spirits, a realm of effect and countereffect, an invisible harmony, a purpose to human striving, and a true good. I was lost to my professional work from the moment I found this beautiful land—I abandoned it. For before I determined an area in which to be active, I wanted to know: who was I? what should I be? what position befitted me? and which laws ruled in the realm whose citizen I wanted to be?

First I considered my nature and vocation separately, and only with regard to myself. I found that the welfare of my spirit could not exist without wisdom and virtue. I found that wisdom and virtue, the objects of my highest striving, could be attained by mastering sensuality [and] the passions, and by the exercise of my forces in noble and useful activity. If I considered myself a citizen of the moral realm, I found myself obliged to promote its welfare just like my own, with all my forces, to sacrifice everything to it, and to consider myself its property.

With what joy I stepped out of the narrow circle of my allotted daily work into the free activity of a thinking being that sets its own purpose for its conduct; out of limited personal self-interest into the great fraternity of all human beings for the good of all. The merely mechanical and animal life that I had escaped lay behind me like a musty dungeon; I stepped into the world in every sense and exercised my forces in many a self-conquest, in many a difficult virtue. Through meticulous consideration I soon came to know everything human in human beings—but the divine was still not manifest to me.

My proud reason soon claimed sole rulership within me: it wanted everything to be reasonable. This demand of course entangled me in perennial disputes with myself and the world: the intractability of my own nature to its [reason's] commandments made me dissatisfied with myself; the perennial struggle of the world against its demands confused me; sophisticated criticism found everything blameworthy—nothing could satisfy this reason.

Once, I had brought it [reason] a great sacrifice. For a long time I was lost in contemplation of this; finally, an inner voice spoke to me: Why, then, is everything on earth good except human beings? Why should they alone become different than they are? Is a person only virtuous if they stand on the ruins of their own spirit and can say: Look, these rebelled, but they fell, I have become victor over them all!—Barbarian! Do not rejoice in your victory; you have waged a civil war: those you have conquered were children of your own nature, you have killed yourself in your victory, you have fallen in your battle.

I could offer no reply to this voice other than the disorder that the moral world would get into if no one was willing to struggle against their inclinations. But this answer did not satisfy me; the peace bought with such sacrifices was too expensive, and I could no longer bear the thought of partly annihilating myself in order to—partly—better preserve myself. How can I know, I proceeded to think, what belongs to the actual nature and harmony of my essence, and what is transferred to me through upbringing and circumstances? Perhaps, if my mind were still unalloyed by foreign additions, perhaps there would then be in me no *should*, no killing of *one* so the *other* would thrive better. Certainly only the world, its confusion, the flow of its deep decay, the cowardly indulgence that it often imposes upon us, had transported me from myself and made me into a being of contradictory nature.

From the moment this became clear to me, I wrested myself away from all relations with human beings; I even left Europe and went back to my fatherland. There, in quiet contemplation of my soul, I wanted to purify myself from everything alien and become wholly myself again.

With what joy I saw Asia again! A balmy air carried the finest scent of the spices of the orient to me. Syria's quiet coast bathed in the warm Mediterranean, and evening clouds rested on the peaks of the mountains: a meaningful inscription at the entrance to this land, in which earthly and heavenly, human and divine, have always converged so closely.

I chose a palm forest on the Persian Gulf as my residence. This quiet place served me as a haven against the shoals and cliffs of the world; but it is not so easy to separate oneself from it. Thousands of secret bonds tie us to it, and the decision that separates us from it is not much smaller than the step from this life into the one beyond.

I can, Lubar interrupted the storyteller, call this step good as little as I can suicide. Both are equally detrimental to human society, and what would become of it [society], if everyone were allowed to kill themselves to it?

Young friend! responded Almor, not everyone can and will do what I did. It does not befit everyone, for as various as is the outer formation of people, just as various is their inner nature, their life, and their wishes. The world shapes one [person], its entanglement makes them adept, its resistance exercises their force. Another shapes the world, and their acts continue to have an effect in it even when they have long stopped acting. These and other similar natures belong to the world, they cannot and may not withdraw from it. It is completely different with me: I never belonged to the world; there was only a bargain, as it were, according to which it gave me those of its goods that were indispensable to me, and I gave it what I could. This bargain is at an end: the world can give me nothing more, its noise makes me deaf to the speech of my own spirit, its circumstances bewilder me, I get lost in it uselessly. Here in this quiet solitude I have found my individuality, my peace, my God, and a thousand spirit voices speak revelations to me, which I cannot hear in the tumult of life.

The struggle (Almor continued in his narration) of the individual with society, of freedom against freedom, of individuality against general laws, and of morals against their impediments, stopped occupying and tormenting me so much. For a long time it had been clear to me that justice is the basis of civil society and morality the basis of human society. These two relations had once satisfied me; I had sought to bring all the points of my mind into contact with them. Now I discovered aptitudes within me that these finite relations would no longer satisfy. My understanding always wanted to know more, insatiably; my power of imagination sought a wider scope for its creations; my appetite sought an infinite object for its striving; and my inner sense intimated an invisible and mysterious connection with something that I did not yet know, and to which I would gladly have given a shape and name. I looked up at the stars and found it sad that my eyes so gladly would have looked further, and yet were chained to the earth. I loved the dawn, to whose embrace I would gladly have flown, and the surging sea, into the depths of which I wanted to throw myself.

In this longing, in this love the spirit of nature spoke to me. I heard its voice, but I did not yet know where it came from; but the more I listened to it, the clearer it was to me that there was a fundamental force in which everything, visible and invisible, was connected. I named this force primal life, and sought to bring my consciousness into connection with it (for a mysterious and unknown descent from it seemed certain to me); I sought all kinds of paths to ascend to it, from the earthly to the heavenly. Finally, religion seemed to me to be this path.

A saying from the Koran that occurred to me one day led me to this thought; with love and eagerness I studied Muhammad's teachings and his life. My spirit passed over into contemplation of him: I saw how the consciousness of divine things germinated early in his soul, how a powerful longing drove him to inject this branch from the eternal tree of life into the weatherbeaten stem[16] of his people, but how this tender plant, which can only bloom and bear fruit in a soil purified by morality and culture, adopted an altered and foreign shape and nature. I saw his attempts, through law, through hope in heaven and fear of hell, to lay a basis for morality in their raw minds; saw, finally, how ambition, an unrestrained power of imagination, and the force of circumstances misled him to combine unholy means and purposes with holy ones.[17] After I had thus seen how the world-spirit had been reflected in this individual, I passed over to the contemplation of its image in the spirits of other representatives of religion. I went through the teachings of Zoroaster, Confucius, Moses, and Christ, the remnants of the wisdom of the Egyptian priests, and the Hindus' holy myths.

As variously as spirit spoke from all these, I still found only one meaning in these forms, with which mine connected most deeply, by which it was broadened and reinforced.

You ask me, young friend, to lead you in through the gates of the eternal temple of religion. Know that its inscription is infinity and speech is finite. But I will attempt to unveil before you the holy statue of Isis at Saïs (under which stand the words "I am what is, what was and will be"); but so your inner sense does not completely come undone before the goddess, you will not see her, neither through your reason, nor through your knowledge.[18]

There is an infinite force, an eternal life, that is everything that is, that was and will become, that engenders itself in mysterious ways, that remains eternal during all change and dying. It is at the same time the ground of all things and the things themselves, the condition and the conditioned, the creator and the creature, and it divides and separates itself in various figures, becomes sun, moon, stars, plants, animal, and human being together, and flows through itself in fresh streams of life and contemplates itself in human beings in holy humility. This intuition of things, the intuition of their original primal ground, is the deepest soul of religions, variously individuated in each individual. But go through all the religious systems yourself: in all

---

[16] The word Günderrode uses here is *Stamm*, which means both "stem" and "tribe."

[17] Günderrode's play *Muhammad, the Prophet of Mecca* develops this claim in more detail: as her character Muhammad gains more worldly power, he becomes increasingly tyrannical and the purity of his message is corrupted. See Ezekiel, "Introduction to *Muhammad*."

[18] The veiled statue of Isis in Saïs has often been used as a metaphor for the secrets of nature.

of them you will find something infinite, invisible, out of which emerged the finite and visible, something divine that becomes human, a transition of temporal life into the eternal. The sense for this eternal life already arose in me here in religious contemplation; for this reason, the temporal has, in a certain sense, become so meager to me and my spirit has organized things completely differently.

The philosophy that considers every individual as a means for the whole has now become hateful to me, [the philosophy] that is still only comprised of individuals, that always asks what use this or that is for the others and considers each as a fruit that has bloomed and ripened in order to be consumed by the whole; [the philosophy] that plants the most various natures in one garden, and wants to grow the oak and the rose according to one standard. To me, each individual is holy, it is God's work, it is its own purpose. If it becomes what it can become according to its nature, then it has done enough, and what it profits the others is a side issue. Each peculiarity is holy to me; whatever of us belongs to the world, our actions within it may be directed according to its laws and according to its order, but no alien law may touch the inner freedom of my spirit, may disturb the distinct nature of my mind which, if it were perfected, would be a pure harmony without an off-tone.—Yes, a time of perfection must come, when each being will be harmonious with itself and with the others, when they flow into each other and become one in a great unison, when every melody throws itself into the eternal harmony.

Just like health, preservation, propagation are the highest for merely animal life, humanity in the broadest sense of the word (according to which it also includes morality and culture) is the highest for human beings as human beings; as such they have humankind as their object.[19] Their pure relationship to it, morality, consists in itself, satisfies itself, and needs no other motive nor prospects than itself and humankind. Anyone who needs some sort of religion as a buttress to their morality, their morality is not pure, for according to its nature this must consist in itself. Thus a human being can do without religion and, considered merely as a human being, does not attain its prospects in religion's territory. But the spirit seeks the spiritual, its thirst searches for the source of life, it seeks its forces, which find no proportion on earth, something unearthly, an infinite object of contemplation for its spiritual eye, and it finds all this in religion. To spirit, religion is what is highest, and spirit's life

---

[19] Cf. Herder, *Ideen*, vol. 3, 438.

in religion is a purely spiritual one. Thus the human being lives in a threefold way: animally—this is its relationship to earth; humanly—this is its relation to humankind; spiritually—this is its relation to the infinite, divine. Whoever does not live in these three ways has a gap in their existence, and something is missing in their aptitudes.—

This new view of things brought my mind perpetual peace. The Persian palm forests were an Elysium[20] to me, but a certain longing drove me to see India. I wandered up towards Tibet, through the chasms and valleys of the Mustagh[21] and down the Ganges to where it disgorges its holy water into the Bay of Bengal, and back again to Delhi, the old capital of the Mongolian Sultans.[22] Not far from this city I met a wise Brahmin who soon became fond of me, took me in to his dwelling on the bank of the Ganges, and educated me in the Sanskrit language. Together we wandered to the more remote regions of India and searched for monuments of the past splendor of this land.

An ardent love of his people animated the Brahmin, he grieved over its fall as if it were his own and reveled in its former greatness, and the lively interest I took in it made me ever dearer to him. He taught me the story of his fatherland in greater detail, and with astonishment I saw that India's culture reached into an antiquity in which other peoples' calendars were not yet born. If, he once said to me, the proud Europeans boast of being the midpoint of the civilized and enlightened world, the sun that illuminated and warmed the earth rose in the orient; later and paler it sends its beams to the occident.[23] The fog of forgetfulness veils the graves of our primeval world, only a few great figures shimmer through; our victorious gods have fled, we are trodden down by the crude Mongols, we die slowly through the profit-seeking Europeans. Each people's greatness appears to be a spring that comes only once and then escapes to bless other areas.

The more I got to know this man, the more I found in him a true priest, a mediator between God and human beings. Divine and human were intertwined in his mind in the deepest and most beautiful way. The earth

---

[20] In Greek mythology, Elysium, or the Elysian Fields, is a pleasant afterlife for those related to or chosen by the gods. In modern times, these terms are used analogously to "paradise."

[21] A range of mountains in the Himalayas, also known as the Karakorum.

[22] Günderrode uses "Mongols" to refer to the Mughal (also spelled "Mogul") Empire, which ruled much of what is now India, Pakistan, and Bangladesh as well as parts of Afghanistan and Myanmar from 1526 until the British conquered most of the region in the mid-nineteenth century. The Mughal rulers were descended from Genghis Khan's Mongol dynasty; Günderrode's spelling emphasizes this connection.

[23] Cf. Günderrode's play *Udohla*, in which India's fall from former glory is lamented in similar terms (SW 1:223).

was holy to him as a forecourt of heaven, its colorful tumult did not confuse him, everything developed clearly before his spirit, and he remained pure and innocent in the whirl of perdition. He stood like Moses on a high mountain where no one could follow him, and God spoke to him, and through him to human beings. Soon he forgot I was a stranger and inducted me into the wisdom of the Brahmins. He taught me how in each part of the infinite spirit of nature lies the aptitude for eternal perfection, how the forces wander through all forms until they develop consciousness and thought in human beings; how from human beings on an infinite series of migrations leading to ever higher perfection awaits souls; how eventually, through mysterious ways, they will all unite with the primal force from which they emanated and will become one with it, and still at the same time remain themselves, and thus unite the divinity and universality of the creator with the individuality of the creature. He taught me how a community exists between human beings in whom the inner sense has arisen and the world-spirit.

"I spent," he said to me, "Months and years in which the spirit was simply silent,[24] but suddenly it spoke to me in high revelations, and then in one moment things became comprehensible to me that for years I had striven in vain to understand. The phenomena around me then had a new and completely different meaning, a fresh source of life flowed through my breast, my thoughts flew more boldly, more rapidly. I was like someone who, in bleak solitude, had almost forgotten the tones of speech, and whom a good and great person approached and spoke kindly to. But when the voice fell silent, when the window of heaven closed, through which divine clarity had come into my dark soul, then I was very sad, and I could not take joy in anything but in the memory of the light that I had seen."

A twofold life seemed to dwell in the old man when he spoke thus, and a spark of his spirit passed over into mine. I could not leave him. I accompanied him everywhere, except some summer nights that he spent with an old Brahmin in the ruins of an Indian temple on the Ganges in mysterious devotions and ceremonies of his religion. One day, he came back from one of these wanderings very weary and pale, and bade me and his seven year old daughter Lasida to accompany him into the shadow of some palms that stood on the Ganges and over which leaned a high cliff decked with inscriptions. He sat down in the shadow of the trees and for a long time did not have the strength to speak. Eventually, he said with a weak voice:

---

[24] The Morgenthaler edition has "was silent to me" (*mir geschwiegen hat*) (SW 1:313).

"Almor! Be the father of my Lasida when I am dead. Live with her and tell her of me; I would like to live on in her love. You, Almor, farewell; I will not die for you because my spirit continues to have an effect in you. Once more, farewell, and leave me by myself: I would like to die in undisturbed contemplation of death, would like to breathe my spirit silently back into silent nature."

I left him, and when I returned in the evening found him dead. His friend, the old Brahmin, came the same evening; he claimed to have known of his death, and buried him at midnight in the place where he had died.

I stayed in Lasida's house, lived like a Brahmin, and trained the girl very little; I left her instead to her own lovely nature. Ten years have elapsed since her father's death and he still lives among us; yes, Lasida leaves this house reluctantly to follow her beloved, because she fears to be shut out from close community with her father by a little distance. And I will never leave this hut, these palms, this stream; I am spellbound here as if in a magic circle and peace never leaves me.

Tiann.

11

Fragments on Ethics and Aesthetics

Introduction

Although Günderrode did not create a fully developed ethics or aesthetics, the short texts translated in this section yield interesting reflections on these topics. This is particularly the case if they are considered in the context of Günderrode's other writings, for instance, her remarks on virtue, beauty, and other "excellences" in "Idea of the Earth" and "Letters of Two Friends." The five poems and fragments translated here all focus on love, beauty, and the spiritual life, and suggest that these three things share an orientation to an ideal beyond the objects and individuals of the everyday world.

The only published piece among the texts translated in this section, the poem "Change and Constancy," appeared in 1804 in Günderrode's first collection, *Poems and Fantasies*. Of the unpublished pieces, "Only One and One to Serve" was probably written in 1804 or 1805, while the other three pieces were written before the publication of *Poems and Fantasies* and possibly as early as 1799.

The untitled fragmentary thoughts beginning "Excellence is a whole ... " consider how to choose and live the right kind of life. The reflections on these questions fall into two categories. The first consists of claims regarding an opposition between an inner and an outer life, which Günderrode also calls a "higher" and a "common" life or a "heavenly" and an "earthly" life. She presents these as contrasting options for how to live, which require a choice between "serv[ing] and benefit[ting] the world" and "contemplating the eternal, infinite, [and] striving for it."

The choice between a worldly and a spiritual path is a common theme in Günderrode's writings. This choice features in "Story of a Brahmin," "The Manes," *Magic and Destiny*, and *Muhammad, the Prophet of Mecca*. Günderrode was likely influenced in this respect by the theologian and biblical scholar Friedrich Schleiermacher (1768–1834), who also wrote about

Karoline von Günderrode. Anna Ezekiel, Oxford University Press. © Oxford University Press 2026.
DOI: 10.1093/9780190089177.003.0013

the contrast between an "outward," worldly life and an "inward" life of spiritual contemplation.[1]

In "Excellence is a whole . . . ," Günderrode praises the inward or heavenly life, referring to it as the "higher" way of life. She devotes much more space to considering this way of living than she does to the "common" or "earthly" life. This is perhaps what has led scholars to conclude that Günderrode advocates a contemplative lifestyle over a lifestyle that engages with the everyday world. Some have aligned this aspect of Günderrode's thought with the Romantic "turn inward"—that is, a supposed shift from considering questions of community and social transformation to a focus on subjectivity and individual interiority.[2] However, Günderrode's thought is not as black-and-white as this interpretation would have it. In "Excellence is a whole . . . ," she states that the earthly and heavenly lifestyles are both "ways of living rightly." She gives examples of people (such as nuns and the Apostles) who follow the spiritual life by living in communities organized around a shared orientation to the infinite. In other words, Günderrode presents the turn to a spiritual lifestyle, not as a rejection of community, but as a different way of choosing community members and organizing one's life together. Essentially, the "heavenly" way of life is a *way of life*: not an escape from living, but a particular way of doing so. It is a way of living focused on one's inward, spiritual development, which prioritizes relationships with others who are engaged in the same project.

The second category of reflections in "Excellence is a whole . . . " relates to the idea that virtues or "excellences" (*Vortrefflichkeiten*) are defined by the relationship of individuals to a whole. This refers to the relationship between virtues as embodied in individuals and the same virtues considered as ideals, e.g., the relationship between individual beautiful objects and the ideal of beauty.[3] This point is also important in the other four pieces in this section.

These texts all present either artistic creation or love (or both) as expressing an orientation toward the universal. They describe love, not as love for an individual, but as love for something these individuals embody or instantiate. For example, in "Excellence is a whole . . . ," Günderrode writes that "there is

---

[1] Schleiermacher, *Monologen*, 12, 20, 22, and *passim*. Günderrode excerpted this text in her notebooks (see her notes on Schleiermacher translated later in this volume). For a comparison of Günderrode's and Schleiermacher's views of the "inner" and "outer" realms, see Hugo E. Herrera, "Urgrund and Access to the Urgrund in Karoline von Günderrode's Discussion with the Thought of Friedrich Schleiermacher," *European Journal of Philosophy* 32.2 (2023): 378–393.

[2] Christmann, *Identitätsgewinn*, 235; Dormann, *Kunst des inneren Sinns*, 74.

[3] It may also refer to the relationship between virtuous actions and the harmonious whole that Günderrode thinks such actions help establish (see the main introduction to this volume and Nassar, "Human Vocation").

no personal love, only love of the excellent," and in "Change and Constancy" Narcissus claims "Love [...] wants to contemplate all excellent things. / When it has recognized the light in one image, / It hurries to others." In theory, any kind of excellent or virtuous characteristic—understood as the embodiment of an ideal of this virtue in an individual—could arouse love in others. However, in the pieces translated here, Günderrode focuses on the ideal of beauty.

In "Love and Beauty," Günderrode claims that love is the longing for beauty, as embodied in another human being: "To see beauty is what love's longing wants." Or, put another way, love, aroused by the beauty of an individual person, reflects an underlying desire for connection with the infinite realm of the beautiful. This claim recalls Plato's concept of *eros* ("love" or "desire") as a force that pulls individuals toward union with the divine. In Plato's account, ordinary, "earthly" love is focused on individuals, but "divine" love transcends this kind of attraction. Instead of physical attraction to individuals, divine or "Platonic" love is attracted to the excellences, especially beauty, that the individuals embody.[4]

The influence of Plato also features in "Tendency of the Artist," in which Günderrode presents works of art as imitations of (Platonic) ideas in material form. Like the figure of Prometheus in "Love and Beauty," the artist in this poem takes something from the ideal realm and implants it in "matter," or the physical realm. In both cases, the resulting physical images (the human being and the work of art, respectively) are inadequate representations of the ideal on which they were based. Nonetheless, these inadequate embodiments help us access the ideal in some way. "Love and Beauty" describes how we are drawn to the ideal of beauty through its embodiment in human beings. And in "Tendency of the Artist," the artist's works express the artist's visions of things from the realm of ideas, allowing others to perceive these ideas in concrete form.

The poem "Change and Constancy" also explores the idea that love is a striving for an ideal of beauty embodied in the individuals who are loved. This poem is a dialogue between two characters, Violetta and Narcissus, whose debate about love is framed by the question of the nature of constancy or faithfulness. Violetta accuses Narcissus of unfaithfulness, because he is

---

[4] Another possible connection to Plato is Günderrode's claim that "Life [...] / does not forget its high origin." This recalls Plato's idea of *anamnesis*, according to which human beings are born with innate knowledge that they can recover through learning. Günderrode suggests that human beings innately possess the knowledge that they originated from "the beautiful" (Raisbeck, *Philosophical Romantic*, 141).

always falling in love with new objects of desire, while Narcissus argues that he is faithful because he consistently pursues the embodiment of beauty in new objects: "I do not love people, and not things, / Only their beauty."

Violetta is advocating something like Plato's idea of "vulgar" or earthly love: a love focused on individuals rather than the excellences they embody. Narcissus, on the other hand, advocates divine or Platonic love, which involves attraction to the infinite that is embodied in finite beings. Narcissus seems unfaithful because he repeatedly abandons one lover for another, but in fact he is devoted to the ideal that lies behind its manifestations in these individuals.

Günderrode's choice of characters in this poem is interesting. She is drawing on a Greek myth in which the beautiful hunter Narcissus falls in love with his reflection.[5] He becomes so absorbed in contemplating his own beauty that he eventually starves to death or, in some versions of the story, kills himself from despair at being unable to touch his image on the water's surface. In Günderrode's dialogue, too, Narcissus perishes because of his complete self-abandonment to love. In this case, however, he does not perish from becoming too absorbed in his own beauty, as in the original myth; rather, he perishes from throwing himself too wholeheartedly into love of the beautiful in general, pursuing one beautiful object after another until he is totally spent. The poem ends: "The stream of life surges up and down / And sweeps me along in its eddies. [...] Oh stream! In you all my life gushes out!"[6] In other words, Günderrode's Narcissus becomes so absorbed in his devotion to the multiple manifestations of the infinite object of his desire (beauty) that he loses himself in them.

The poem beginning "Only One and One to Serve" portrays a similar desire to lose oneself in enjoying multiple objects of desire. Here, the adoration of beauty in multiple objects, reflecting an orientation toward "the beautiful" itself, paves the way to viewing all individual beings, including oneself, as parts of a single, infinite, ever-changing "life" (or, here, "vastness"). This shift in viewpoint allows one to participate in this infinite nature, overstepping

---

[5] Because of the importance of reflection in the original story, Ruth Christmann argues that Günderrode uses Narcissus to represent "the Early German Romantic method of self-knowledge through contemplation of the I in the other" (*Identitätsgewinn*, 159). Another interesting aspect of Günderrode's adaptation is that in the original, Narcissus' fate is a punishment for rejecting the nymph Echo, but Günderrode replaces Echo with Violetta. This is probably because violets historically symbolize faithfulness (Licher, *Mein Leben*, 300–301).

[6] This image of Narcissus swept away in an infinite flux should be read in the context of Günderrode's metaphysics, according to which all finite life forms are transient manifestations of eternal life itself: "See all life!" Narcissus exclaims, "It is not persistence, / It is an eternal wandering, coming, going, / Living change!"

one's boundaries as a finite being: one can step "into the vastness / Out of narrow, stifling life." Like in "Change and Constancy," faithfulness to an ideal is contrasted with devotion to a single beloved object, which is presented as a turn away from the infinite, toward finite things. The result of such devotion to "only one" transient thing would be a meaningless existence "Without a center."

Other philosophically interesting topics emerge in the pieces in this section and await closer investigation. For example, in "Excellence is a whole . . . ," Günderrode describes dying as becoming poetry for one's friends, inviting exploration of her ideas about poetry, language, and the narrative construction of identity, perhaps in comparison to the work of other philosophers.[7] It would also be interesting to study the connection of this claim to Günderrode's idea of a continuing influence by the dead in "The Manes." And it could be illuminating to cross-reference the fragment beginning "They still grow on the world like an apple on the tree . . . " with the passage in "Story of a Brahmin" in which Almor complains about a view of individuals "each as a fruit that has bloomed and ripened in order to be consumed by the whole."[8]

(Excellence is a whole ...)

Excellence is a whole. We do not have it: it is like the blue of the sky above us, and our excellence is only a striving towards it, a view of it; therefore there is no personal love, only love of the excellent.

*

Let yourself live as you are without playing tricks on yourself, i.e., without trying to force yourself to love things that you cannot love. Your lamentation that you do not love is a longing for love; this longing is a thought which (because it has no object upon which to rest) gazes into the infinite. Now my thought comes across your formless gazing upwards and cultivates it, gives it its form, its ground and purpose in consciousness. Now, when I have brought all your thoughts that have no form into contact with mine and have formed

---

[7] On the use of language and memory to construct identity in Günderrode's work, see Allingham, "Countermemory." On the relationship between Günderrode's ideas about narrative and identity and those of early German Romantic thinkers, see Ezekiel, "Narrative and Fragment."
[8] For reference, see the translations of "The Manes" and "Story of a Brahmin" and their introductions earlier in this volume.

them, then I take my thoughts in another direction; you then believe I have abandoned you. But I would be arrogant if I were to impose myself on those fortunate ones that do not need me.

*

I have experienced everything that I tell them: I was in their condition, but to a higher degree. I struggled through superstition and doubt and returned to faith; they must have faith too, for everything is faith—even the newest and worthiest philosophy turns to faith.

*

There are only two lives: the common (which is worse than we are) and the higher. Many people hover between the two; the true artist stands wholly in the latter. It is true bliss, and anyone who has once entered it—to them, the world is lost without salvation.

*

There are only two ways of living rightly: earthly, or heavenly. One can serve and benefit the world, hold office, conduct business dealings, raise children—then one lives in an earthly way. Or one lives in a heavenly way, in contemplating the eternal, infinite, in striving for it (a form of nunnery). Anyone who would like to live differently than in one of these two ways is debauched.

*

They still grow on the world like an apple on the tree, but when the fruit is ripe it falls from the stem; then it has its specific shape, is perfected. They, too, must wrest themselves free from the world and become wholly themselves; then they are perfect. One law rules in the whole of nature.

*

They have torn apart a sacred image, and therefore may not pray: this is their condition. They linger in contemplation of their flaws and neglect what is highest.

*

They appear to me like someone who sings badly with a beautiful voice, they live badly with good aptitudes.

*

People say I am useless because I do not conduct business dealings, and yet I work for the eternal through the influence I have on some minds. Anyone who would like to be a priest among men may not be a hypocrite; for this reason I cannot deal with the Pharisees,[9] for this reason I cannot conceal the truth. I do not care that my contemporaries do not esteem me for this; anyone who espouses a better teaching[10] must always undergo that, I will not perish from it; the Apostles gave up wife and child and everything and followed Christ.

*

True, genuine love is mostly an unhappy phenomenon: one tortures oneself and is mistreated by the world. Coquetterie has always interested me; it is at the same time the most spiritual game and the greatest training for the spirit; through it, one belongs to oneself without losing oneself. It is a peculiar assemblage in them that they must understand how to separate,[11] not through thoughts (for their thoughts are precisely the mixture) but through separate occupations. They poeticize with their imagination, work with their arms, dance with their feet, read Goethe and Homer and study these, i.e., read them with joy, until they have integrated the persons in their thoughts, i.e., until Ajax[12] is no longer only a hero to them, no, until they cognize in him infinite thought (which is presented in human form through art). So far all their needs have been transferred and pressed into that of love, that is why their love is no longer free, necessary not lovable.[13] But when they have done all that they will feel sophisticated, and happy. Furthermore they are more determinate in their being, they tolerate nothing of poor quality, do not go around much with common people, for that would be to trample excellence underfoot.

*

My view of dying is the most peaceful. In life, a friend is to me what grammar is—if he dies, he will become poetry to me. I would rather know nothing of my best friend than not know some beautiful artwork.

---

[9] The Pharisees were a religious group in Palestine that flourished around 2000 years ago. The New Testament portrays them as opponents of Jesus; this portrayal informs Günderrode's statement here.

[10] The Morgenthaler edition has "a newer, better teaching" (SW 1:437).

[11] The Morgenthaler edition has "must try to separate" (SW 1:438).

[12] This may refer to Ajax the Great or Ajax the Lesser; both are mythical ancient Greek heroes.

[13] The Morgenthaler edition has "therefore their love is not free, not lovable," and "more necessary" added as a footnote after "free" (SW 1:438).

(Love and Beauty)

Prometheus had perfected humanity,
But the dead matter remained inert,
Until he stole the sun's sparks;[14]
(A drop that fell from beauty's sea)
Yet this spark catches fire in the image
In which the artist's wisdom cloaked it.

Life emerged from beauty,
But does not forget its high origin;
It strives towards it, and love is this desire,
That eternally contends for the sunlight.
Love is wanting, memory of the beautiful,
To see beauty is what love's longing wants.

That's why love can never be sufficed,
That's why it's always rich in its realm;[15]
That's why it seeks to join to beauty
And begs eternally before beauty's realm.
But ah! infinite is the realm of the beautiful
And as infinite our love's longing.

(Tendency of the Artist)

Say! What drives the artist to draw his ideal
From the land of ideas, and entrust it to matter?
His shaping would succeed better in the realm of thoughts,
If it were more fleeting, still it would be freer,
And more his own, and not subservient to matter.

Questioner who asks this! You don't understand spirit's task.
Don't see what it strives for, nor what the artist craves.
They want to act immortally, all the mortal men.

[14] In Greek mythology, Prometheus created human beings from clay, then stole fire from the gods and gave it to them, thus founding human civilization.
[15] This line includes a wordplay on the words *reich* ("rich") and *Reich* ("realm"). The Morgenthaler edition has "never" (*nimmer*) instead of "always" (*immer*) (SW 2:377).

They want to live forever, in the posthumous fame of heroes.[16]
The pious to live in heaven, the good in good deeds,
The artist wants to endure in the realm of beauty,
So he presents his thoughts in lasting form.

Change and Constancy

Violetta.

Yes, you are unfaithful! let me hurry from you;
You can divide your feeling like threads.
Who, then, do you love? and to whom do you belong?

Narcissus.

Nature taught me to love so:
I will always belong to the beautiful
And never waver from beauty's course.

Violetta.

So your loving, like your life, is wandering!
From one beautiful thing you hurry to another,
Get drunk on its cup of trembling,[17] until
What's new, more beautiful, beckons you –

Narcissus.

Then contemplation sinks in higher charms
Like bees' lips in flowers' calyxes.

Violetta.

And then the flower will wither sadly
Being thus abandoned by you!

Narcissus.

Oh no! the sun has kissed it.
The sun has sunk, and evening fog bedews.

---

[16] This line is omitted from the Hirschberg edition of Günderrode's works but included in the Wolf and Morgenthaler editions (*Schatten eines Traumes*, 81; SW 1:378).

[17] In the Bible, the "cup of trembling" (*Taumelkelch*) is a cup filled with intoxicating liquor, symbolizing the wrath of God and/or human fear and suffering (Isaiah 51:17, 52:22; Zechariah 12:2).

Though it can no longer behold the brightness,
Its night is sweetened by starlight.
Did it not often see the day burn up in the east?
Did it not see the night escape, mutely weeping?
And day and night are more beautiful than I.
But one day flies, another returns;
One night dies, a new one descends
For nature gives comfort in everything beautiful.

Violetta.
What, then, is love, has it no subsistence?

Narcissus.
Love only wants to change, not wither;
It wants to contemplate all excellent things.
When it has recognized the light in one image,
It hurries to others, where it burns more beautifully,
It will hunt down what is excellent.

Violetta.
Then I will receive your love as a guest;
For it absconds like a sated desire,
My heart no longer its homeland.

Narcissus.
Oh see the spring! Does it not resemble love?
It smiles blissfully, kindly, and the dull
Clouds of winter, no one sees them any longer!
It's not a guest; it rules in all things,
It kisses them all, and a new wrestling
And stirring will awaken in all beings.
And yet it tears itself from Tellus'[18] arms
Its breath shall warm other regions too;
To others, too, it brings new, beautiful day.

Violetta.
Have you never known holy faithfulness?

---

[18] In Roman mythology, Tellus is a name for Mother Earth.

Narcissus.

To me, faithfulness is not what you call that,
To me, unfaithful is not what unfaithful is to you! –
Someone who shares the moment of highest life;
Who lingers blessedly in love, without forgetting;
Who still judges, and still calculates, measures;
I call them unfaithful, not to be trusted
Their cold consciousness will look clear through you
And be the judge of your self-forgetting.
But I am faithful! To be suffused with the object
To which I give myself in bonds of love
Will be all, will be my whole being.

Violetta.

Is there no love, then, that compels you?

Narcissus.

I do not love people, and not things,
Only their beauty, and am thus true to myself,
Yes, another faithfulness would be unfaithful to myself,
Cause me discontent, strife and regret,
Only thus are my inclinations ever free.
The ordering powers, which devised
Hardship only for corruption, will never
Destroy the harmony of the inner patterns. –
So leave me as the moment bore me.
In eternal circles the Horae[19] turn;
The stars wander without firm footing,
The brook hurries from its source, does not return
The stream of life surges up and down
And sweeps me along in its eddies.
See all life! It's not persistence,
It's an eternal wandering, coming, going,
Living change! Colorful, active striving!
Oh stream! In you all my life gushes out!
I rush into you! Forget land and port!

---

[19]   In Greek mythology, the Horae are the goddesses of time and the seasons.

(Only One and One to Serve)

Only one and one to serve
That would tire my soul.
Roses only and always roses –
Other flowers bloom more brightly;
Like the bees I'd like to swarm[20]
Be drunk on glowing grapes
Cool myself in the lily's white
Repose in the bushes' night.

In the serene free blueness
In the unbounded vastness
I want to wander, want to float
Nothing should shackle my steps
Light bonds are chains to me
And my homeland becomes a jail.
So on and on into the vastness
Out of narrow, stifling life
Actively grasped with active senses
Everything fair, everything beautiful
Devoted wholly to none
No limit to sensing.

Woe to those with narrow senses
Dedicated to one, only one
Everything they sternly spurn
Will be avenged on the poor souls.
The vastness will not become a homeland,
Shapeless in the distance,
Dissolved in empty longing
Life's purpose thus becomes.
The beautiful limits and suffices itself,
Faithfully circles one thing

---

[20] The German verb translated as "to swarm" is *schwärmen*, which also means "to rave" or "to be enthusiastic about." It forms part of the noun *Schwärmerei*, meaning "enthusiasm" or "infatuation," which was often used in Günderrode's time to describe someone carried away by religious or other ideas.

Is renewed in one thing
Like the pulse's stirring beats
Always circling the heart
Always returning to the heart
Always renewed in the heart,
Ignited by its glowing.

Woe to those who stray
From their heart, questing downward.
The vastness will not become a homeland,
Life remains shapeless
Without a center for all striving.

12

Fragments on Music

Introduction

Günderrode left only short reflections on music in the form of fragmentary notes and poems, most of which she did not publish. Six of these are translated here: the poems "The Tones" and "The Cathedral in Cologne" and four short sections of prose: "The Realm of Tones," "Music," "Music for Me," and "The Nightingale."[1]

Günderrode's short writings on music suggest a creative and revitalizing role for music, but she did not develop this topic in depth and gave little or no indication of whether or how her ideas about music might connect with the rest of her work. Nonetheless, the pieces translated here hint at a possible role for music in Günderrode's thought as a generative or resurrecting force and as something that connects human beings to nature.

The connection of music to birth or rebirth appears in all six pieces. In "The Realm of Tones," Günderrode describes a "mysterious life" that "inhabits all materials, but it is trapped within them." After being touched by "an external impetus," the tones are unbound and "emerge from their prisons." Similarly, "The Tones" begins by describing the "soul" of musical tones as "imprisoned in matter" before it is released into nature—first into the movement of air and water, then manifesting in the song of the nightingale. Eventually, the tones are heard, absorbed, and gestated by human beings. In both "The Tones" and "Music," Günderrode describes the human being as an artist made pregnant by and giving birth to music. This association of the artist-musician with pregnancy reflects an idea that was in circulation at the time Günderrode was writing, in which artistic creation is seen as a form of male pregnancy and birth.[2] In order to highlight this connection,

---

[1] Singing and music also feature in some of Günderrode's pieces not included in this volume, including "The Prisoner and the Singer," "The Mourner and the Elves," and "The Apparition."

[2] This idea appears, for instance, in work by the early German Romantic writers Novalis (e.g., *Schriften* 3:569 #97) and Friedrich Schlegel (KFSA 5:61). For critiques of the way Novalis and Schlegel compared pregnancy and (male) artistic creativity, see Ezekiel, "Women, Women Writers and Early German Romanticism," 483–484; Schrage-Früh, "Subversive Weiblichkeit?" 375–376.

Karoline von Günderrode. Anna Ezekiel, Oxford University Press. © Oxford University Press 2026.
DOI: 10.1093/9780190089177.003.0014

for these pieces only, I have translated *Mensch* as "man" rather than as the universal "human being."

In "Music for Me" and "The Cathedral in Cologne," Günderrode associates music with resurrection, rather than birth. In the first of these pieces, she describes music as "a true awakener of the dead." However, it is in "The Cathedral in Cologne" that the regenerative function of music emerges most powerfully. Günderrode begins this piece with a claustrophobic description of the tombs in the cathedral, using language that recalls the description of the "sleepers" in her fragment "A Dream" and the entombment of "life" in matter at the start of "The Realm of Tones." Notably, she describes the dead as silent. Halfway through the poem, a shift occurs as singing and organ music begin, revitalizing the cathedral and its deceased inhabitants: "the tones transform [. . .]. / And everything is glorified to heaven [. . .], / For entranced eyes the graves, the dead, disappear." Günderrode then claims, "I have seen the resurrection with the eyes of spirit."

"The Cathedral in Cologne" is also interesting for its subtitle: "A Fragment." The poem cannot have been describing the current Cologne Cathedral, which was completed in 1870 following renewed works begun in 1842. In Günderrode's time, the building was an unfinished medieval construction, its towers incomplete and topped with a crane. The subtitle "fragment" can, therefore, be read as referring to both the poem and the cathedral.

This use of the term "fragment" takes advantage of eighteenth- and nineteenth-century associations of fragmentariness. At the time, both fragmentary texts and architectural fragments (ruins) were celebrated for their ability to recall a "vanished whole." These fragments reminded people of a lost civilization or great culture of the past, or alternatively indicated the continued greatness and vitality of such a culture, enduring in spirit despite its material collapse.[3] The idea of a ruined building or city or a fragment of text evoked wreck, loss, and incompleteness, but also hidden or yet-to-be-realized promise. Thus, the poem's subtitle of "a fragment" reminds us that, however awe-inspiring Cologne Cathedral may be, it is only a hint of what medieval Europeans planned.

In some of the pieces translated in this section, music also appears as a means of connecting human beings to nature. Günderrode uses a nightingale to symbolize this connection. The nightingale was a popular literary trope in Günderrode's time, drawing on a long history of symbolic

---

[3] Elizabeth Wanning Harries, *The Unfinished Manner: Essays on the Fragment in the Later Eighteenth Century* (Charlottesville: UP of Virginia, 1994), 360, 56f.

depictions of nightingales. These appeared in European literature since ancient Greece[4] as representations of love (especially young love and lost love), death, and melancholy, as embodiments of poetry or muses, and as symbols of the primordial unity between human beings and nature.[5] In Günderrode's "The Nightingale," which seems to have been a draft opening for a short story or reflection, the vocabulary suggests that she planned to take up the association of the nightingale with youth, birth, spring, and morning. In "The Tones," the nightingale appears as the embodiment of tones in the realm of living nature, just before the tones pass into "the ears of man." The nightingale's song, therefore, is depicted as something that links human beings to nature.

Considered in the context of Günderrode's metaphysics, which present human beings as continuous with and the same in kind as the rest of nature, it is possible that Günderrode was beginning to sketch a role for music as an animating force that runs through all things. Drawing on the pieces translated here, it seems she saw this force as present but muffled or constrained in bare matter, more evident in moving nature (such as water and air), and, in the life of animals—such as the nightingale's song—given a form that can inspire human beings and awaken them to artistic and spiritual life.[6]

Although Günderrode's writings on music are brief and unfinished, they hint at an exciting role for music within her philosophy as a whole. The pieces translated here connect in tantalizing ways with her thinking on the connection of human beings to nature and the continuity between those things we consider alive (such as animals and plants) and those we consider

---

[4] Most famously in Ovid's *Metamorphosis*, in which the princess Philomela is transformed into a nightingale after gaining revenge on her sister's husband for raping her and cutting out her tongue. The nightingale also appears in work by Sophocles, Aeschylus, Chaucer, and Shakespeare, as well as in texts by famous writers of Günderrode's time such as Friedrich Schiller (1759–1805), Friedrich Hölderlin (1770–1843), Clemens Brentano (1778–1842), Ludwig Gotthard Kosegarten (1758–1818), Christoph Martin Wieland (1733–1813), and many others.

[5] Günter Butzer and Joachim Jacob, eds., *Metzler Lexicon literarischer Symbole* (Stuttgart: J. B. Metzler, 2008), 246.

[6] The model of music that Günderrode seems to have been developing may have been influenced by the work of Romantic writer Wilhelm Heinrich Wackenroder (1773–1798). Wackenroder's 1799 collection *Fantasies about Art for Friends of Art* includes chapters titled "The Miracle of Musical Art [*Tonkunst*]," "The Specific Inner Essence of Musical Art," "The Tones," and "On the Various Genres in Each Art, and in Particular on the Various Kinds of Church Music" (Wackenroder, *Phantasien über die Kunst für Freunde der Kunst*, ed. Ludwig Tieck [Hamburg: Friedrich Perthes, 1799]). Wackenroder relates music to several concepts, including nature, death, life, resurrection, and transfiguration, in ways that may have inspired Günderrode. However, his account of music differs from Günderrode's in significant ways, including the role he grants music as an expression of human emotions and his locating of the origins of music in the national spirit of primitive peoples, neither of which feature in Günderrode's work, and the latter of which would probably have conflicted with her syncretistic view of nations and cultures (for an example of Günderrode's efforts to syncretize diverse religions, see "Letters of Two Friends" and its introduction earlier in this volume).

dead or inert (such as rocks).[7] As such, they are an exciting supplement to Günderrode's more well-developed metaphysical work in pieces such as "Idea of the Earth" and "Letters of Two Friends."

The Realm of Tones

A mysterious life inhabits all materials, but it is trapped within them, snared in matter's firm bonds, from which it cannot wrest itself on its own. But when an external impetus touches the material, then the bonds are undone. The tones emerge from their prisons, embrace the air with trembling joy, and spill over into each other in harmonious vibration. So, once, when all things were still mingled in crude masses, the living spirit hovered over these materials, and when it embraced them a series of harmonious figures emerged from their mingling.

Music

But when the errant tones rush over the ears of man, he absorbed them in his inmost core, carried them under his heart,[8] and after he had breathed into them from his spirit, he let them wander and speak to related souls. Thus every artist of tones carries the realm of tones under his heart once more, nourishes it from his spirit and then births it again, and it wears his features, and wanders until a new rebirth.

Music For Me

I cannot understand the essence and weave of music; its inner laws remain hidden to me, and my judgment of what is excellent in it and what is not is wavering and fallible. My attention cannot follow the course of a beautiful piece of music; I listen for a while, but soon my spirit loses itself in a series of images that come and go. They come like shifting representations of colorful dreams; soon I see dark clouds of roaring storms carried scurrying forth, then a dark ocean illuminated by pale moonshine, which breaks, foaming,

---

[7] For details on these aspects of Günderrode's thought, see the section on metaphysics in the general introduction to this volume.

[8] In old-fashioned English and German, the term "to carry under one's heart" (*tragen unter seinem Herzen*) means to hold something close or, if what is carried under the heart is a child, to be pregnant.

on black rocks. This and many other representations—partly from my life—
pass quickly, surging up and down, over my soul. And this life that the music
awakens in me becomes so powerful that I no longer hear it; and a piece
of music that does not work on me like this gives me little joy. To me, the
storm is a true awakener of the dead. For when I hear its roaring, the images
of the past emerge from their graves before me, and I wander once more
among them.

The Nightingale

(Fragment)[9]

I awoke to a sweet life in the womb of aromatic bushes; a brook murmured
quietly through flowery meadows, and the blue sky showed peacefully and
clearly through the foliage, when, for the first time, I looked around myself in
the world,—

The Tones

Your deep soul, imprisoned in matter,
Grapples for life's breath, for liberation;
Who will loosen the bonds of your yearning,
To rise melodiously from muteness?
Who, tones, will open your prison's bars?
And unchain your ether-wings?

Once, when violence met resistance,
Shattered the tones' old prison's night;
Straying here and there, in wide spaces
They fled, awoken from muteness,
And wandered through the blue arcs
And exulted in the wild waves' storm.

They slipped, whispering, through the treetops
And breathed from the nightingale's breast,
With bold streams they plunged from cliff

---

[9] The subtitle "fragment" seems to have been added by Hirschberg.

Peaks, in wild lust for freedom.
They rushed past the ears of man,
He drew them into his deepest core.

And when he had carried them under his heart,
He bade them wander the breezes' path
And say to all related souls,
How lovingly his spirit nursed them.
Harmoniously they sweep from their cradle
And wander forth and bear human traits.

The Cathedral in Cologne

A Fragment

Five times the ceiling vaults on groups of gothic columns,
The choir rises still higher, borne more proudly aloft,
Beautiful within, adorned with bronze, marble and carpets
And a crimson day breaks through colored windows. –
But there, where darkness weaves denser through the columns!
A musty smell breathes dully from the depths,
There the heroes of the church sleep in covered coffins
And their effigies rest upon them, hands folded in prayer,
And their staring gaze is turned to heaven.
Amazed, I watch them; it seems they must speak,
But they stare on as they have for centuries
And I shiver deeply, for the dead are so silent.
But then song rises, and organ tones; they float,
Celebrating, up into the domes, where resplendent saints pray
But the tones transform, and into the wings of angels
And sweep, surging melodiously, around the holy images.
And everything is glorified to heaven—music, and colors, and forms,
For entranced eyes the graves, the dead, disappear,
And from the silent crypts a joyful cheer rises. –
Yes, I have seen the resurrection with the eyes of spirit.
And the life of art leads the soul to heaven.
Poetry! You soul of the arts, you that bore them all,
You ensoul the grave, ascend to heaven aloft.

13

The Aeronaut

Introduction

The unpublished poem "The Aeronaut," written between 1802 and 1804, uses a metaphor of hot air balloon flight to depict a struggle to escape the bonds of earthly existence. The poem deploys images of air, water, ascent, and descent to portray the self as continuous with and bound to nature. "The Aeronaut" can be read as describing the nature of life and death, as illustrating Günderrode's social and political views, as a critique of Romanticism and German idealism, or as an attempt to conceptualize forms of experience beyond ordinary human consciousness.

The start of the poem places the narrator in a realm of space, air, or "ether," described metaphorically as an ocean: "I traveled in a wavering barge / On the blue-lit ocean / That flows around the shining stars." At the time Günderrode was writing, the sky was often represented as an ocean ripe for exploration in the new era of hot air balloon flight. For example, the French author Paul-Philippe Gudin de la Brenellerie (1738–1812) celebrated the first crewed balloon ascent 20 years earlier with a poem dedicated to the "new Argonauts" who, he wrote, would sail the "new ocean" and surpass the voyages of Columbus and Captain Cook.[1]

In Günderrode's work, the ocean appears as a symbol of wholeness. She uses this symbol to represent the idea of individual living beings merging together, like drops of water in the sea, before and after their embodiment as individuals—i.e., before birth and after death.[2] In the context of Günderrode's other work, it is possible that the beginning of "The Aeronaut,"

---

[1] Gudin de la Brenellerie, "Sur le Globe Ascendant," in *Journal de Paris* (28 August 1783): 989–990. Wieland cited this poem in a piece on hot air balloons (Christoph Martin Wieland, "Die Aëropetomanie" [1783], in *C. M. Wielands sämmtliche Werke*, vol. 33 [Leipzig: Georg Joachim Göschen, 1840], 125).

[2] On this use of ocean imagery in Günderrode's writing, see "An Apocalyptic Fragment" and its introduction earlier in this volume; see also Anna Ezekiel, "Introduction to 'Piedro,' 'The Pilgrims,' and 'The Kiss in the Dream,'" in Karoline von Günderrode, *Poetic Fragments by Tian*, ed. and trans. Anna Ezekiel (Albany: SUNY Press, 2016), 87–103.

Karoline von Günderrode. Anna Ezekiel, Oxford University Press. © Oxford University Press 2026.
DOI: 10.1093/9780190089177.003.0015

in which the narrator is immersed in an oceanic whole, represents the state of existence before birth and after death, or perhaps only a memory or a prophetic glimpse of this situation.

The idyllic opening of the poem is followed by a violent rupture and descent. The narrator is "dragged down" to earth, failing to escape the "law of gravity." The poem generalizes this fate to all mortal beings: "None may elude it [gravity] / Of the earthly race." Despite all our efforts, and notwithstanding occasional glimpses of the "heavenly" and "holy," human beings cannot ascend to the heavens; we remain bound within the circumference of our ordinary existence.

Although the connotations of the poem seem clear in general outline, closer investigation of what the ascent to the heavens represented for Günderrode yields complex answers. The German title of "The Aeronaut" (*Der Luftschiffer*) makes it clear that the ascent she depicts here is accomplished in a hot air balloon (*Luftschiff*), placing the poem in a literary tradition of using hot air balloons and their navigators as metaphors for a wide range of social, political, and philosophical phenomena. At the time Günderrode was writing, hot air balloons were a very modern and current topic. The first ascent, in Paris in 1783, immediately captured public imagination. Balloons, balloonists, and ascents in balloons swiftly became symbols for, among other things, the triumph of human reason or free will,[3] the immortality of the soul,[4] the attempt to reach beyond the ordinary bounds of human knowledge to make divine things or things that exceed reason and language comprehensible,[5] and the German idealist philosophy of Kant and Fichte.[6] Hot air balloons were likened to celestial bodies and gigantic eyes, with the view from above that they provided said to be a God's-eye view previously unavailable to mere mortals.[7] In general, balloon flight was seen as allowing human beings to expand their perspectives beyond previous limits that had seemed fixed. For critics, the danger and disaster that

---

[3] Eickenrodt, *Augenspiel*, 195–196, 218.

[4] Eickenrodt, *Augenspiel*, 199; Jean Paul Friedrich Richter, *Das Kampaner Tal, oder über die Unsterblichkeit der Seele nebst einer Erklärung der Holzschnitte unter den 10 Geboten des Katechismus* (Berlin: Hofenberg, 2019 [1797]), 40–59.

[5] Victoria Niehle, "Die ästhetische Funktion des Raumes. Jean Pauls 'Des Luftschiffer Giannozzo Seebuch,'" in *Raumlektüren. Der Spatial Turn und die Literatur der Moderne*, ed. Tim Mehigan and Alan Corkhill (Bielefeld: transcript, 2013), 82–83; Trop, "Arts of Unconditioning," 422.

[6] Heinz Brüggemann, "Luftbilder eines kleinstädtischen Jahrhunderts. Ekstase und imaginäre Topographie in Jean Paul 'Des Luftschiffers Giannozzo Seebuch,'" in *Die Stadt in der europäischen Romantik*, ed. Gerhard von Graevenitz (Würzburg: Königshausen & Neumann, 2000), 135.

[7] Brüggemann, "Luftbilder," 127–128; Eickenrodt, *Augenspiel*, 195–196, 214.

often accompanied balloon flights was a fitting analogy for human hubris: a new Icarus motif and an indication of the crises of modernity, especially the crisis of human subjectivity.[8]

Günderrode would certainly have been aware of these symbolic uses of hot air balloons. One of her favorite writers, the satirical author Jean Paul Friedrich Richter (1763–1825), wrote allegorical depictions of balloon flights in two works: *Kampaner Valley, or On the Immortality of the Soul* (1797) and *The Aeronaut Giannozzo's Logbook* (1801).[9] In these texts, Jean Paul explores new forms of perception and subjectivity and mounts a critique of contemporary society and politics as well as philosophical idealism, especially the work of Kant and Fichte.[10] Other texts that Günderrode may have had access to and that develop similar themes include Friedrich Hölderlin's poem "To the Ether"[11] and Christoph Martin Wieland's short histories of ballooning published in 1783 and 1784.[12] Hölderlin and Wieland were both very popular at the time and much admired by Günderrode's circle of friends.

In light of these discourses around balloons, scholars have suggested that Günderrode's "The Aeronaut" can be interpreted as a critique of Fichte's philosophy[13] or of new, Romantic ideas of subjectivity that aimed to expand "imaginative and existential possibility" beyond ordinary experience.[14] That is, as Gabriel Trop notes, while the Romantics dreamed of broadening the possibilities for how we live, think, and imagine, Günderrode's poem reminds us of the intractability of many of the real, concrete conditions that limit our lives, including our physicality as well as social conditions.[15] Similarly, Günderrode's biographer Margarete Lazarowicz claims that "The Aeronaut" depicts the impossibility of escape from socially imposed limitations, including the limitations of gender.[16] By contrast, Gerald Bär connects the social transgressiveness of ballooning, especially for female balloonists,

[8] Brüggemann, "Luftbilder," 136; Eickenrodt, *Augenspiel*, 206.

[9] Eickenrodt, *Augenspiel*, 257–269; Trop, "Arts of Unconditioning," 421–448. The language in the balloon scene in *Kampaner Valley* is noticeably similar to Günderrode's.

[10] Brüggemann, "Luftbilder"; Eickenrodt, *Augenspiel*, 197.

[11] Friedrich Hölderlin, "An den Äther," *Musenalmanach für das Jahr 1798*, ed. Friedrich Schiller (Tübingen: Cotta, 1797).

[12] Wieland, "Die Aëropetomanie"; "Die Aëronauten" [1784], in *C. M. Wielands sämmtliche Werke*, vol. 33 (Leipzig: Georg Joachim Göschen, 1840), 131–191.

[13] Eickenrodt, *Augenspiel*, 260–261.

[14] Trop, "Arts of Unconditioning," 440.

[15] Trop, "Arts of Unconditioning," 440–443.

[16] E.g., Lazarowicz, *Porträt einer Fremden*, 194.

with the warrior heroines of Günderrode's Ossian-inspired dramas.[17] For Bär, in "The Aeronaut," Günderrode plays with a topic that was considered out of reach for women like herself, thus pushing against social boundaries. In general, however, there is a consensus that "The Aeronaut" is meant to suggest that the lack of boundaries and direct encounter with the celestial and ethereal, which is remembered in the first part, is transient and unsustainable: in the end, human social, bodily, intellectual, and perceptual limitations cannot be evaded. Despite our best efforts, as individuals, we are cut off from communion with the wider realm of nature and the eternal truths of the universe.[18]

The latter interpretation fits well with the idea that "The Aeronaut" presents Günderrode's claims about individuality, consciousness, and epistemology in an imaginative form. Günderrode acknowledges Kant's claim that human experience of the world is limited by our physical, cognitive, and perceptual properties.[19] But, she maintains, this is not the only form of existence we can experience. In several pieces, she explores possibilities for extending our knowledge of the world beyond the perceptual and cognitive limits of ordinary experience. Furthermore, she claims that although we are currently human, we have been, and will again be, otherwise: to Günderrode, we are part of an eternal cycle of ever-changing beings. In line with this account, the first part of "The Aeronaut" may depict a memory or a vision of our existence before birth, when, instead of existing as individuals, we were merged with the rest of cosmos. Once we are born, we lose this immediate immersion in nature and find ourselves limited by the constraints of individuated, mortal, embodied, conscious existence. On this interpretation, "The Aeronaut" describes how the "earthly race"—those already born as individuals—are separated from the "harmony" of undifferentiated existence and from knowledge of this form of experience: the "writings of the stars" are obscured by "clouds" and "fog."

The various interpretations of "The Aeronaut" mentioned above are not mutually exclusive; it is very possible that Günderrode intended the poem to

---

[17] Gerald Bär, "Ossianomanie und Aeronautik. Karoline von Günderrode zwischen populärem Zeitgeist und kritischer Selbstbespiegelung," in *Noch Zukunft haben: Zum Werk Karoline von Günderrodes*, ed. Frederike Middelhoff and Martina Wernli (Springer, 2024), 135–162.

[18] See, e.g., Birgit Wägenbaur, "'habe getaumelt in den Räumen des Aethers.' Karoline von Günderrodes ästhetische Identität," in *Frauen: MitSprechen. MitSchreiben. Beiträge zur literatur- und sprachwissenschaftlichen Frauenforschung*, ed. Marianne Henn and Britta Hufeisen (Stuttgart: Heinz, 1997), 210, 215.

[19] Günderrode, Letter to Gunda Brentano, 11 August 1801 (translated in the Letters section below).

function simultaneously on multiple levels. Despite its brevity, this is a rich and complex poem that highlights the depth of Günderrode's philosophical thought.

The Aeronaut

I traveled in a wavering barge
On the blue-lit ocean
That flows around the shining stars,
Greeted[20] the heavenly powers
Was sunk in their contemplation,
Drank the eternal ether,
Wrested myself wholly from the earthly,
Above, knew the writings of the stars
And in their circling and turning
Saw figured the holy rhythm
That drags every sound
Forcibly into harmony's surging urge

But ah! I am dragged down,
Fog veils my gaze,
And I see again the earth's borders
Clouds drive me back.[21]

Alas! The law of gravity
Asserts its right anew,
None may elude it
Of the earthly race.

---

[20] Instead of *begrüßt* ("greeted"), the Morgenthaler edition has *gekrüst*, which could be a variant spelling of *gegrüßt* ("greeted") or *gekreist* ("circled") (SW 1:390; see SW 3:230).
[21] The Morgenthaler edition has "Clouds drive me back to it/her [the earth]" (SW 1:390).

14

Once I Lived Sweet Life

Introduction

The unpublished poem "Once I Lived Sweet Life" was written between 1802 and 1804, around the same time as "The Aeronaut."[1] The two poems share similar themes, but "Once I Lived Sweet Life" more obviously aims to convey Günderrode's views on metaphysics and the nature of life, and to vividly describe types of experience beyond ordinary human consciousness. In particular, scholars note the promise of this poem for imagining new forms of transcendence that avoid sharply separating mind from body, spirit from matter, and the human individual from nature. The poem uses imagery of air and water to portray the self as continuous with nature, transient, and changeable, communicating Günderrode's ideas through metaphor and a sense of vertical movement.

"Once I Lived Sweet Life" begins with the narrator floating in a space identified with the sky, featuring clouds, air, wind, and celestial bodies, but described metaphorically as "a deep blue ocean." Günderrode often uses the ocean as an image of a whole in which individuals are dissolved before they are born and after they die, like drops of rain dissolving in a body of water.[2] The water cycle—ocean to clouds to rain (or sometimes dew or tears) and back to rivers and the ocean—features in Günderrode's work as an analogy for the cycle of birth and death. It is therefore possible that the opening lines of "Once I Lived Sweet Life" are meant to depict a period before the birth or after the death of the narrator, when he or she is integrated with the (oceanic) whole of nature.

This peaceful opening is followed by a descent, but unlike the abrupt fall in "The Aeronaut," "Once I Lived Sweet Life" describes a gentle turn downward marked by love, parting kisses, and sorrow. The narrator is accompanied in

---

[1] See previous chapter.
[2] See esp. "An Apocalyptic Fragment." On Günderrode's use of ocean imagery, see also Ezekiel, "Introduction to 'Piedro.'"

Karoline von Günderrode. Anna Ezekiel, Oxford University Press. © Oxford University Press 2026.
DOI: 10.1093/9780190089177.003.0016

their descent by "playmates," which appear as "colored lights." This moment marks the beginning of a play of ascent and descent and a complex interaction between the earthly realm and the space of sky or heaven. After the playmates have "soared down," they begin to fade and disappear. The narrator describes a "great hurrying shadow / that followed them / to snatch them"—the shadow of death, stealing the narrator's friends and loved ones. The narrator then "raised little wings" and returned to an easy existence in the "clear ether." This time, this aerial space is presented unambiguously in terms that signify heaven: Günderrode describes it as the "holy deep" and "unnamable space of heaven" and populates it with gods, heroes, and mythical animals. Finally, the narrator remembers that "I had once / torn myself away / from a sweet body" and "turn[s] to the earth" once more in a final movement of descent, or rebirth.

One reading of the poem is that these alternating descents and ascents metaphorically describe birth, death, and rebirth. The narrator moves from immersion in the whole (the situation before birth, on Günderrode's account), through birth as an individual in the company of other individual beings (the playmates), then death and a return to the heavenly realm, and finally to rebirth.

However, "Once I Lived Sweet Life" can also be read in a way that inverts this picture. Alice Kuzniar and Karin Obermeier argue that the "heavenly" spaces described in the poem represent, not immersion in the whole as I have just suggested, but moments of individuation, characterized by intellectual reflection. And, they claim, the "earthly" spaces do not describe embodiment as an individual living being but depict moments of union with nature, in particular the mother's body. On this reading, the lines "I had once / torn myself away / from a sweet body" do not represent a memory of dying, as I suggested above, but instead the memory of birth. The "sweet body" is not the narrator's own body but that of their mother, from which we tear ourselves when we are born. These scholars suggest that the body of the mother also functions as a metaphor for nature as a whole. On their interpretation, "Once I Lived Sweet Life" presents the act of becoming a human individual (through birth and the development of consciousness) as an act of tearing oneself apart from nature through a "violent rupture."[3]

---

[3] Alice Kuzniar, "Labor Pains: Romantic Theories of Creativity and Gender," in *"The Spirit of Poesy": Essays on Jewish and German Literature and Thought in Honor of Géza von Molnár*, ed. Richard Block and Peter Fenves (Evanston: Northwestern UP, 2000), 84; Karin Obermeier, *Private Matters Made Public: Love and the Sexualized Body in Karoline von Günderrode's Texts* (Diss., University of Massachusetts Amherst, 1995), 55–56, 58.

On this view, the narrator's encounter with celestial and mythical beings in the poem does not describe the period after the death of the individual, as I presented it above, but rather the "reflective and highly conscious phase" of existence as an individual human being. The encounter with what Kuzniar and Obermeier see as the highly conceptualized realm of gods and heroes is read as a moment of individuation and consciousness, not of integration.

Kuzniar and Obermeier claim that this moment of individuation is the middle part of a movement away from and back to integration in the whole. They argue that the return to the "source of life" (also described as the "womb of the mother") at the end of the poem is not a description of rebirth, but rather shows spirit and body being reintegrated, this time at a higher level of self-awareness. Thus, according to these scholars, "Once I Lived Sweet Life" presents a three-part movement from unity with nature and the mother's body, through birth, individuation, and the development of consciousness, to an incorporation of mind and body into a higher sense of self.[4]

While these opposing interpretations are quite different in many respects, they share the claim that in "Once I Lived Sweet Life," Günderrode suggests that there is no uncrossable gulf between the individual and the whole, the mind and the body, spirit and nature, or heaven and earth. In this poem, "the earth" is not radically cut off from the spiritual realm but intimately embedded in it: it is "rocked in the arms of heaven," as Günderrode puts it. Kuzniar and Obermeier interpret "the earth" as signifying immersion in nature while "heaven" represents the individualized, conscious life of the mind, and claim that Günderrode believes we should integrate these in order to develop better forms of self-awareness. The alternative view that I described first is that "the earth" represents embodied existence as one individual being among many, while "heaven" represents immersion in the whole of nature, and that the poem describes a repeated movement back and forth between the two—the cycle of life, death, and rebirth. Either way, "Once I Lived Sweet Life" illustrates how easy Günderrode thinks it is for individuals to move back and forth between these states.

"Once I Lived Sweet Life" thus illustrates Günderrode's non-dualistic account of mind, body, and nature. This aspect of Günderrode's work has been explored by Christine Battersby, who draws particular attention to the function of the repeated, organic movements inward and outward, up and down in this poem. "Günderrode," Battersby claims, "counterpoise[s] 'male' positions of transcendence (up in the heavens) by an emotional interpenetration with

---

[4] Kuzniar, "Labor Pains," 83; Obermeier, *Private Matters*, 60.

the earth (which she describes as a womb)."[5] By doing this, Günderrode creates a model of the self and its relation to nature that undermines what Battersby calls "the masculinist model of the 'I' as separate from nature."

Battersby claims that in the process of doing so, Günderrode also undermines "masculinist" concepts of the sublime, which involve "transcendence of materiality and the earth."[6] She writes: "Günderrode develops a female sublime, which refuses many of the oppositional categories of Kantian aesthetics that were so central to the Romantic sublime. In particular, she collapses the Kantian distinctions between mind and body; self and other; individuality and infinity."[7] Unlike in the Kantian sublime, for Günderrode, there is "no struggle for domination" involved in the experience of the sublime; "the 'I' nowhere exalts itself by a process of overcoming matter, body or the earth."[8] Instead, claims Battersby, "Once I Lived Sweet Life" describes an interweaving and eventual integration of self and other and mind and body through repeated movements between "heaven" and "earth"—that is, between individuation and immersion in nature. This process might be described as a new model of transcendence or instead as asserting the richness and spiritual depth of the physical world.[9]

"Once I Lived Sweet Life" articulates an alternative to dualistic systems of thinking that draw a sharp contrast between body and mind, self and other, earth and heaven, life and death, and immanence and transcendence. As such, it is a valuable part of Günderrode's philosophical work and an important contribution to early nineteenth-century debates regarding personal identity, life after death, the nature and significance of connections between the self and others, and even aesthetic concepts such as the sublime.

Once I Lived Sweet Life

Once I lived sweet life,
for it seemed as if I were suddenly
only a filmy cloud.
Above me nothing to see

[5] Christine Battersby, *The Sublime, Terror, and Human Difference* (Oxford: Routledge, 2007), 127.
[6] Battersby, *Sublime, Terror and Human Difference*, 127.
[7] Battersby, *Sublime, Terror and Human Difference*, 120–121.
[8] Battersby, *Sublime, Terror and Human Difference*, 124.
[9] Anna Ezekiel, "Metamorphosis, Personhood and Power in Karoline von Günderrode," *European Romantic Review* 25.6 (2014): 773–791.

but a deep blue ocean
and I sailed around easily
on the waves of this ocean.
Merrily in heaven's air
I fluttered all day long,
then settled glad and fluttering
there at the rim of the earth
as it tore itself, steaming and full of fervor,
from the sun's arms,
to bathe itself in nighttime coolness,
to refresh itself in the evening wind.
Then the sun embraced me,
seized by parting's sorrow,
and the beautiful bright rays
loved all and kissed me.
Colored lights
soared down,
skipping and playing,
rocked in the air's
filmy limbs.
Their garments
purple and golden
and like the fire's
deeper glow.
But they became
paler and paler,
the cheeks more wan
the eyes dying.
Suddenly my playmates
disappeared from me,
and as I sadly
gazed after them
I saw the great
hurrying shadow
that followed them
to snatch them.
Yet in the west
I saw the golden

seam of the garments.
Then I raised little wings,
fluttered now here, now there,
was glad of the easy life,
at rest in the clear ether.
Saw now in the holy deep
unnamable space of heaven
wonderfully strange images
and figures moving.
Eternal gods
sat on thrones
of gleaming stars,
looked at each other
blessed and smiling.
Sounding shields,
ringing spears
raised by powerful,
contesting heroes;
Before them flew
enormous animals,
others twined
in broad rings
Earth and heaven,
following each other
forever in a circle.
Blooming full of charm
among the brutes
stood a virgin,
ruling all.
Lovely children
played amidst
poisonous snakes. –
There to the children
I wanted to flutter,
to play with them
and also to kiss
the virgin's soles.
And a deep longing

within me caught me.
And it seemed to me I had once
torn myself away
from a sweet body, and only now
did the wound bleed from old pain.
And I turned to the earth,
as it, sweet in drunken sleep,
rocked in the arms of heaven.
Quietly now the stars rang out,
so not to wake the beautiful bride,
and the heavens' breezes played
lightly around her tender breast.
Then it seemed as if I had sprung
from the deepest life of the mother,
and had tumbled
in the spaces of the ether,
an errant child.
I had to weep,
flowing in tears
I sank down to the
womb of the mother.
Colored calyxes
of perfumed flowers
caught the tears,
and I penetrated them,
all the calyxes,
trickled downwards
down through the flowers,
deeper and deeper,
down to the womb
of the enclosed
source of life.

15

Mora

Introduction

In 1760, the Scottish writer James Macpherson published the first of his volumes of works by Ossian, a legendary Celtic bard whose work Macpherson claimed to have translated into English.[1] The stories were an instant hit and were quickly translated into other languages, including German, where they had an enormous effect on literature. Among other things, Ossian is noted as an important influence on Johann Wolfgang von Goethe (1749–1832), the emotionally expressive literary (and musical) movement known as *Sturm und Drang* ("Storm and Stress"), and Romanticism.[2] It was soon discovered that Macpherson had written the volume himself based on Gaelic folk tales, but this did nothing to diminish their popularity, and more volumes and editions were published over the next several decades.

Günderrode's short play *Mora* is one of three pieces,[3] all from her first collection *Poems and Fantasies*, that overtly engage with the works of Ossian. Ossian's influence is also clear in many of Günderrode's other texts, especially in her depictions of nature as turbulent and emotionally laden. Storms, surging waves, rasping ravens, howling winds, ghosts, graves, and towering cliffs are characteristic of Macpherson's writing and feature often in Günderrode's work.

The story of *Mora* does not follow the plot of any particular Ossianic tale, although it has similarities to several, especially "Fingal" and "Oithona."[4] These stories furnish many elements of Günderrode's *Mora*, including the setting by a cave, the love triangle, the heroine's use of a weapon, and

---

[1] James Macpherson, *Fragments of Ancient Poetry, Collected in the Highlands of Scotland, and Translated from the Galic or Erse Language* (Edinburgh: Hamilton and Balfour, 1760).
[2] Gerald Bär, "'Ossian fürs Frauenzimmer'? Lengefeld, Günderrode, and the Portuguese Translations of 'Alcipe' and Adelaide Prata," *Translation and Literature* 22.3 (2013): 343–360.
[3] With her adaptation of the poem "Darthula" and her short story "Timur."
[4] James Macpherson, "Fingal: An Ancient Epic Poem. Book I" and "Oithona," in *Morison's Edition of the Poems of Ossian, the Son of Fingal*, Translated by James Macpherson, Esq., vol. 1 (Perth: R. Morison Jr, for R. Morison & Son, 1795), 1–22 and 291–300.

Karoline von Günderrode. Anna Ezekiel, Oxford University Press. © Oxford University Press 2026.
DOI: 10.1093/9780190089177.003.0017

her death at the hands of her unwanted suitor. The device of bards singing about the characters is also taken from Ossian. In addition, the names in Günderrode's piece are identical or similar to names in Ossian's work.[5]

Mora illustrates Ossian's importance for Günderrode's thought on gender, which she developed in more detailed form in later, longer works such as *Hildgund, Magic and Destiny*, and *Udohla*. But already in *Mora* we see her working through issues related to gender and gender roles. In this early piece, Günderrode uses the trope of the warrior woman or virgin in arms to push back against gender norms that, in her time, excluded women from the arenas of war and politics. The poem also indicates the importance to Günderrode of the possibility of a meaningful and honorable death for women, which Mora embodies by dying in defense of her lover and her own right to choose.

Günderrode's featuring of warrior women also connects with a literary tradition of the "virgin in arms": idealized women who fought in wars or killed tyrants. This trope achieved new popularity after the French Revolution, in which real women participated in violent revolt, bringing to public awareness the question of the compatibility of violence—even justified violence—with "feminine" values.[6] Many works of literature from this period feature warrior women, including Friedrich Schiller's *The Maid of Orleans*, Heinrich von Kleist's *Penthesilia*, and Christine Westphalen's *Charlotte Corday*. These works often portray the deaths of these women: violent female characters were socially unacceptable and therefore had to be tamed in some way, often by dying.[7] In addition, warlike women tended to be shown relinquishing their femininity, rejecting marriage, motherhood, and other supposedly feminine features to take up arms.[8]

Helen Watanabe-O'Kelly has argued that, in contrast to male writers of the time, women writers used the trope of the woman warrior to explore women's capacity for agency, leadership, and violence and to consider "how a woman reconciles her destiny as wife, mother, daughter, or sister with the exceptional situation that is war."[9] In other words, rather than presenting

---

[5] Ossian's characters include Frothal (King of Scandinavia), Torlath, Carmor, Morna, and a bard called Carril, who may correspond to Günderrode's Karul in Mora. Ossian also mentions a chief called Car-ul. Another chief, Ton-thormod, may have inspired the name of Günderrode's bard Thormod.

[6] Hoff, "Dramatisch Weiblichkeitsmuster"; Licher, *Mein Leben*, 119, 147.

[7] Hoff, "Dramatisch Weiblichkeitsmuster," 102.

[8] Watanabe-O'Kelly, *Beauty or Beast?*, 34–35.

[9] Watanabe-O'Kelly, *Beauty or Beast?*, 212–213.

warlike behavior and "feminine" attachment to family as mutually exclusive, women writers tried to imagine whether and how these could be made compatible.

Günderrode worked through some of these same issues in several texts, including *Mora*, "Darthula," "Timur," and *Hildgund*. In *Mora*, Günderrode blurs categories of traditional masculinity and femininity while calling attention to the ways these categories are socially constructed.[10] Mora does not renounce her femininity to take up arms; instead, she adopts "masculine" characteristics of bravery, ferocity, protectiveness, and honor while retaining "feminine" characteristics such as beauty and gentleness. However, once dead, Mora is remembered in stereotypically feminine terms. Although the bards claim she has entered Valhalla, the afterlife of fallen male warriors, all their descriptions highlight her femininity: she was, they say, "beautiful," "lovely," and "gentle." Günderrode creates a strong contrast between this exaggeratedly feminine memory of the dead Mora and her more gender-fluid characteristics while alive. As a living woman, Mora was recognized as a competent hunter: Frothal urges her to arm herself and repeatedly asks her to go hunting with him. She also showed herself to be a fierce but reasonable warrior, first trying to talk Karmor out of fighting and then, when he insists, declaring that she "thirst[s] for battle." But after her death, only her beauty and gentleness are remembered. In the end, despite Mora's strength and heroism, the identity that is retroactively constructed for her by the bards is as a tragic, beautiful woman.

Some scholars argue that Günderrode's women who die in battle represent a fantasy of dying, especially for the sake of love. Gerald Bär writes that Ossian's work was popular with women, including Günderrode, for enabling "the projection of female fantasies, laden with […] notions of erotic fulfilment in death."[11] Michaela Schrage-Früh claims that "in the idealization of romantic love and of romantic dying for the sake of love [Günderrode] found the possibility of bringing her gender and urge for heroism and meaning into harmony."[12] This reading fits with attempts to interpret Günderrode's work in relation to her suicide, which was triggered by the end of her affair with Creuzer,[13] and presents *Mora* and "Darthula" as expressing a death wish.

---

[10] Allingham, "Countermemory," 53; Krimmer, *Company of Men*, 134.
[11] Bär, "Ossian fürs Frauenzimmer."
[12] Schrage-Früh, "Subversive Weiblichkeit?," 385; my translation.
[13] For details, see the section on Günderrode's life and works in the general introduction to this volume.

There is some support for this interpretation in Günderrode's letters. For instance, in 1801, she wrote to a friend:

> Yesterday I read Ossian's "Darthula," and it had such a pleasant affect on me: the old wish to die a hero's death seized me with great intensity; it seemed intolerable to me to still be alive; even more intolerable to die a peaceful and common death. I had already often had the unfeminine wish to throw myself into, to die in, the wild thick of a battle.[14]

However, as Liesl Allingham notes, while scholars have focused on the supposed death wish in Günderrode's writing, "less attention has been paid to Günderrode's desire for a *meaningful* death."[15] Günderrode's female characters who die in battle or, like the titular character in *Hildgund*, risk death by taking up weapons against their enemies, do so in order to defend their honor, their homeland, the lives of loved ones, or for the sake of revenge. This also applies to some of Günderrode's female characters who die by suicide, such as Thia in the short story "Timur," who pulls Timur off a cliff to avenge her father's murder and the usurpation of his throne. Some of these motivations also apply to Mora: she puts on her lover Frothal's armor to protect him and, at the same time, to defend her right to choose whom she marries. Along with a desire to defend Frothal's honor after Karmor accuses him of being unwilling to fight for Mora, and after trying to talk Karmor out of fighting, these motivations push Mora to violent action.

Günderrode's Ossian-inspired pieces, including *Mora*, center on women who take an active role in the masculine spheres of battle and political action in order to obtain their goals. Their motivations in risking violent death are to protect or avenge loved ones and to uphold their personal, familial, and national honor. Günderrode's warrior- and politically active women blur or trouble gender boundaries, resist women's objectification, and promote women's right to pursue their own self-determination, including through violence.

---

[14] Günderrode, Letter to Gunda Brentano, 29 August 1801, in Weißenborn, Ich sende Dir, 78–79.
[15] Allingham, "Countermemory," 42 (my emphasis).

Mora

Frothal, King of Scandinavia
Mora, his beloved
Karmor, a warrior
Thormod ⎫
        ⎬ bards
Carul ⎭

Carul. Waft, you breezes of spring! Play with maidens' locks, whisper in the high grass of the meadow and rustle in the treetops of the copse! But stop your wings sweeping off in the storm and abducting my voice unheard, when I sing of spring. Beautiful are you, oh spring! Your steps soft over the fields! Flowers germinate, springs burst from you! The birds rejoice when you come, those melodious bards of nature, and they hush when you hurry away, you lovely, whispering son of heaven.

Thormod. Did you see the evening descend on the hills of Scandinavia? You lovely singer of spring! Slow are its steps, dark its robe of clouds. It ascends over the forests and mountains like the spirits of the dead from their graves. Then the birds hush; cool shivers tremble through all life; damp mists gather. Only the echo sighs through the night, only the marsh toad and the rasping owl converse with it.

Carul. But the stars come and smile kindly, and the gleaming locks of the moon; its greenish beams illuminate the earth. Not all life falls silent in the night; the evening breezes whisper, the waterfall murmurs melodiously, and the land of dreams opens its gates and the sweet children of the mind flutter up and kiss the brows of the slumberers.

Thormod. Hark! What blusters through the forest? What heaves so the churning sea? The winds have loosened their shackles. Abundant rain crashes down, clouds tower up! Lighting splits the night! The star of evening weeps in its clouds, the hurricanes run wild, churning the bosom of the foaming sea and ripping the sails of struggling ships. Thunder rolls! And the son of the cliffs calls after it with a hundred voices.

Carul. Frothal, King of Spears,[16] wanders alone and astray in the wood. Dark is the night, and his feet do not tread the way home.

Thormod. The thunder rolls dreadfully, the earth trembles—but Frothal does not tremble.

Carul. See! Through the night a friendly light sends its pale shimmer. It is Mora's light, the beautiful daughter of Torlat. Her cozy hut receives the straying wanderer, and her beauty envelops the heart of the king. For Frothal was not astray when he strayed to the lovely maiden.

Frothal. Your singing is pleasant to my ear, you bard of song.

Mora. Thormod! Your singing is like the eagle's flight. Carul! Your song is as lovely as the voice of love.

Frothal. My soul is aroused; my arm starts for my spear. Come with me to hunt on the forested island, daughter of Torlat.

Mora. Don't go to hunt on the forested island! My soul trembles, for a dream warned me: I saw you slain by hunting spears. So avoid the hunt, oh King!

Frothal. I should avoid the hunt! Never, maiden, never do I avoid danger, for if I gain love and glory, then my dying is no death. What then should I fear, daughter of Torlat?

Mora. If you die with glory and love, Frothal, you still die for me.

Frothal. Come to the merry hunt! Take the weapons of the kings of Scandinavia so that you shine in the steel of heroes, and follow me, maiden.

Mora alone, then Karmor.

Mora. The night has blustered itself out on the forested heights, and Frothal slumbers so sweetly in the cliffside cave. Ah! the hunt gave me no joy,

---

[16] Ossian uses the term "King of Spears" to describe various heroes (Macpherson, *Morison's Edition*, vol. 1, 180, 267, 307).

exhaustion no slumber. My soul is sorrowful, my heart beats fearfully, and Frothal slumbers so sweetly.

Karmor. Yes, he must be here, here in the cave. Frothal! Come!

Mora. What do you want from Frothal? Why does your voice chase off his slumber?

Karmor. I call the King to duel.

Mora. Why do you call him?

Karmor. He robbed me of the soul of my bosom: I loved the daughter of Torlat, and she chooses him.

Mora. She chooses him, and not you. What use is fighting to you? How does victory help you?

Karmor. You are Frothal! This is his sword, this the shield of the kings. Come to fight for Torlat's long-haired daughter. Or do you fear the sword of Karmor, as your hesitation betrays? Won't you fight for the maiden you love?

Mora. Come! I thirst for battle, my courage rejoices at the danger! Come!

Frothal, then Thormod and Carul.

Frothal. What racket awoke me! It was as if I heard the distant clang of arms! But now it is so silent, only the morning breeze slips through the leaves.— Hark! What rustles in the forest? It is Mora's light footstep. Mora! Come, come my beloved!

Carul. Mora is not coming to you, oh King of Spears!

Thormod. Mora will meet you no more: no more in the hall of shells,[17] nor on green meadows. She wanders in Valhalla's dream-rich groves; her bosom so white is pierced through; her dark locks swim in blood.

---

[17] The "shells" mentioned here are drinking shells, which Ossian describes being served during feasts. The "hall of shells" is therefore a feasting hall (see Macpherson, *Morison's Edition*, 31, 218).

Frothal. Grief benights my soul, you sons of song! Eternal grief embraces me.

Carul. Karmor, the grim warrior, loved the maiden, and wanted to challenge you to battle. But Mora's shield shone like that of the kings, her sword was that of the ruler. Frothal! She fell for you.

Frothal. Sing, you bards, praise of the beautiful daughter of Torlat! Sing the maiden's glory, so her easily withered beauty should bloom immortally. And call to battle the dark Karmor: he shall fall, even if his arm were as mighty as the arm of Thor, his sword like Odin's.

Carul. Mora, you fell in your beauty, sank in your prime! You were lovely as the evening star, gentle as the departing sun.

Thormod. Roaring mountain streams plunge from their peaks, waves roar! Raging winds howl over the plains. But mountain streams, waves and storms do not awaken Mora, for she sleeps the long sleep. Mora! Mora, the blooming spring does not wake you, nor the radiance of morning, nor the purple of evening, nor the call of love. It is fair to wander in the light of life, but narrow and gloomy is the grave, eternal the sleep. So weep for Mora, for she will not turn back to the light.

16

Udohla

Introduction

Udohla was published in 1805 in the journal *Studien,* along with Günderrode's play *Magic and Destiny.* Set in India ("Hindustan") during the Mughal Empire,[1] *Udohla* deals with a clash of cultures between the Muslim Mughal rulers and the subjugated population of Hindus. While the emperor (the "Sultan") considers whether to marry a woman he believes is his sister, an act contrary to Islamic law, his Hindu advisor Sino hopes for a revolution and the restoration of India's past glory. The theme of revolution makes *Udohla* relevant to Günderrode's political philosophy and (since these are closely related) her metaphysics. At the same time, the play contains interesting reflections on gender, agency, power, cultural difference, and colonialism.

Udohla is one of Günderrode's most political works, along with *Muhammad, the Prophet of Mecca.* Both plays present revolution as a form of revitalization—something Günderrode claims is periodically necessary to counteract natural processes of entropy, which lead any given culture or nation to gradually lose strength, vigor, creativity, and cohesiveness. Eventually, this makes political bodies collapse or become vulnerable to conquest by younger, more vigorous cultures. In *Udohla,* the character Mangu claims that this process underlay the Mughal conquest of India, and warns that the conquerors are now at risk of something similar happening to them:

> [Hindustan] sank into enervation's arms;
> That's why it yielded to the Mongols'[2] sword.
> A like fate threatens the proud victor.
> Desire rocks him in its arms,

---

[1] The Mughals ruled a large area across India, Pakistan, Bangladesh, Afghanistan, and Myanmar from the sixteenth to nineteenth centuries.

[2] Usually spelled "Mughals" or "Moguls." Günderrode's spelling highlights the descent of the Mughal dynasty from Mongolian conquerors.

Karoline von Günderrode. Anna Ezekiel, Oxford University Press. © Oxford University Press 2026.
DOI: 10.1093/9780190089177.003.0018

And softness lulls him into deep slumber,
That old subjugator of the world. –

For Günderrode, this cyclical process of enervation, decay, collapse, and revitalization characterizes not only the political field but also the physical realm, including both living and inanimate objects. Like political bodies, objects like rocks, plants, and animals are formed temporarily through the interconnection of their constituent parts, which eventually break down and break apart, after which the elements that constituted them are reused to create new forms.[3] Due to the analogy Günderrode draws between the political and metaphysical realms, *Udohla* can be read as considering the possibility, not only of a political revolution, but also of a future recreation and revitalization of the physical world.

It is worth noting two further aspects of Günderrode's treatment of revolution in *Udohla*, both of which take up ideas regarding "the east," especially India and North Africa, that were prominent among her contemporaries. The first is the connection of enervation and loss of vitality to the heat of the sun. In his analysis of Goethe's "Muhammad's Song" (a major influence on Günderrode's poems "Egypt" and "The Nile"), Kevin Hilliard notes that "it was a commonplace of the medical literature that the oriental sun dried out the body's humours and the blood," leading to "heavy, viscous, sluggish" blood and a tendency to melancholy.[4] This theory underlies Mangu's statement in *Udohla* that "The sun has conquered Hindustan, / It has consumed its channels' inner core: / That's why it sank into enervation's arms."

Second, the idea that civilization arose first in the east and gradually moved westwards, while dying out in its original location, was relatively widespread in Günderrode's time. For instance, this idea informed the Romantic position that India was the birthplace of human culture and still the location of vestiges of hidden knowledge, the original human language (Sanskrit), union with the divine, and connection to our natural origins.[5] In *Udohla* Sino declaims:

---

[3] See the general introduction to this volume and Ezekiel, "Revolution and Revitalisation."

[4] K. F. Hilliard, "Goethe and the Cure for Melancholy: 'Mahomets Gesang.' Orientalism and the Medical Psychology of the Eighteenth Century," *Oxford German Studies* 23 (1994): 84.

[5] Similar views feature in Günderrode's "Story of a Brahmin" and "The Adept." For a classic account of the development of these views in German thought, see A. Leslie Willson, *A Mythical Image: The Ideal of India in German Romanticism* (Durham, NC: Duke UP, 1964), esp. 3–48.

Yes, to us all gods are well-disposed.
They rock this land as if it were a cradle
For it was the first to rise from the ocean,
And now lamentingly it sighs in chains.

In *Udohla* Günderrode links this idea of an eastern origin for human culture with revolution. She suggests that civilization first arose in India before moving westwards, leaving India withered and vulnerable to conquest; this civilizing tendency will eventually circle the globe and return in a restoration of indigenous Indian culture. Sino continues his above monologue with: "When will the morning dawn on better times? / Patience my heart! Eventually they must come." In his final speech he repeats the claim that a new dawn awaits India:

Easily deceived, I often thought I saw
The purple seam of morning in the east,
Announcing India's day after long night.
Often it seemed I heard the call of birds
Greeting the sun early, full of portent.

Much more could be said about the role of the sun, and of the interplay of day and night, in *Udohla*. For instance, we might ask what the connection is between the ideas, both present in this play and apparently contradictory, that the sun dries out and exhausts a people and that the revitalization of India is associated with the rising sun. And in this context, what should we make of Nerissa's claim that she is "like those flowers / That sorrow in the long glow of midday, / And deeply rejoice when the night sinks down"? Nerissa, although posing at the Sultan's sister, is in fact a Hindu woman, Ewana, whom the palace servants put in Nerissa's place to hide the fact that the real Nerissa had run away. As others have noted,[6] Nerissa/Ewana's longing for the night—along with her yearning to escape the palace and return to nature, to her former hiding place in caves, and to a life of carefree wandering along the Ganges—connects women and Hindus to stereotypes of childlike innocence, pre-enlightenment mysticism and superstition, and pre-civilization naturalness.

---

[6] Christmann, *Identitätsgewinn*, 219–220.

Günderrode's use of stereotypes in *Udohla* is worth a closer look. Above, I mentioned the eighteenth- and early nineteenth-century belief that the hot sun dried out "the humors"; this claim was associated with negative stereotypes of "easterners" as lazy, sleepy, and passive.[7] This stereotyping is present in Günderrode's representation of Hindus in *Udohla*. Both Sino and Nerissa/Ewana suffer from melancholy, revealed in the mournful quality of much of their speech.[8] Meanwhile, the character known as the Dervish describes Hindus as sensual, indolent, and childlike: "Temptation threatens us from the Hindu people," he tells the Sultan; "They [...] seek to lure us from the victorious course / Of virtue to their lazy voluptuousness." He claims the Mughals "have always sought / To form this tender people [Hindus] into men; / Alone they would stay children, immature." Udohla's rapid changes in emotion also depict Hindus as childlike and impulsive. And Sino's repeated expressions of hope for someone else (Udohla) to free the subjugated Hindus presents him, and Hindus generally, as passive and lacking agency.[9]

These characterizations associate Hindus with children and dangerous femininity, presenting them as lazy, unpredictable, sensual, and lacking political maturity. Consistent with this portrayal, the threat the Hindu people offer the Mughals in *Udohla* is primarily one of temptation or seduction, away from the enlightened, morally rigorous, and rational path of Islam toward dissolution, sloth, and surrender to physical and emotional impulses. While the threat is overtly framed as assassination, revolt, and revolution, the bigger danger is assimilation into the culture of the indigenous population and the associated loss of Mughal power and influence—that is, the loss of the vitality that allowed them to conquer India in the first place.

In contrast to the Hindus, Günderrode presents the Mughal conquerors as active, vigorous, and embodying values of rationality, autonomy, and self-control. As others have noted,[10] these values are male-coded and correspond to

---

[7] In "Muhammad's Song," Goethe presents the cure for this torpor and melancholy as Islam, metaphorically depicted as a refreshing river ("Cure for Melancholy," 95–98). Similarities between this piece and Günderrode's poems "Egypt" and "The Nile," and Günderrode's portrayal of Islam as revitalizing in *Muhammad, the Prophet of Mecca*, support reading the Mughals in *Udohla* as a reinvigorating force that, at least initially, counteracted what Günderrode presents as the torpor and dissipation affecting the Hindu people.

[8] E.g., Sino cries "Woe is us! Woe is us! Born into slavery / Nothing breaks the heavy chains but death," while Nerissa/Ewana frequently refers to negative emotions ("sorrow," "wretched," "dull," "lamentation").

[9] See also Sino's description of Hindu priests, who "live in seclusion" and "are not concerned with human deeds." Instead of pursuing worldly or political activity they focus on contemplating nature and the divine.

[10] Christmann, *Identitätsgewinn*, 220; Obermeier, "Ach diese Rolle," 104.

European enlightenment ideals, which Günderrode places in conflict with the supposedly feminine "Asian" values represented by the Hindu characters and customs in the play. As Karin Obermeier puts it, "the Sultan's political power is rooted in the masculine behavior of rational control over his bodily desires and moral superiority. Acknowledging and yielding to (sexual) desire for his sister Nerissa/Ewana implies a weakening of the foundations of that control."[11]

However, Günderrode also subverts the opposition she has created between the masculine, rational, active Mughals and the feminine, emotional, passive Hindus. In the first place, Günderrode highlights what Obermeier calls "the limitations of a purely rationalist, moral code that denies the non-rational and sensual."[12] This is consistent with Günderrode's claims elsewhere regarding the need to realize both the rational and emotional sides of human nature in order to live a fulfilling, authentic life.[13] In *Udohla*, the paralysis and self-loathing that result from separating the rational and emotional aspects of human nature are represented in the Sultan's efforts to navigate the conflict between Islamic law (Mughal culture) and his desires (which are consistent with Hindu cultural values, as these are represented in the play).

Furthermore, while Günderrode characterizes Hindus as sleepy, sensual, immature, and passive, she presents them as possessing agency and political will. Stefani Engelstein argues that although Günderrode accepts stereotypes of Hindus as "emotional, sensuous, and spiritual" she "reverse[s] the valence of these traits and she implies that they are consistent with political subjecthood."[14] Günderrode does this by modifying prevailing ideas regarding agency and political participation to incorporate emotion, gentleness, flexibility, and spirituality in her model of what it is to be an agent.

Accordingly, it is not the enlightened male Sultan but the Hindu woman Nerissa/Ewana whom Günderrode presents as embodying agency, self-determination, and activity in the political arena. In fact, Nerissa/Ewana is the only character in the play to display real agency.[15] The Sultan dithers

[11] Obermeier, "Ach diese Rolle," 104.

[12] Obermeier, "Ach diese Rolle," 104.

[13] E.g., in "Story of a Brahmin," Almor states: "My proud reason soon claimed sole rulership within me: it wanted everything to be reasonable. This demand of course entangled me in perennial disputes with myself and the world: the intractability of my own nature to its commandments made me dissatisfied with myself [...]—nothing could satisfy this reason. / [...] Is a person only virtuous if they stand on the ruins of their own spirit and can say: Look, these rebelled, but they fell, I have become victor over them all! [...] Do not rejoice in your victory; you have waged a civil war: those you have conquered were children of your own nature."

[14] Stefani Engelstein, "Sibling Incest and Cultural Voyeurism in Günderode's *Udohla* and Thomas Mann's *Wälsungenblut*," *German Quarterly* 77.3 (2004): 289.

[15] This is similar to the titular character in *Hildgund* (Anna Ezekiel, "Introduction to *Hildgund*," in Karoline von Günderrode, *Poetic Fragments by Tian* [Albany: SUNY Press, 2016], 39–55).

about whether to marry her until the revelation of her true identity seems to decide the matter; he then changes his mind when Nerissa/Ewana's cultural taboos push in the other direction. Sino waits for someone else to orchestrate the revolution he hopes for, and it fails to materialize. And Udohla oscillates wildly between hope, despair, murderousness, and joy, thrust this way and that by external events rather than determining his own course. Only Nerissa/Ewana comes to a firm resolve about how she will act and, furthermore, is able to implement her decision, gaining her freedom (and Udohla's) and determining her own destiny.

This portrayal of Nerissa/Ewana challenges prevailing ideas about heroism and agency, which are often construed as masculine, dominating, and individualistic. "With the character of Nerissa/Ewana," writes Obermeier, "Günderrode creates a different kind of female hero, whose heroism allows the qualities of nurturance, love, and concern for others to co-exist with self-reflection and active independence."[16] In this way, Günderrode provides an alternative to a view of agency as a masculine trait associated with personal power, domination, rationality, and imposing one's will on others. Instead, Nerissa/Ewana's agency is based on loving consideration of one's own and others' needs, concern for the various (possibly conflicting) moral imperatives of one's situation, and careful negotiation with those affected by one's decision. These characteristics of Günderrode's ideal political and moral agent are consistent with supposedly "feminine" qualities and the stereotypical representation of Hindus in *Udohla*.

To be clear, these stereotypes are still problematic and orientalizing. What is interesting is that Günderrode attempted to grant these stereotypes a positive value and incorporate them in an ideal for agency. This model of agency has significant political ramifications, as it underpins a call for the self-determination of oppressed groups (here, women and Indians, who at the time were subjected to European colonialism) *whether or not they are considered to possess the traits associated with enlightenment ideals for political maturity.* We will return to this point below.

The play also highlights another key element of Günderrode's model of agency: the claim that the ability to act freely is a function of one's social situation, including the way one is treated by others.[17] The Sultan is

---

[16] Obermeier, "Ach diese Rolle," 101. On Günderrode's reinterpretation of gender, agency, and heroism, see the section on gender in the general introduction; introduction to *Mora*; Allingham, "Countermemory."

[17] On Günderrode's account of the dependence of agency on how one is treated by others, see Ezekiel, "Metamorphosis, Personhood and Power."

an all-powerful ruler who could marry Nerissa/Ewana without her consent and/or execute Udohla, who is both his rival and an old enemy's son. However, he instead allows Nerissa/Ewana and Udohla to leave, even though, he says, this means he will die of a broken heart. Without the Sultan's consent, Nerissa/Ewana would not be able to act on her decision to leave the palace and return to a life wandering the country with her family. Thus, her agency is dependent on the Sultan's recognition[18] of both her autonomy as a woman and the validity of her customs as a Hindu (according to which she may not marry her father's murderer).

At the same time as contributing to her unique model of agency, Günderrode uses this decision by the sympathetic character of the Sultan to promote self-restraint, care and respect for others, including for their autonomy, and recognition of cultural values that are different to one's own. In this respect, Günderrode is drawing on the European literary trope of the "enlightened Sultan" or "enlightened despot." At the time, this trope was often used as part of a call for intercultural tolerance[19] and, sometimes, to critique European colonial aspirations, especially when these were associated with a demonization of an Asian "other."[20] Günderrode presents the Sultan as gentle but firm, inclined to listen to others' opinions and consider their wishes, and respecting both his own Muslim culture and Hindu customs. He employs both Muslim and Hindu advisors and considers different cultural mores with respect to his own marriage.

It is questionable whether Günderrode's use of an enlightened despot in *Udohla* engages with Indian culture or imposes European ideals on a supposedly Asian character. On the one hand, Günderrode's Sultan reflects the reputation of some of the real Mughal Emperors. In particular, Akbar I (1542–1605) and Shah Jahan (1592–1666) are considered to have been enlightened rulers, tolerant of different religions and cultures, encouraging

---

[18] This aspect of Nerissa/Ewana's agency is shared by female protagonists in other works by Günderrode, especially Hildgund and Darthula in the texts of the same names (see the section on gender in the general introduction to this volume; Ezekiel, "Introduction to *Hildgund*").

[19] E.g., in Gotthold Ephraim Lessing's 1779 play *Nathan the Wise*, where the Muslim Sultan Saladin, a Christian Knight Templar and a Jewish merchant come to respect the equality of their respective religions. Lessing's text also features hidden sibling identities and was likely a direct influence on *Udohla*.

[20] E.g., Benedikte Naubert's 1786 novel *Walter of Montbarry* also features Saladin as an enlightened despot and uses this framing to criticize European colonial aspirations and assumptions of moral superiority (Julie Koser, "Looking East: Cross-Cultural Encounters in Benedikte Naubert's *Walter von Montbarry*," in *The German Historical Novel Since the Eighteenth Century: More than a Bestseller*, ed. Daniela Richter [Cambridge: Cambridge Scholars Publishing, 2016], 15–44).

the arts, and giving prominent government roles to individuals from different backgrounds. There are also Indian literary precedents for this type of character. Notably, the fourth/fifth-century Sanskrit author Kālidāsa's play *Śakuntalā* (published in German translation in 1791) features an enlightened king and shares other features with *Udohla*, such as a romance involving concealed identities and concern for issues of family and caste in relation to marriageability. We know that Günderrode was familiar with this play: one of her frequent correspondents, Georg Friedrich Creuzer, even explicitly connects it with *Udohla*, writing: "You can, indeed *should* write dramas in the sense of *Sakontala*, and your Udohla inclines in this direction."[21]

On the other hand, the Sultan clearly embodies European enlightenment ideals, including rationality, tolerance, mercy balanced with firmness, and respect for others.[22] As a result, it is possible to read *Udohla*'s Mughals as an analogy for European colonial rulers and, especially, British rule in India.[23] On this reading, the final rapprochement between the Sultan, Nerissa/ Ewana, and Udohla is a call not just for intercultural understanding, but for better treatment of Asian nations by Europeans, possibly including an end to colonization itself. *Udohla* presents the colonizer with a choice. On the one hand: the liberation of colonized people and a more equal relationship between former colonizing and colonized populations.[24] This must be initiated by self-restraint, respect, and self-sacrifice on the part of the colonizer, as represented by the Sultan's decision to die of a broken heart rather than deny Nerissa/Ewana the right to self-determination. On the other hand, the colonizer may choose to continue the status quo, which imposes on colonized people oppression, death, loss of liberty, and forced assimilation to the colonizer's culture.[25] This course of action, according to *Udohla*, justifies revolution. A truly enlightened ruler, the play suggests, would choose to liberate their colonial subjects regardless of cost to themselves.

[21] Creuzer, Letter to Günderrode, 20 February 1806, SW 3:144.
[22] Christmann, *Identitätsgewinn*, 220.
[23] Engelstein, "Sibling Incest," 283.
[24] See also "The Frank in Egypt" and the introduction to this piece included in this volume.
[25] Despite the enlightened attitudes of the Sultan, all these elements of colonialism are clearly outlined in *Udohla*. For example: Mangu notes that the Sultan has become "the yoke by which [Hindus] are oppressed"; the rebel Bahadur is executed; Udohla has been imprisoned and Sino begs him to think of friends and relatives "Who languish in dark dungeons' night"; Nerissa/Ewana laments her incarceration within the palace where "all flowers sorrow"; the Dervish notes that the Mughals have tried to impose their culture on their Hindu subjects.

In this respect, *Udohla* is a rejection of tyranny[26] and a call for a more equal and mutually respectful relationship between Europeans and Asians.

Some elements of *Udohla* tantalizingly seem to almost connect with real individuals and circumstances. The name of the play and its titular character are likely derived from the Arabic "al-Dawla," often spelled "ud-Daulah," meaning "dynasty" or "nation." This term was used in the titles of rulers and senior advisors in the Islamic world, including Mughal India. For example, Mir Syed Jafar Ali Khan Mirza Muhammad (1733–1757) and Najmuddin Ali Khan (c.1747–1766), both Nawabs of Bengal, were known as "Siraj-ud-Daulah" and "Najm-ud-Daulah," respectively. At the time Günderrode was writing, India was ruled by the British East India Company, who began their administration in the mid-eighteenth century by deposing Siraj ud-Daulah and replacing him with someone they hoped would be more pliable. Günderrode's Udohla states at one point that he was raised in Bengal and was close to the Nawab there. Although the characters and plot of *Udohla* do not map precisely onto real people and events, it is possible that Günderrode was imagining alternative events surrounding or preceding the rise of British power in India.[27] This took place in the context of significant revolts and counter-revolts between members of ruling and high profile families in Bengal, which left the region vulnerable to Company interference. Ironically, Sino's hope for the overthrow of the Mughal rulers would, in the real world, bear fruit only in the form of further colonization, this time by Europeans.

Udohla

In Two Acts

Characters:
The Sultan of the Mongols in Hindustan.
Mangu, Grand Vizier.

---

[26] The theme of tyranny was a live issue in Europe in Günderrode's time, largely due to Napoleon's increasingly autocratic and expansionist approach to power. Günderrode features tyrants in four plays (*Udohla, Nikator, Hildgund*, and *Muhammad, the Prophet of Mecca*), and Lucia Maria Licher argues that these characters are all foils for Napoleon, allowing Günderrode to critique what was often perceived as Napoleon's increasing despotism (Licher, *Mein Leben*, 188, 202; see Ezekiel, "Introduction to *Muhammad*"). Of these characters only *Udohla*'s Sultan is an enlightened despot; the other three rulers are more obviously tyrants.

[27] Günderrode does something similar in her short story "Musa," which is loosely based on events during the Ottoman Interregnum (Anna Ezekiel, "Karoline von Günderrode, 'Musa,'" *Trail of Crumbs*, January 2021).

Sino, at the court of the Sultan, and
Udohla, Hindus.
A *Dervish*.
Nerissa, in the Harem of the Sultan.
Elpa, Overseer of the wives of the Sultan.

First Act.

Room in the palace in Delhi.
Mangu and *Sino*.

Mangu.
Have you carried out what I commanded?
Has everything been readied for the feast?

Sino.
It has been done; hail the new morning
Of the brightest, the most joyful day.
The rich sea has given its rich treasures,
Laid out beautifully, shining, in the palace;
The diamond from the depths of the mountain,
The chasms' child, which adorns the brown hair
Of the night with light's sparks, has been wrested
From the dark earth, and arranged upon the breast,
The silk hair of the beautiful Sultanas;
And everything that richly blooming time
Bestows on all the regions is combined.
In our gardens, in the bushes' night,
The tender Amra shrub exhales its spice,
And balsam mixes with the rose's scent
And exchanges its sweet breath with the air.

Mangu.
And is the air pervaded, too, with tones?
And the scorching day with cool brooks?

Sino.
The midday cools its hot cheeks
In the fresh rock-springs of cool caves,

And young birds sing upon the breezes
And áre rocked on tender flowers' twigs. –
Thus well prepared are we for that feast
That oft should have begun, but never did.
Three times already has the morning broken
On which Nerissa should have wed our lord
And joined the ranks of the Sultanas;
Fair women whom the Ruler of the World –
The fortunate! – favors with his love;
And always, when the splendid day arrived
That should have given him the one he loved,
He darkly said: "Today it may not be;
Another day may give me my beloved,
Inauspicious signs loom over my joy."
Now tell me, Mangu, what that signifies?
He loves her, but to him too early comes
Each day that should give her to him;
Indeed I do not understand such conduct.

Mangu.
Don't speak of it. He loves what he should not.
It does not befit a follower of Muhammad
To wed his blood relation, his own sister
Contrary to duty and the law,
And that he falters is his bosom's voice
Which, rebuking, warns him of his crime.
But hush, our role is only to obey,
And our opinion on this comes far too late.

Dervish enters.

Dervish.
Vizier, is it true what I have heard?
The Sultan will marry his sister?

Mangu.
Where have you been, friend? In which mountain chasms,
In what faraway seclusion?

That you only heard this rumor today?
Nerissa will be led into the house
In which the royal women live;
The Sultan's sister will become the Sultan's wife.

Dervish.

Oh shame, you've weaned yourself from blushing!
And boldly thrust yourself upon the throne,
And decked your forehead with the crown.
No, such a deed is against God and law
Unheard of in the race of Ishmael.[28]

Sino.

May what is rare then never come to pass?
And that alone is right which always is?
The times may change; human deeds
Drive in steady, repeating circles.
What you denounce as crime, look! Hindus
Are allowed by Brahma's holy law.[29]

Dervish.

I know well that the Koran's pure teaching
Does not suit the erring Hindu folk.
You yourself—for your speech betrays you—
Still cleave to your fathers' ancient folly;
Thus you rejoice that the Lord of the Mongols,
Born to protect the law,
Now exchanges it for your customs,
And thus elevates your sins as right.

Sino.

Hear, priest! Long before the Mongols' name was known,
When they, a pastoral folk, wandered

---

[28] A term for Muslims who, according to Christian, Islamic, and Jewish traditions, were originally descended from the prophet Ishmael.

[29] As Stefani Engelstein notes, the claim that Hinduism (or eastern cultures generally) permitted sibling incest is false, but was widely thematized in German literature in Günderrode's time (Engelstein, "Sibling Incest," 280). Engelstein suggests that this aspect of *Udohla* may have been influenced by Goethe's 1779 play *Iphigenia in Tauris* (284–285).

Through Asia's steppes, without a homeland,
This land was a state bounded by fame;
And great princes ruled it,
And many noble deeds were done,
Before you or your wisdom had been thought of,
Or your Muhammad wrote the Koran.

Mangu.
The Sultan consulted the priesthood,
Whether it befitted him to take
As a wife his own natural sister?
And they replied that he was allowed to do
Whatever his own heart might permit.
And he took this answer for a Yes.

Dervish.
So may it be, when desire interprets
And flattery acquiesces to its claims.
But the Sultan shall hear my voice,
The truth shall reach the ruler's ear.

Sino.
Oh blind fool! Destiny has decided,
And you want to throw yourself in its way?
By heaven! Even Allah has approved it,
It is opposed now only by your priests.
With us, priests act completely differently:
They live in seclusion.
Removed from earthly noise and activity.
There, nothing disturbs holy contemplation,
Hard-hearted zeal is unknown to their souls,
They are not concerned with human deeds,
The peace of God is in their breasts
And holy nature speaks to them
Through her children, who are still undefiled
By the mad striving of brazen caprice.
The speech of holy animals, and the plants'
Still undeveloped tender silent minds;

To divine these and understand their life:
To them that is a worthy calling.

Mangu.
My Sino! You have lost yourself in idle fables
And your country's childhood dreams.

Dervish.
For many years the Mongols have ruled
In Hindustan, and they have always sought
To form this tender people into men;
Alone they would stay children, immature.

The Sultan enters. All prostrate themselves.

Sultan.
Rise, Vizier, what do you have to say to me?

Mangu.
My lord, the traitor has now been punished,
Bahadur's head has fallen at the hands
Of the executioner, though his children escaped death.

Sultan.
In truth he has made the best trade,
As freedom ends his long imprisonment.

Mangu.
Should we also have the son pursued?
Admittedly he fled six months ago.

Sultan.
If he bears his father's firm soul
And his hatred for the Mongols' realm,
Then the youth's death would indeed serve us well.
But leave him, for we'd have too much to do,
If we were to hunt for all the insects
That only scratch us, but do not wound us. –
Now Sino! Dervish! did you want to say something?

Sino.

My King! Shall the festivities now begin?

Sultan.

No! No! Not yet, my heart pounds in my breast
And intimations of ill luck surround me. – –
Now Dervish, if you want something from me, then speak.

Dervish.

My King! Worry drives me to you;
Worry for the welfare of your soul
Which you have endangered through this choice,
Forbidden by convention, of your sister;
Temptation threatens us from the Hindu people,
They hate the earnest strictness of our life
And seek to lure us from the victorious course.
Of virtue to their lazy voluptuousness.
That's why we need strictness and firm sense.
Our ruler must provide a great example
Of how the holy precepts are revered.

Mangu.

The sun has conquered Hindustan,
It has consumed its channels' inner core:
That's why it sank into enervation's arms;
That's why it yielded to the Mongols' sword.
A like fate threatens the proud victor.
Desire rocks him in its arms,
And softness lulls him into deep slumber,
That old subjugator of the world. –
The eyes of the people are turned to you.
The Hindus wish for victory for their ways,
They weep that their ruler is at ease
Becomes the yoke by which they are oppressed,
And the Mongols hope that Tamerlane's
Grandson,[30] son of the Lords of the World

---

[30] The Mughal Empire was founded by Babur (1483–1530), the great-great-great-grandson of the Turko-Mongol conqueror Timur, known in English as Tamerlane. Through his mother, Babur was also descended from the Mongol Emperor Genghis Khan.

Will never shame the throne of Muhammad
Through a crime learned from strangers.

Sultan.
Enough of that. I have heard you;
Remove yourselves. Sino! You stay with me.

Mangu and Dervish off.

Why, oh destiny, must she be the one I love?
The only one you have forbidden me.
The earth adorns itself lavishly with flowers,
And richly holds its treasures out to me,
In vain fortune exhausts itself to please me
For I must give up hope for this one wish.
In my house are many lovely women,
But none stirs and none delights my heart.
For everything beautiful that my eye sees
Only awakens my longing for her charms;
And when she's near and I could embrace her,
Then a deep shudder holds me back,
A gentle quake runs through my limbs, as if
There stood an angel of death by her side,
My arms sink, my lips tremble
And my deepest senses are confused.

Sino.
Custom daunts you, the crowd's reproof,
The prejudices of Muhammad's disciples.

Sultan.
I had not seen her for five years, and how
Astonished I was when, after this time
Aga guided her into my arms,
She had changed, but her dear features
Still reminded me of childhood days
Of kinship's deep understanding.
I surrendered to the holy feelings,
But she held back with frightened shyness.

My love wanted to subdue her fear,
But my love overpowered even me.
What should I do now? I cannot renounce her,
And possess her? Ah! I do not dare.
My breast is like the tempestuous sea,
Whether regret or longing consume me,
Whether I flee her or take her as my spouse,
I will be ruined whatever course I choose.

Garden of the palace.
Nerissa and *Elpa.*

Nerissa.
Look! Elpa, twilight is already falling,
Yes, it enfolds the hot, tired day,
Only now am I well, like those flowers
That sorrow in the long glow of midday,
And deeply rejoice when the night sinks down,
And caress it with their sweet perfume.
I am like that; I sorrow when the sun
Stands high at midday with its radiant eye.

Elpa.
Then, oh fair one, may you never rejoice?
For your fortune's sun indeed stands high.

Nerissa.
Oh Elpa! If you saw my quaking soul,
How painfully deception weighs me down.
If I might only sink at my King's feet,
Say to him that I am not Nerissa,
Not his sister, that I, a stranger
Took his sister's place when she escaped.
Why did I let myself be talked into lies?
Oh! this role grows all too hard for me. –

Elpa.
Well then! Confess to him: the Sultan's daughter,
His sister, ignominiously escaped

With a slave, that she thus betrayed
And shamed her house
And her parentage; that we hid it,
That we set you in her place,
For of all women you were the most like her.
Confess it to him, though it would cost my head,
And Aga's too, for with our lives we stand
For the daughter of the Kings.
But if you want we'll plunge ourselves in ruin:
Two lives are not worth any lies to you.

Nerissa.

I could save your life as well as Aga's,
And still confess the truth to our lord.
I do not fear that; I fear his love
That would rejoice about this swap;
He would marry me this hour
If he only knew I am not Nerissa.

Elpa.

What? Do I hear aright? You fear his love
And the marriage for which the Sultan hopes?
So little do you know how to grasp fortune's favor,
Determined for you by the King of the World?

Nerissa.

I don't know why, but when I look into his eyes
A deep fear descends upon me,
As if my soul would like to warn me about him.
And yet there is nothing in his countenance
That frightens me; his smile is so gentle,
Yes, his words of love are sweet to me;
And yet I cannot and will never love him
Because my soul tells me to flee him.

Elpa.

The peacock has a hundred radiant eyes
With which to show his feathers' loveliness,
And you, Nerissa, should have none to see

The splendor of your fortune?
I don't believe it; you must nourish other wishes,
How else could you trust such vain unease?

Nerissa.
You err, and yet with silent, murky longing
I think of my glad, free youthful days,
When I pilgrimaged with my good father
Through Hindustan, masked and unknown.
Now we followed the Ganges' silver flow
Down from Tibet's mountains to the sea,
Then we entered Asia's splendid cities,
That lay before us in the evening's blaze.
Fugitives were wandering through the alleys,
Music and dance and desire were everywhere;
So bright and happily flexible was my life,
A rapid stream that gushed out from the clouds
And now! When I recall those lovely hours
Memory floats from the free world
Over to me between these narrow walls
Thus I call wretched my splendid lot.
I long to go back to the night and its dangers,
To that homeless pilgrimage.
Between these walls all flowers sorrow,
The tender stems whisper to themselves
How they are consumed by locked-up longing;
Yes, even the strong palm sinks its head,
And limp and dull is all the life around me,
And here nature bestows herself grudgingly
For none listen to her holy voice,
Her service spurned by an uncultured race.

Sultan and Sino enter.

Sultan.
Nerissa, you! How are you? Fair one! Love!
You drop your gaze? Sweet woman, are you sad?

The women of India are wilting flowers
Even in life's first youthful radiance;
Only Nerissa is always like the fresh rose
Quickened by heaven's eternal dew.
Except today, drawing gloomily around her,
Jealous clouds would quell her lovely eyes.

Nerissa.
If India's women are always wilting flowers
Then let me weep for their unhappy lot.

Sultan.
No; my love will be the breath of spring
That breathes joy and fresh life into you –
What did I say there? My love is diseased,
And it is sicker than your gloomy gaze.
Now a longing draws me to your arms,
Then an old curse wrenches me from you.
I flee; the flame ignites anew,
A cold shudder snuffs it out again.
Now I want to hush, then lament to you,
Exulting in joy, then despairing in pain.

Nerissa.
Why must I be the one to give this pain?
Oh, flee me, seek another happiness.

Sultan.
Escape! Ha! Escape the breath of breezes,
They follow you from the Indus to the pole.
Try it, wander out into the west,
To see if you may avoid the sun's beams.
In vain; they always rise anew from the shadows.
Wherever you wander, the east goes with you.
Thus my love like heaven's breezes
And like the sun pursues me everywhere.

Nerissa.
Woe to me and you! I fear your love,
And your hatred is as awful as your grace.
What should I do? Devise what salvation?
Is there no further help, no advice?

Mangu enters.

Mangu.
A stranger asks if he may see your face
My King. Shall I tell him that he may?

Sultan.
It is granted him to come to us immediately,
Call him, he may speak before me now.

*Sino steps into the background and beckons; Udohla appears and
prostrates himself before the Sultan.*

Mangu.
Speak, stranger! For the Sultan will hear you
Rise and speak, say who you are.

Udohla (rising before the Sultan).
I am called Ahmed, am your servant, born
In Hyderabad, Salim's sister's son.

Sultan.
My friend! You are related to the Nawab?
To the worthy, powerful; I greet you.

Udohla.
The Nawab bade me bring you this letter
And greetings and submission to his lord.

He passes him a piece of paper.

Sultan.
You've done so. *(after he has read it)* You are a good messenger.
Ask for a reward; it will behove me

To give you what you ask for.
So right away choose freely what you please.

Udohla.
On my way from Hyderabad, as I drew near,
In the mountains I fell into robbers' hands.
I would surely have been lost,
Except a young man rescued me,
And when I bade him choose a reward he said:
"If you appear before the Lord of the World
Throw yourself at his feet, pleading
That he may spare my father's life,
Bahadur's, who was captured in an insurrection."
So said the youth. *(kneeling.)* Lord! hear him.
I have no request but his
Oh great king! do not scorn it.

Sultan.
You ask too late; his head has already fallen.

Nerissa.
What will become of me! Elpa! lead me from here.

off with Elpa.

Sultan.
Come, Mangu! Let us hurry to the princess,
And Sino, you explain to him what happened.

off with Mangu.
Long pause. Udohla remains a while on his knees, then stands up slowly.

Udohla.
So the dear head has already fallen,
The downfall of our house is decided!
What can I do now? Since I have lost everything
I am relieved of any fear.
You heard what I said, go! reveal me.
I am Bahadur's, your enemy's, son.

Sino.
Oh youth! I weep for your misery,
For I am Sino, a Hindu just like you.

Udohla.
You Sino? Then I'm not abandoned
By all the gods, because I found you here.
I know you, although I have never seen you,
For you have always been my uncle's hope.

Sino.
Oh Usbek! He still lives! The dear! The good!
He alone was spared his house's fall.

Udohla.
He was my second father; for my own
I have not seen, I think, in many years.
My uncle took me with him to Bengal,
When Bahadur easily persuaded
The outraged people to make him their chief.
Thus I grew up far from my father.
But when he lost his only daughter,
He summoned me to share his fate.
I went; only my father was imprisoned,
I was caught and sent away from him. –
How unbearably long, cheerless hours
I languished alone like that in gaol,
Without hope, and I faced death
With gloomy, deeply depressed courage.
Then my dungeon's doors opened
And I escaped to my uncle's guest,
To the Nawab, who kindly took me in
Like a son, and unwillingly let me go.
But my inner spirit drove me to find out
Whether my father could still be saved;
Either by pleading before the Mongols' ruler;
Or, if not, then with sharp bold steel.
So I came here, and I live still to decide

If this dagger will run us both through;
Whether it will first pierce the Sultan's purple
Or whether I bring only myself as an offering to the dead.

Sino.
You are no Hindu. No, for in your breast
Boils the Scythian's wild, untamed blood.
Everyone knows that insurrection is punishable by death.

Udohla.
Well then! In that case may the Sultan live
May the light of the sun still bring him delight;
But it befits me better now to die.
My father's spirit beckons me down to him,
He'd like to see the son he never knew,
Press him once against his father's heart.
Oh sweet joy down there among the dead!
Come, ascend! Black out for me the light
Of that dear day that I hardly saw
From which I now must, grieving, part.

> *He draws the dagger; Sino holds him back.*

Sino.
Stop and live! What do you want from your father?
The dead are not awaiting us beyond.
They transform through many, many shells
Until the great day of resurrection.
You know this well; so live the days
As long as the gods' will grants them to you.

Udohla.
Should I live just so as to survive?
What is left for me to wish, to do?

Sino.
Have you no friends and blood relations
Who languish in dark dungeons' night?

Well then! Seek to rescue them.
The Sultan has a heart easily moved,
His ruler's defiance melts in love's delight,
He has in truth a human sentiment. –

Udohla.
I have already reached the edge of life,
Now the future's door opens for me.
My eye that was surrounded by grave's night
Closes against the unaccustomed light.

Sino.
Come! Let me seek, find paths for you,
I will lead you on a more level way.

Second Act.

Garden.
Nerissa and *Elpa.*

Nerissa.
Go! Seek him! call him! for I must see him,
I must speak to him; lead him here.

Elpa off.

What will befall me now? Woe, woe is me
Unhappy one! The gods of India
Abandon me, because I first, disloyal,
Abandoned them, and the God of Muhammad
Sees angrily the prayers I, doubting, send him,
The false service, devoted unwillingly to him,
That always still half means the ancient gods.
Thus all heaven's powers threaten me,
And nameless lamentation has become my lot. –
Here he comes! Ah, how my sick heart pounds!

Udohla and Elpa enter. Elpa steps back.

Udohla.

What sporting destiny, oh King's Daughter,
Bestowed on you the name of one unknown?
What is it that, out of the colorful crowd
Of thousands, calls me to the sight of you?

Nerissa.

I saw you kneeling down before the Sultan
And pleading for a head already lost.
Speak, did you know the youth whose father
You wanted to save from the Lord of the World?

Udohla.

Princess! What happened I explained
And more than I explained I do not know.

Nerissa.

You evade me, your gaze
Strays sheepishly, and a traitorous blush
Tells me too well what you would like to hide,
Your lips themselves, which could lie, quake.

Udohla.

And if I knew the destiny of the youth,
Might I trust it to you, then, Princess?
The sister of the Sultan who pursues him,
Who thirsts for the unlucky one's blood?

Nerissa.

You know Udohla, then? Yes, you've revealed it.
But do not tremble for him or for you,
No, go on and boldly trust in me:
For I'm thinking of a way to save the youth.

Udohla.

You know his name? Then know:
He wanders back and forth along the Ganges,
And seeks his grave with a life-weary gaze:

There remains nothing more for him to wish on earth.
So if you want to save someone, oh King's Daughter!
Then do not think of him. No! Save those
Of the Hindu people who are languishing
In gaol, take pity on their long distress.

Nerissa.
Then has Udohla no brother, no sister?
And nothing on the earth that is his own?

Udohla.
He never saw his only sister, who
Was abducted from her father by robbers.

Nerissa.
They say Bahadur saved her
And no-one knows the exact circumstance.
Why did he not escape before he was captured,
Delivered into his enemies' hands?

Udohla.
He did not want to leave his fatherland.

Nerissa. Passes Udohla a chain.
Take this chain and think of me
As I will think of those unlucky ones
Whom you would like to see me save.

                                        off with Elpa.

Udohla.
Oh sweet tones! From such sweet lips!
Now the first day of my life begins,
A day invigorating as the dawn
And balmy and intimate as midnight.
To which god will I now make pilgrimage
To absolve me from my thoughts of death?
Oh all you gods! Most gravely I blasphemed,
For life is more beautiful than death.

Room in the palace.

The Sultan stands[31] thoughtfully. After a long pause
Mangu and Sino appear.

Mangu.
My ruler! Ahmed, who at your court –

Sultan.
At my court? Ahmed? Then speak!

Mangu.
His name is not the name he gave you;
He is the son of Bahadur, the traitor.

Sultan.
Who says so? And how will you prove it?
Bahadur's son? It's almost unbelievable.

Mangu.
I was present, Lord, when he was captured
Through your loyal servants' eagerness,
And when he knelt pleading before you
I recalled this youth dimly;
But, doubting, I did not dare accuse him;
Whereas today I'm certain of his crime:
His features emerge from the distance, distinct
And recognizable to my searching eye.

Sultan.
Then seek him out and bring him to me,
But until then I want to be alone.

off.

Sino.
You may well be wrong, how easily the eye deceives!
What would the youth be doing in the Sultan's court?

---

[31] The Morgenthaler edition has "sits" (SW 1:221).

Mangu.
Bahadur's blood flows in the youth's veins,
His poisonously proud, untamed blood.
What can he do except plan malice?
And what act is too brazen for that house?

Sino.
You hope to find something damnable;
Unjust zeal has carried you away.

Mangu.
Ha! I forgot with whom I spoke of this.
You are a Hindu. Well, we know you, then;
We may not trust in your loyalty,
You will always lean towards our foes.

Sino.
I know that you will never get to know me,
It is impossible; why did I hope for it?

       Mangu remains a while standing thoughtfully, then goes off.

Then break at last your bonds of silence
My long tamed only all-too patient heart!
Woe is us! Woe is us! Born into slavery
Nothing breaks the heavy chains but death.
We've sunk so deep that of the renown
Of this country's old magnificence
Only a saying reaches our ears,
Ah! A saying that we hardly understand –
Heaven loves us, yes the sun itself
Sends its beams down lovingly to us;
And may never turn its eye away from us
While stinting of itself to other folks.
Yes, to us all gods are well-disposed.
They rock this land as if it were a cradle
For it was the first to rise from the ocean,
And now lamentingly it sighs in chains. –

Oh, when will the earth reshape itself again?
When will the morning dawn on better times?
Patience my heart! Eventually they must come,
Your old gods still live.
They live, to generate the world anew,
Perhaps more lovely hours are already near.

Mangu enters.

Mangu.
I wanted, oh Sino, to trust something to you
That is odd, but extremely pleasing.
A trusted messenger came from Aude[32]
And brought this signet ring and letter,
In which Nerissa, the Daughter of the King,
Writes to me how deeply she now regrets her flight,
How she longs to come back to her brother,
If he can forgive her for her act.
So says the letter, and so that I'd believe it
She encloses the King's signet ring.

Sino.
Incredible deceit! Who would believe it!
Whom may one believe, and whom accuse of lies?

Mangu.
Aga has let me in on the secret,
That fear of death led him to deceit;
That he compelled a girl who had been kidnapped
And persuaded her to take the step
Of appearing as our Sultan's sister;
And how Elpa backed him up.

Sino.
I know indeed how changed she seemed to us,
Nerissa, so different from before.

---

[32] This may be an alternative spelling for Awadh, or Oudh, a historical province in northern India.

Mangu.
Yes, even to the Sultan she seemed changed.
His spirit was soon inflamed with love for her;
In that, however, his heart did not betray him
For in drawing him to this stranger
It did not lead him to commit a crime.

Sino.
Then go! Reveal to him what you have learned,
Do not delay the hour of his joy.

Garden.

Nerissa.
My destiny, it must now be decided.
Do I escape alone, and seek that path,
The old, well-known, that I so often trod
By starlight, veiled in midnight?
It will be. I part; but with a cheerless soul.
I seek the silent fissures of that cliff
In which, long hidden with my father
I lived in lonely contemplation;
There the past shall become my future,
I'll see again the great primeval world,
Seek again the lost aptitudes,
Reconcile anew with the old gods. –
By the Ganges my brother wanders up and down,
And seeks his grave with a life-weary gaze;
So Ahmed said. Yes, I will seek him,
And share his fortune like I did with my father.
Before my eyes there swims a lovely image
That I would so gladly call brother.

Elpa enters.

Elpa.
You are sought: the Sultan wants to see you,
He seeks you himself with great haste.

Nerissa.

He will seek me often and not find me.
Go! Tell him that I cannot see him now.

Elpa.

How is it that you may resist your ruler?
He seems so urgent and so deeply moved!

Nerissa.

Oh heaven! Must I go through this too,
Must I look upon the murderer's face!
Hear again the voice that I find worthy
And think that it uttered those cruel words,
Pronounced the dreadful sentence of death,
That forever separates me from his love.

Elpa.

Your crazed senses have driven horrible words
Out from the bottom of your soul
Which, like poisonous plants, sow disaster;
It would be better for me if I had not heard them:
Therefore I will forget them, unremarked,
Buried, before they bear terrible fruit.

Nerissa.

Did you not outrageously tear them from me,
The words that my lips tremblingly spoke?

Elpa.

Come, before the Sultan finds you in this mood,
You may not appear like this before him.

Both off. Udohla enters.

Udohla.

Only a few words did she have to say,
Why did they not fill all the times,
All the times until the final days? –

Heaven seems to rejoice with her name,
It's whispered lightly by all the airs of spring.

Sino enters.

Sino.
You're still here? Udohla! Don't you know,
That you're betrayed completely to the Sultan?
That he knows you are Bahadur's son?
You might consider all you have to fear,
So flee, before the worst happens.

Udohla.
Escape, my friend! For me the earth is small.
For only where she wanders is my life,
And where she is not, there is barren emptiness. –
These trees have seen her, and this air
Has cooled her caressingly, and so to me
They are my homeland and my world.

Sino.
I still don't know to whom your words allude.
But stay, I'll still find a way to save you:
Nerissa will be married to the Sultan,
The night specter of fear has disappeared,
That long separated his love from her.
In this joy he will forgive you.

Udohla.
I know enough. Do not seek to save
He whom those words forever damn.
I give myself up willingly and gladly
For lost, but I have seen life's brilliance.
It surrounded me, lovely, like a bride,
Who reveals herself only shyly and in part,
But I have guessed its sweet charm,
And give it steadfastly a parting kiss;
And if the Sultan sends me to my death,
He only steals a life already ending.

Sino.

My heart was moved lovingly to you;
I hoped to be revived by your youth,
Offer you the ripe fruits of my life
And join you through me to the world of old,
Me to posterity; yes through your lips
I wanted to entrust much to the future.
Now that will not be; for you are wearing out
Your youth in wild drives and mad striving.
I saw you sacreligiously call gods of death,
Then exult again in life's delight:
Now already you renounce life rashly,
Too sluggish and proud to dare something for rescue.

Udohla.

What do you want from me? My bloom is past
And has left no fruits behind.
Can I demand of heaven's winds
That they do not bend my life's stem?
Leave me, so I do not tear your heart apart
And drag it with me down into the crypt.
Do not entrust your crops to my breast,
They will not blossom beautiful and strong,
No, with me they will molder in the grave,
And, like me, go under without trace.

Sino.

Then that intuition did indeed deceive me
In which you seemed so meaningful to me!
I falsely thought destiny must intend something
Because it led you here so wonderfully.
So I erred; you came only to go again,
You were only a guest in my love;
And nonetheless I must still think how to save you,
And give you up as unwillingly as myself.

The Sultan, Mangu and retinue enter.

Sultan. To Mangu.
Go! Hurry, and I will await her here,
I can no longer bear this hesitation. –   *(pause)*
You, Ahmed! Say: is it true, what I heard,
They tell me you're Bahadur's son?

Udohla.
Lord! It is true, what you heard about me.

Sultan.
Then it is also true that death is your due.

Udohla.
If you command it, Lord! then I must die.
I know it, and I am prepared for it.

> *Nerissa and Mangu enter.*

Sultan (facing them).
My love, the separating wall has crumbled
And you are mine. Yes, love, you are mine.
How could you cruelly torment me for so long,
And hide from me such blissful happiness?

Nerissa.
Where can I find the tones for these words,
At which my pale lips hesitantly shake?
So know then, I am separated from you
Forever by your own act:
My father's blood incriminates your soul,
It is Bahadur's daughter who stands before you.

Sultan.
Oh Allah! *(He covers himself with his cloak)*

Udohla.
What sweet dream gently surrounds my soul?
Say, Sino! Will the lovely dream pass by?
Oh be silent so that I may never wake!
Is she Ewana, my sister?

Nerissa.

What? Do I hear right? Is Ahmed not your name?

Sino.

He is your brother, Bahadur's son.

Udohla hurries to her, she sinks into his arms. Long pause.

Sultan.

The way she rests in this youth's arms,
A sight that is like hell's torments to me!

Nerissa.

It was your word that spilled my father's blood;
I do not judge whether he earned it;
But this one here does not share in his crime,
He has never raised his sword against you.
Therefore have mercy on him, for my sake,
And let me go peacefully with my brother.

Sultan.

Do you forget what it could cost me,
If I, oh dear one, must now let you go?
You do not see the deep, grave wound
That you strike past cure against my heart.
You hurry forth in glad, swift courage,
While I slowly, painfully bleed out.
In vain does pride imprison the deep pain,
It springs its fetters to attain freedom.

Nerissa.

It is not so, lord! My soul is clouded
By your memory, wherever I may be.
And I feel deeply, when I part from you
That I must violently rip myself away.
Yet I must; for I am separated from you
By everything that is holy to human beings,
By the laws and customs of my people.
Therefore let me go; I may not stay.

Sultan.
Farewell then, you, whom I shall never see
Again. You lovely eyes! Graceful star
That rose over my life;
Foretelling light! that promised me delight,
That flatteringly steered all my destiny
That faithlessly now plunges into clouds. –
Nerissa, go! You've torn my heart to pieces,
I will go grieving to the dead.

off.

Udohla.
Ewana come! We'll go to Bengal,
To delight our uncle's lonely old age.

Sino.
Your destiny, young friend, is now decided,
But ours the distant future still conceals,
The future that I will not live to witness,
The rising that these eyes will never see.
Easily deceived, I often thought I saw
The purple seam of morning in the east,
Announcing India's day after long night.
Often it seemed I heard the call of birds
Greeting the sun early, full of portent.
I erred, the day is not yet here.
But you, oh friend! you will perhaps behold it,
And if it comes, youth! then remember me,
And help to spring the people's heavy chains;
And thus repay me for my stolen love.
Then I will gladly bear the parting from you,
If I only knew I gave you the future. –
Through signs heaven will reveal
When it is favorable to the great work.
Until then bear silently its will,
And hope for the returning of the god.

PART 2

NOTEBOOKS

17

Introduction to Günderrode's Notebooks

Günderrode's notes are useful for identifying texts that influenced her thought and understanding how she modified or sometimes rejected the ideas she studied. This information can alter how we interpret published pieces. For instance, Günderrode is often thought to have based her metaphysics on the work of Friedrich Wilhelm Joseph Schelling (1775–1854), a key thinker in the development of German idealism; however, the dating of Günderrode's notes on Schelling tells us that she had already developed the outline of her metaphysics without his direct influence. This information encourages more careful examination of how Günderrode's thought differs from Schelling's, as well as of her adaptation of ideas from other thinkers including Immanuel Kant (1724–1804), Johann Gottlieb Fichte (1762–1814), François Hemsterhuis (1721–1790), Johann Gottfried Herder (1744–1803), Friedrich Schleiermacher (1768–1834), and the early German Romantics Novalis (1772–1801) and Friedrich Schlegel (1772–1829), who are referenced frequently in her work or excerpted in her notebooks.

Günderrode's notes give an incomplete picture of her readings, not only because she may have filled other study books, now lost, but also because she tended not to take notes on texts she owned.[1] Nonetheless, the notes we have give valuable information about many of Günderrode's sources, as well as her study habits. Günderrode's notes often begin by following her source closely before gradually departing from her material, summarizing, modifying ideas, and sometimes adding clarifications or critique.[2] Some of the notes are not in Günderrode's handwriting, possibly due to problems with her eyes, which led her to rely on friends for transcription. We also know from her correspondence that she enjoyed discussing philosophical and literary texts with her sisters and friends, and her notes confirm the sociable nature of much of her study.

---

[1] Hopp and Preitz, "Umwelt. III," 228.
[2] Hopp and Preitz, "Umwelt. III," 226n18.

Karoline von Günderrode. Anna Ezekiel, Oxford University Press. © Oxford University Press 2026.
DOI: 10.1093/9780190089177.003.0020

Günderrode's notes are not passive copies from her reading material, but show engagement with the texts—minimally in her selection of text, but also including significant modifications that often indicate disagreement with her source. Some scholars have assumed that differences from the original texts reflect a lack of understanding of the material,[3] but this is not supported by a close reading.[4] Nonetheless, this assumption has likely contributed to the fact that, although parts of Günderrode's notes have been available in German since 1975 and more were published in the critical edition in 1991, there has been relatively little work done to uncover her original thought in these writings.

The excerpts from Günderrode's notebooks translated here include translations of Günderrode's notes on Schelling,[5] Schleiermacher, Hemsterhuis, Novalis, and Schlegel. They also include an index of philosophical terms titled "Philosophical Dictionary," a short passage beginning "Reason and understanding . . . ," scattered notes on philosophy and mathematics, and the introductory section of Günderrode's notes on chemistry. Also translated are short quotations from Jean Paul Friedrich Richter's novel *Hesperus* taken between November 1799 and summer 1801, and a set of notes taken between summer 1804 and early 1806.[6]

I have omitted Günderrode's notes on Fichte, as these have already been published in English translation elsewhere.[7] Also not included here are translations of Günderrode's lengthy excerpting of two volumes authored by the philosopher Johann Gottfried Karl Christian Kiesewetter (1766–1819), which aimed to explain and popularize Kant's ideas.[8] I have also omitted transcriptions of several poems and works of literature.[9] In addition to Günderrode's philosophical and literary interests, her notes include work on many other topics, which are not translated here. These include her studies

---

[3] E.g., Christmann, *Identitätsgewinn*, 67; Hopp and Preitz, 231n31.

[4] As Dalia Nassar has shown in relation to Günderrode's notes on Fichte (Nassar, "Human Vocation").

[5] Diagrams are omitted.

[6] The notes are translated from Günderrode's handwritten manuscripts. For details, including published German transcriptions, where available, see the appendix "Sources for Günderrode's Notebooks."

[7] Karoline von Günderrode, "On Fichte's *The Vocation of Humankind*," trans. Anna Ezekiel in *Women Philosophers in the Long Nineteenth Century: The German Tradition*, ed. Dalia Nassar and Kristin Gjesdal (New York: OUP, 2021), 70–74.

[8] J. G. K. C. Kiesewetter, *Grundriß einer reinen allgemeinen Logik nach Kantischen Grundsätzen...* (Berlin: F. T. Lagarde, 1795) and *Grundriß einer allgemeinen Logik nach Kantischen Grundsätzen.... Zweiter Theil welcher die angewandte allgemeine Logik enthält* (Berlin: F. T. Lagarde, 1796). SW 3:328–331.

[9] See Hopp and Preitz, "Umwelt. III."

of ancient geography, Greek history, history of religion, metrics, Latin, and physiognomy, as well as a chronology relating to Phoenicia, Egypt, Greece, Rome, the Middle East, Mongolia, China, and the European Dark Ages. I also omitted a short biography of Achille François Marquis du Chastellet (1759–1794), a collaborator of the French philosopher and politician Nicolas de Condorcet.[10]

---

[10] Günderrode spells the name "Achill du Chatelet."

18

Notes on Philosophy of Nature

Introduction

The writings in this section are translated from Günderrode's notes on the philosophy of Friedrich Wilhelm Joseph Schelling (1775–1854), which emerged from her intensive study of Schelling's writings between the middle of 1804 and 1806.[1] The notes show independent work, not just in collating and summarizing ideas from a range of Schelling's writings, but also in reformulating and in cases diverging from Schelling's ideas. While the connection to Schelling is clear in the concepts, terminology, and outline of the texts, for most of these notes, it has not been possible to identify specific passages to which they correspond.

To varying degrees, the beginnings of the four sets of notes run parallel to each other, providing alternative formulations of the same or similar ideas. These opening passages have strong similarities to Günderrode's philosophical essay "Idea of the Earth" and may have been preparatory work for this piece, which Günderrode worked on further and published as part of "Letters of Two Friends."

The notes beginning "The true idea of materialism . . ." are based on a passage in Schelling's dialogue *Bruno, or On the Divine and Natural Principle of Things*.[2] Whereas Günderrode's other notes on Schelling seem to relate to his early period on the philosophy of nature, *Bruno*, published in 1802, belongs to the period of Schelling's work on identity philosophy. In the passage reflected in Günderrode's notes, Schelling's character Alexander argues that the usual idea we have of matter is of something inorganic, whereas in fact we should see matter as existing "at the point where the organic and the inorganic are together and are identical."[3] This view of things, Alexander

---

[1] SW 3:336–343. Günderrode's notes relate to texts from both Schelling's earliest period on philosophy of nature (before 1801) and his period of identity philosophy (approximately 1801–1809). In titling this chapter "Notes on Philosophy of Nature," I have followed the critical edition of Günderrode's writings (SW 3:336).

[2] Schelling, *Bruno*, trans. Michael G. Vater as *Bruno, or On the Natural and the Divine Principle of Things* (Albany: SUNY Press, 1984), 205f.

[3] Schelling, trans. Vater, *Bruno*, 206.

Karoline von Günderrode. Anna Ezekiel, Oxford University Press. © Oxford University Press 2026.
DOI: 10.1093/9780190089177.003.0021

claims, is not perceptible to our senses, but can only be discerned by the use of reason. He continues that, in itself, matter is a single, undifferentiated source of potential: "In itself, matter lacks all multiplicity. It contains all things in an undivided and therefore indiscriminable manner, as if they were one infinite self-enclosed possibility." We see similar ideas in "Idea of the Earth" and "Letters of Two Friends," where, however, they are embedded in Günderrode's account of a world comprised of indestructible "elements"— a term that does not appear in *Bruno*. Also, Günderrode omits Schelling's appeal to the ancient Greek gendering of the matter-form distinction; this is very characteristic of Günderrode's work, as she consistently rejected gender dualism.[4]

The passage beginning "Nature is an eternal activity . . . " seems to be Günderrode's reflections (with a friend, who wrote some of the notes) on the early Schelling's ideas in general.[5] The editor of the critical edition of Günderrode's works, Walter Morgenthaler, suggests that the first paragraph may relate to parts of *First Outline of a System of the Philosophy of Nature* and that the subsequent list of "potencies" approximately follows Schelling's 1800 article "General Deduction of the Dynamic Processes of Categories of Physics."[6] However, Günderrode's inclusion of geometrical factors in the third potency is not found in the latter piece. The notes present a model of opposing forces that interact to produce natural phenomena, which are then traced in descending order from broad natural laws to more concrete phenomena. This model is developed in more detail in the next set of notes, titled "Idea of Nature."

"Idea of Nature" begins with very similar text to the previous set of notes and shows Günderrode moving from a systematic philosophical presentation of (a modified version of) Schelling's ideas to a more poetic form, especially in the first three paragraphs. Like "Nature is an eternal activity . . . ," "Idea of Nature" describes a productive spirit of nature manifested in infinite

---

[4] European philosophy has a long tradition of conceiving of the physical world, nature, or "matter" as female, and the realm of the intellect, mind, spirit, or "form" as male. For an example of Günderrode's rejection of this idea, see her poem "The Frank in Egypt" and the introduction to this poem, included earlier in this volume.

[5] SW 3:340; Hopp and Preitz, "Umwelt. III," 321–322.

[6] F. W. J. Schelling, *Erster Entwurf eines Systems der Naturphilosophie* (Jena: Christian Ernst Gabler, 1799); *Einleitung zu dem Entwurf eines Systems der Naturphilosophie*, vol. 2 (Jena: Christian Ernst Gabler, 1799); "Allgemeine Deduction des dynamischen Processes oder der Categorieen der Physik," in *Zeitschrift für spekulative Physik*, vol. 1 (Jena: Christian Ernst Gabler, 1800), book 1, 100–136 and book 2, 3–87; *Vorlesungen über die Methode des akademischen Studiums* (Tübingen: Cotta, 1803 [1802]).

numbers of finite products in time. The piece begins with an overview of the "struggle" of conflicting forces that underlie the products of nature before beginning a pseudo-scientific derivation of specific natural phenomena—especially gravity, light, magnetism, and electricity—from the two original, opposed forces.

Despite the focus on basic laws of physics, the text retains hints of a more organic model. For example, the line "Light is the generative [erzeugende] principle; gravity that which conceives [das Empfangende]" associates physical forces with conception and pregnancy. At the time Günderrode was writing, it was common for both literary figures and philosophers to reduce phenomena in all areas to a gendered dichotomy, which could then be overcome through a process analogous to human activities of love, pregnancy, and birth.[7] Although this gendering of natural phenomena appears in Günderrode's notes here, it is not found in her published works.

The passage beginning "All things are . . . " is the longest of Günderrode's notes from her studies of philosophy of nature and the least similar to the other sets. Parts of this passage freely follow (and occasionally quote) sections of Schelling's Ideas[8] but with lengthy insertions that may be derived, in modified form, from other of Schelling's writings or may be Günderrode's own reflections.[9] The passage includes the characterization of natural phenomena as "finite presentations of the infinite" that appeared in the previous notes, but adds much more detail. It also more explicitly explores the relationship between matter and consciousness, especially the question of how the latter can emerge from the former. The passage relates these ideas to the nature of knowledge in the forms of intuition, reflection, philosophy, and "absolute knowing." Here we see Günderrode noting the claim that "reflection" (i.e., conscious or representational knowledge) separates the knower from what is known: reflection "separates intuiting from what is intuited, myself from objects." This claim occasionally emerges in Günderrode's published work, for example in "The Wanderer's Descent."[10]

---

[7] On the role of this type of analogy in early German Romanticism, see Ezekiel, "Women, Women Writers."

[8] F. W. J. Schelling, Ideen zu einer Philosophie der Natur (Leipzig: Breitkopf und Härtel, 1797).

[9] SW 3:340–341.

[10] This claim is also important in work by the Romantic writer Novalis (the pen name of Friedrich von Hardenberg [1772–1801]) and the German idealist philosopher Johann Gottlieb Fichte (1762–1814). For details, see the introduction to "The Wanderer's Descent" earlier in this volume.

Notes on Philosophy of Nature

(The true idea of materialism ...)

The true idea of materialism was lost early. According to [this idea], matter itself is that which is simply unchangeable, eternal; the One that is elevated [*erhaben*] above all opposition, and from which the oppositions develop that we designate variously according to their various potencies.

Matter and body are often mistaken for each other. We have no intuition of matter but we do of bodies, i.e., of determined matter.

The way the manifold emerged from the oneness of matter can be grasped like this: matter contains all things; now, that through which they are all one thing is matter, while that through which they are different and separated from each other is their form. But the forms are various and finite, except that first necessary and eternal form, the principle of all forms, without which matter itself cannot be thought, and which cannot be separated from it but is absolutely one with it; it is totally imperishable, simple and eternal. That primal form is, as it were, the possibility of true matter, the reality of the absolute.

If we were to call the primal form the worldsoul, then we would be wrong to oppose *this* to matter, like spirit is usually opposed to the body. For this worldsoul or primal form only *is* because it is inseparable from eternal matter, and one with it and indistinguishable [from it].

In absolute matter, form and essence are identical. But, again, the absolute form contains the possibility of all forms, and thereby fertilizes the essence. The product of these two things are finite things: in these, the essence is possibility, so to speak, and their form is reality (i.e., their particular reality accrues to them through this particular form). Essence and form are not identical in them; [rather,] their essence is infinite (in that it bears within itself that identity of essence and form in eternal matter), [whereas] their form is finite, and more restricted than their essence, disproportionate to it. Therefore finite things change their forms, while their true essence forever seeks the imperishable and absolute form, which it would only find in the totality of all forms, i.e., at the end of all evolutions of the principle of form, that is, at the end of times. But through the infinity of its evolutions it becomes similar to the infinite essence again: an infinity in time, an infinite finitude.

Thus matter is that which is eternally one, and, however it may be separated for appearance—into what we call possibility and reality, form and essence, finite and infinite, body and spirit, repulsion and attraction—all these oppositions are not within it; rather, they are its various revelations. But the organic body—the most complete synthesis of form and essence, thinking and being, spirit and body—is its most similar copy.

(Nature is an eternal activity...)

Nature is an eternal activity [*Tätigkeit*], a self producing product, an ever enduring becoming—for if it were a being then its productive activity would be cancelled out by this completion. But it is an activity, infinite in time, a continuum that would develop with infinite velocity (and thus have no state) if its activity were not inhibited at all points by something just as infinite: repulsion and attraction. These two activities converge so that they do not cancel each other out; instead, the inhibition changes the infinite velocity into a finite one, whereby a product emerges. And although the same thing always repeats itself under the same conditions, and thus adopts the appearance of subsisting, the activity out of which it sprung would be negated by this subsisting. Thus there can be as little rest in the product as there is in the producing force of nature, which (only held chained in a determinate form by the inhibition) strives to create ever new conditions, and opposes itself to the inhibition. Both forces, therefore, are contending in all products, and all things only exist through their permanent struggle. But that pure action [*Aktion*]—the primal connection of the two forces—is not what appears in space; the visible appearances of nature are, rather, only the outer expression—the various connections—of the primal activities [*Urtätigkeiten*]. These primal activities contain the principle of all products, but never emerge themselves. Space is not filled, no material is brought forth, by the two first dimensions of the first potency; they are ideal primal actions [*Uraktionen*]—principles of material, but yet not material.

1 Potency

1 *Dimension*. Preponderance of attraction. Principle of magnetism.

2 Dim. Preponderance of repulsion. Principle of electricity.

3. Dim. Synthesis of gravity. Principle of products.

2 Potency

1 D. If, through a new contestation of the actions, attraction is victorious, then magnetism emerges: the first concretion, the principle of cohesion (length).

2 D. If repulsion overcomes attraction, electricity emerges, the principle of breadth.

3 D. If magnetism and electricity bind together, then chemical process emerges, or activity pervading all sides (principle of gravity).

The activities are the dimensions of the 2nd potency, only the phenomena of matter, as it were, which, in the $3[^{rd}]$ potency, congeal ever more towards being through the increasing preponderance of attraction.

3 Potency

1 D. Filling of space by length.

2 D. [Filling of space] by breadth.

3 D. [Filling of space] on all sides, thickness.

Idea of Nature

Nature is an infinite activity, a self-producing product, an ever enduring becoming; if it were a *being* then its productive activity would be cancelled out. But if it were only pure activity then it would develop at infinite velocity, and would therefore have no state and would not bring about any product. But at all points its pure positive activity is opposed by an equally infinite negative activity as an inhibiting factor, and through this opposition products become possible.

The positive and negative activities must be thought of as equal to each other, for nature cannot exist through the victory of either one or the other, but only in their equilibrium. If both activities—equal to each other, different only in their direction—were to meet in one point then they would necessarily cancel each other out (make null), and a common effectiveness, a product, would not be possible. Their meeting must therefore be thought of as occurring in many points, and in each point in a different proportion, so that the necessary equality in the whole does not cancel out the necessary difference in the products.

Thus the way in which the two activities meet is one that changes the infinite velocity of the first one into a finite velocity, i.e., makes a product

214 KAROLINE VON GÜNDERRODE

possible. But within the products there is as little rest as there is in the productive nature-spirit, which strives to present itself in ever new states, and is only held chained in a determinate form by the inhibition, which it resists and from which it seeks to tear itself away. The permanence of this struggle in the whole ensures nature its infinity in time, for time is the succession of the developments of this struggle, and only infinite time (and within it an infinite evolution of its capacity to present itself) is commensurate to it. But, because nature presents itself in all forms and in all times, no single *form* can suffice it, and, because its activity is infinite, it can persist in *none* of these forms. Therefore the individual product is dissolved by the victory of one of the two activities in it, and its essence returns to that from which it sprung, which develops ever new forms from out of its abundance.

If the positive and negative activity come together so that neither is bound by the other, a product emerges that (as it were) only tends towards figuration: *light.*

But if the positive (repulsion) and negative (attraction) activities come together so that repulsion is bound and held firmly by attraction, then *gravity* emerges: it is the condition of material figuration that fills space. Gravity is the first connective relationship of the primal forces; it is the synthetic point itself, in which attraction[11] envelops repulsion.

Light[12] and gravity are the real factors of ideal primal forces: through their various conjunctions, various materials emerge. That which is apparent to our senses as quality,[13] therefore, is only the expression of different connections of light and gravity.

Light is the generative principle; gravity that which conceives. In products where light predominates there will be more life and activity; in those where gravity predominates, more solidification, dead form.

We call materials that, through a conjunction of light[14] and gravity, emerge with a *predominance* of *gravity* "*magnetic*"; those that, through the synthesis

---

[11] Günderrode's note: "Repulsion is infinite extension; attraction is infinite restriction—its tendency is to reduce to a point, and thus to cancel out the world of appearance."

[12] Günderrode's note: "In the world of appearance, light is the factor of repulsion, gravity [that] of attraction."

[13] I.e., the qualities of materials, such as their color, hardness, transparency, etc.

[14] Günderrode's note: "Because light and gravity are the general conditions of matter, no chemical analysis can separate their factors within a product from each other, for through such a process the matter would cease to be. Thus, however analytically the chemist proceeds, their elements are still synthetic products."

of light with gravity, emerge with a *predominance* of *light* [we call] *"electrical"* materials.

If repulsion is absolute extension [and] attraction [is] absolute reduction, then, with respect to space, light is extension in its second potency, whereas gravity is like a point. The point is extended to a line by the addition of light; the line extended to a surface by a further addition of light; surface and line synthesized become a *cube*.

For [the world of] appearance, the unity of nature is divided into two opposed forces that are only synthesized again in the product. This unity and duality is expressed in all products: thus in a line the unifying point is the unity; the two opposing poles [are] the duality.

The line is the first figuration and, insofar as it designates the victory of the factor of gravity, the expression of congealing, of the being-for-itself of the body, of individuality. But because gravity, as the predominance of the attractive factor, is the principle of holding-together, of condensing, the line is at the same time the form of cohesion, for attraction limited to the sphere of a given body is cohesion.

But, just as the opposites in the line may be demonstrated mathematically, so, too, [they may be demonstrated] dynamically and chemically. Dynamically, [the line] decomposes into a negative and a positive pole, for it seems as if nature does not succeed in mixing the factors to the point of indifferentiation, since, however much their union is permitted, they are always revealed as opposites. The positive pole is that within which the factor of light is relatively predominant, which manifests chemically as azote;[15] the negative [pole] is that in which the factor of gravity predominates: for chemistry this is revealed as carbon.

The phenomenon that is commonly only called magnetism is only found (however many bodies are subject to absolute cohesion, that is, magnetic) in lodestones and iron. These two bodies must therefore be seen as the most perfect forms of absolute cohesion.

If we think of a combination of light and gravity in which the former is *not* overcome and held fast by the latter, then the relationship of the two forces will be more like being next to each other than being in each other.

---

[15] "Azote" is an old name for nitrogen.

(All things are ...)

All things are, so to speak, finite presentations of the infinite, and so to a greater or lesser extent all things have a double being: an individual limited being, insofar as they constitute an independent entity for themselves; and a universal being, insofar as they are dependent on and connected with the universe, and therefore are, at the same time, participants in the infinite. This double being is the principle of all entities. Thus all the bodies and materials of the earth are each an individual being for themselves and also, at the same time, a universal being insofar as they are an element that belongs to the great whole of the earth. The earth itself has this double life. Its individual movement is the movement around its own axis: it strives to break away from the sun to become entirely an individual, but the sun, with all its magnetic force, strives to draw it to itself, to unite it with itself, and thus to annihilate its singularity. The double movement of the earth around the sun and around its own axis emerges from the struggle of this attractive force of the sun with the force of the earth, by virtue of which the latter seeks to maintain its selfhood. The moon is much more strongly attracted by the earth than the latter is by the sun: the earth's force upon it works so strongly that it allows it hardly any movement. It is therefore unable to turn around its axis; it only follows its course. The nearer the planets are to the sun, the weaker their individual movement and the more they are mere satellites of the sun. Their life, which thus gains in universality by obtaining a higher and more general tendency, loses in individuality. With the distance of the planets from the sun, their particularity increases in proportion to how their universality decreases. They turn more slowly around the sun, and faster and more violently around their own axis; they have multiple moons and their particular force is far greater than that of the planets near the sun.

That is absolute which is not limited by anything else, which limits itself, and which is in itself cause and effect at once, and consequently has no ground outside itself. The universe is an absolute. All things are absolute in a certain sense, insofar as they participate in the universe; but they are also not absolute, insofar as they have a ground outside themselves (the universe).

Absolute knowledge—i.e., knowledge in general, the knowledge of everything that is—is, at the same time, real (real, being): a spirit that knew everything, all of whose knowledge would also be real. For if I know everything, then nothing is outside my knowledge; but, also, I cannot know of anything that is not. This highest unity of the ideal (of knowledge, thinking) with the real (of what is, of the real) is an absolute again, the universe again.

Nature is the ideal formed in the real.

Knowledge is a transferring of the ideal onto the real.

Acting is a transferring of the real into the ideal.

The first moment of intuition is the unity of the intuiting and what is intuited.

Reflection divides this primitive unity: it separates intuiting from what is intuited, myself from objects, spirit from material. Finally, it dissects my own life into two parts in order to observe one half with the other. It therefore makes me into object and subject at the same time.

Philosophy presupposes this division, and makes it its task—through an act of freedom—to reunite in consciousness that which is separated by reflection (intuited and intuiting, thought and object, object and subject).

Philosophy, therefore, first investigates whether there are really things outside us, whether these things can affect us, and how they can do so.

Thus, concerning the first question, in order to learn whether there are things in themselves, that means things that would exist without our representation, if these so-called things outside us were stripped of all that our representation transfers onto them. And all concept of succession[16] of cause and effect, of space and time, belongs to representation.

But if things are stripped of everything that my representation transfers onto them, what do I have left of them? Nothing, i.e., no more representation—and what are they to me if I cannot represent them to myself?

However, our representations would be absolutely empty, mere forms, if there were not things that corresponded to them. Accordingly, things without representations are not thinkable for us, and representations of things without the things are nothing: empty, insubstantial concepts. But in order for things to have reality for us, and in order for our representations to have reality, philosophy seeks their absolute unity, the identity of the object and subject. But it can take no other path towards this than self-observation: it must descend into the depths of its own mind[17] and seek the ground of our

---

[16] Günderrode's note: "Succession is a concept that necessarily emerges from the finitude of our spirit, by virtue of which we cannot survey a thing at once and at one point, but are compelled to let our representations follow each other."

[17] Günderrode's note: "since, whatever we may perceive and investigate, we perceive only our selves, i.e., our states, in our own mind we can only find constructions of things."

representations within it, find the necessity of their emergence and their unity with their objects there.

Philosophy is therefore nothing other than the natural doctrine of our spirit. It allows the whole system of our representations to develop in front of us, and with it, at the same time, the whole system of outer appearances, or of objects outside us. This philosophy wants to show how nature coincides (not accidentally) with the laws of our spirit and realizes them. Thus, as nature is visible spirit, spirit is invisible nature. If this is demonstrated in the following, the question "how can things outside us work on our representations and generate them?" will need no further discussion.

The insight that the *absolutely ideal* is at the same time also the absolutely real is the condition of all higher scientificity—not only philosophical scientificity but also mathematical and astronomical scientificity—for this unity is the ground upon which they are built.[18]

We first ask: what is the absolute ideal? It is an absolute knowing (a knowing that knows everything), an absolute act of knowledge.

In absolute knowing, the objective must therefore be wholly subjective and the subjective must be wholly objective.

But how does this highest unity of the objective and subjective, the ideal and real, come to be divided?

The absolute in its highest unity (where it is object and subject, ideal and real) is an eternal act of knowledge which is itself material and form; an eternal producing that produces itself, that is itself essence and form. For because this absolute is everything, nothing is outside it, and there is no cause of its being but itself. It can therefore only produce itself, can only itself be material and form.

This absolute (the highest unity) is an eternal, active act of knowledge, the concept of which is at the same time a creating, i.e., the essence of which is that its thought is at the same time real, a *being*.

In this absolute, three actions can be distinguished:

1) Where it brings forth its essence (subject), the general [*das Allgemeine*] or infinite, as a particular, finite form (object). (But every form is finite, as form, i.e., as limited.) Thus in this act the subjective objectivizes itself.

---

[18] Günderrode's note: "The astronomical calculations apply without one having previously experienced their accordance with the movements of the heavenly bodies."

2) Where the objective, the form, the particular finite thing, is dissolved again in the essence of the general or infinite. This act is the subjectivization of the objective.

3) Where the object is not separated from the subject, and the form is not separated from the essence. Thus in the third act an absolute emerges again, i.e., a unity of the object and the subject, of the form and the essence, of the particular and the general, of the finite and infinite.[19]

Now, because the absolute is everything (the ideal and real at the same time), everything that exists must proceed from the absolute. But because the absolute can only produce itself, all its productions must also be an absolute, and these three acts of the absolute must be expressed in everything: 1) the objectivization of the subjective, 2) the subjectivization of the objective, and 3) the indifference of both (absoluteness).

Because it is our purpose to ascend from the real to the ideal, we must first pay attention to the former.

The real side of that eternal acting of the absolute infinite is nature in itself.

Eternal nature,[20] the basic force or the type from which all individual appearances (bodies) proceed, is the spirit of God born in form (objective). This is the general, or the essence, whose particular, or form, all individual appearances of nature are (the body, so to speak, of this invisible force of nature).

Philosophy of nature

Now, this eternal nature is neither only real nor only ideal, neither only essence nor only form, but, again, an absolute unity of both: a realized idea, an essence that molds itself in forms, forms that dissolve themselves in essence, and a unity of both.

In order to further investigate these three acts in nature and in natural appearances, we must consider the invisible type of nature, the all-pervading nature-spirit, as the general. And so we find out how it 1) expresses, molds itself in forms (appearances of nature), 2) how these forms return to and dissolve themselves in the essence, 3) how form and essence are one.

[19] Günderrode's note: "But this unity is not that primal unity, or the eternal, in which the ideal and the real rested, still undivided and indivisible; it is a synthesized unity, a product of opposed activities, an absolute in second potency, the universe."

[20] Günderrode's note: "The ancients called nature the birth of things, because the eternal things, the ideas, are born in nature, so to speak."

In order to detect these three acts in all particular appearances, we must seek the potencies that are always subordinated to the three acts.[21] So, for example, in order to construct nature according to this idea, we must completely abstract from the absolute ideal, and instead of this set the universal (the force of nature) as its factor (representative). And thus we must say: 1) the general force of nature presents itself in particular appearances (forms). 2) The appearances return to the general force of nature. 3) The force of nature and its forms (appearances) are indifferent. If we want to pursue this idea further in terms of how it presents itself in detail, then we must posit, as the factor of the general, a subordinated, relative general (one that is not absolute, but only general within its class) and a relative particular. For example, in descending order towards the real:

> The force of nature as general, subject.
> The heavenly bodies or solar system as particular, object.
>
> A level deeper:
> Our solar system, that which is sun-like, as general.
> The material of the planets as particular.
>
> etc.

On our planet, *light and heat* (the factors of the general, or of that which is like the sun) are incorporated in everything particular, [i.e., in] earthly materials (factors of the particular). In almost all their presentations, these two principles, the general and the particular, appear as contesting [with each other]. In those bodies in which the general [principle] wins, the absolute cohesion of the bodies (or that through which they are individual, that which holds their inner parts together) is overpowered by relative cohesion[22] (that which the general brings to bear against the particular in order to annihilate it) or the attracting force of that which is like the sun (by which it strives to bring the earthly into relationship with the sun and subordinate it to it). This can happen like this: Light and warmth penetrate a body to such a degree that the connection of its parts (absolute cohesion) is disturbed—light and warmth are trying to affect it everywhere, to dissolve it. If the body's absolute

---

[21] Günderrode crossed out a description of these three acts: "of the absolute, ideal: 1) the formation of the ideal in the real, 2) the returning of the real to the ideal, 3) the indifference point of both."
[22] Günderrode adds a note after the word "cohesion," stating simply "attraction."

cohesion cannot withstand this relative cohesion, then in terms of its form it will be drawn back to a surface (fully accessible to light and warmth), but in terms of its quality it will become transparent (fully penetrated by light).

By contrast, bodies whose absolute cohesion is stronger than relative [cohesion] resist the pressure of light and heat more. They do absorb the general in themselves, only its effects are lost in its particularity. They remain hard, cold and opaque, due to the strength of their absolute cohesion.

In absolute cohesion, the factor of the general is nitrogen or light-material[23] (azote) and the particular is carbon. In relative cohesion hydrogen is the general, and oxygen is the particular.

Only those bodies that have an affinity with oxygen are combustible. There are two kinds of combustion: (1) when the body corrodes air and absorbs its oxygen—this is called oxidization or calcification; (2) when the base materials of the body bind with the air and are dissolved by it—bodies combusted like this cannot be reduced like the first. Because oxygen is the condition of all combustion, every process of combustion must end in an indifferentiation of the general (hydrogen) with the particular (oxygen) in relative cohesion, or, in absolute [cohesion], in an indifferentiation of the general (azote) and the particular (carbon) with the particular of relative cohesion (oxygen). From this it is clear that in relative cohesion all bodies are combusted, i.e., are saturated with oxygen or bound with it.

Light and heat are, perhaps, one and the same. One could say that heat is invisible light, and light is visible heat. Light is an infinitely fine fluid, the infinite velocity of which penetrates space without filling it. It is, as it were, the ideal in the real, and also the regression of the real into the ideal, because it [light] appears again in the ideal as the factor of the real. Light can be considered the generative principle, and gravity that which receives.

Atmospheric air is a chemical mixture of azote and oxygen, both of which constituent parts, as with all bodies, are bonded with light and heat. Air is an indifference of the general (azote) of absolute cohesion with the particular (oxygen) of relative cohesion.

In its pure state, water consists of two chemically bonded, combustible types of gas: oxygen and hydrogen. Oxygen is the condition of all negative

---

[23] The idea of *Lichtstoff* ("light-material," "light matter," or "luminiferous material"), a substance that emits light, was used in late eighteenth- and early nineteenth-century chemistry and philosophy of nature, often contrasted with either *Schwerstoff* ("gravity material" or "heavy matter") or *Wärmestoff* ("heat material/matter"), known in English as "phlogiston." These theories are now debunked.

[electricity] and hydrogen of all positive electricity. In water, the general and the particular are fully equivalent: it is wholly like the sun and wholly earthly.

Magnetism is absolute cohesion in its highest activity. That is, if two homogeneous bodies (which, because of their similarity, cannot complete each other, insofar as only something dissimilar can constitute the 2 sides of a totality) are brought near to each other, then each draws more into itself. Thus the being-in-itself of the body, its individual striving, is expressed in magnetism. Magnetism, as the striving for cohesion, is what determines length in the filling of space; it is that which withstands the sun; and, with respect to the earth, the north-south polarity. At the same time, it designates the formation of unity in multiplicity, in which each [aspect] of this multiplicity posits itself as singularity. Magnetism has a negative and positive pole: its positive [pole] must be the one where the general predominates.

If two dissimilar bodies are brought close to each other, they strive to complete each other, to become a totality. This striving is achieved through friction: the uneven contact of the friction disturbs the cohesion of the bodies that are rubbed together, [and] they come out of their resting equivalence. The cohesion is strengthened in one (the particular becomes predominant), reduced in the other (the general becomes predominant). The particular draws its factor (oxygen) out of the air; by contrast, the general binds with its factor (azote) in the air (because the air is mechanically divided by friction), and so a [form of] combustion emerges, the lowest degree of which is electrical phenomena. But combustion is a conversion from absolute cohesion into relative [cohesion] (in which that which is like the sun is subordinated), [and] consequently a function of breadth, insofar as, through combustion, the bodies are penetrated on all sides by light and heat. Electricity is therefore the striving for identity of bodies that are different in relative cohesion, or the activity of relative cohesion. The regression of the particular into the general is expressed in it; with respect to the earth, this manifests as the east-west polarity. But there is a negative and positive pole of electricity: the negative [pole] is that in which the particular attracts the particular (oxygen); and the positive [pole] is that where the absolute predominates—it must therefore be more active because the general is the factor of what is (like the son) active.

The chemical process is the indifference-point of magnetic and electrical activity; it unifies their operations in a third [thing].

Matter is the result of attractive and repulsive forces that fill space. Matter cannot be thought of without forces. Now, if we abstract from all qualities and think of two masses that are similar in quantity, then one will cancel out the force of the other. If we think of two [masses] of dissimilar size, then the greater will attract the smaller and, as it were, devour it. If we think of three [masses] of similar size, they will indeed stand in a certain relationship and mutually hold each other, but no movement will emerge. But if we assume bodies that are different in number and size and similar in quality, then the largest, the predominant weight of which is already a striving for the center, will set itself in the middle. Its effect on the others can then only be thought most completely and accurately if it moves them in circles around itself. It follows naturally that the repulsive force of the smaller [mass] provides weaker resistance to its attraction than [that of] the larger; it will therefore draw the smaller [mass] closer and more strongly than the larger. This movement, the attraction and repulsion, is dynamic, or appropriate to matter (considered apart from any qualities).

Because all satellites demonstrate repulsion against their central bodies, one must consider attraction (by virtue of which they restrain all the bodies found around them) as their own dynamic activity. The central body demonstrates attraction towards its satellites; its repulsion is therefore perhaps directed against a higher central body to which it, in turn, belongs as a satellite.

There are three kinds of movement: dynamic (quantitative); mechanical, or compelled by an external impact; and chemical (qualitative), or inner. But no movement (which is cancelled-out equivalence) can be thought of except as opposed to rest, and no rest except as in opposition to movement; therefore where I perceive movement I must conclude partial rest, and conversely.

Where we see the forces fully equalized (one, so to speak, bound and cancelled out by the other), there is no activity, no movement, no life, but only a being, a constant subsisting in itself. But where the forces are in a certain conflict (in active opposition) there is activity, movement. Where this conflict becomes permanent in a determinate form, there is life.

But the form is the result of this conflict, and the conflict ends with it.

We have followed, in an ascending line, the 3 potencies of the absolute, in the 3 subdivisions, which each has 3 more dimensions.

A) Potency of the formation of the general in the particular. This potency is that of mere being, and its dimensions can be considered dimensions of the filling of space.

  1 Dimension. Absolute cohesion, filling of space in length, being in itself.
  2 Dim. Relative cohesion, filling of space as a surface, returning to or yielding to the general.
  3 D. Indifference point, thickness.

B) Potency of the return of the particular to the general is the potency of the activity of matter, of phenomena.

  1 D. Magnetism.

  2 D. Electricity.

  3 D. Chemical process

C) Potency of the indifference of the general and particular; appears as organism, life.

  1 D. Regeneration drive.

  2 D. Irritability.

  3 D. Formative capacity, reason; at lower levels this shows itself as sensibility.

Nature is the real side of absolute knowledge. Its products are thoughts congealed to being, dark dreams out of which it progressively awakens to consciousness. It presents the laws of our spirit in realities, in being. Just as we must think of matter as the result of the opposed forces[24] of repulsion and attraction, so the conflict of these opposed activities (among other forms) is the condition of nature, of life, and of spirit. We define repulsion as that force by virtue of which a thing strives to extend itself, unconstrained, into the infinite on all sides and to push away everything that resists it. This force is a positive, active, infinite one.

Attraction resists the infinite expansion of repulsion, it seeks to draw the expansion back to one point. It is, therefore, a negative, constraining, finite force.

All forms have proceeded from the conflict of these forces: the first gave things extension, the second gave them limitation, determination. But the product of opposed activities is always a finite, constrained thing. Repulsion strives to fill space on all sides; attraction wants to bring the filling of space back to one point; what emerges from the activity of the two together is the filling of space under determinate limits.

The positive, infinite activity of spirit strives to extend itself on all sides; if left alone to do this it would dissolve in the infinite, so to speak. The negative, finite activity strives to draw its activity back to one point (it is a striving for

---

[24] Günderrode's note: "without these forces, no material, no filling of space, would be conceivable: without attraction there would be no connection at all, without repulsion no expansion."

the center, a leading back into itself, consciousness). From the conflict of the two activities emerges a constrained activity, a determinable, finite thing, an indifference of the infinite and finite: our spirit.

Repulsion is, so to speak, the factor of space, or of unlimited extension, and attraction is the factor of time, or of constraint in successive points (moments of time). Time only exists where circumstances follow each other, where something becomes, is, and was. Time is therefore finite in everything. But where nothing becomes and was, where everything is and remains unchanged, there time cannot be imagined.

That which appears to our senses as quality emerges through the conjunction of attraction and repulsion according to relationships of degree. In the world of physical bodies, the greatest degree of repulsion combined with the least [degree] of attraction is light.

In the form of magnetism (length), the relationship of degree appears as a predominance of attraction (of that which restricts, holds together). Repulsion and attraction have a point of synthesis in the line; from this point the two forces divide and flee in opposite ways, and thus form both poles: attraction [forms] the negative [pole], repulsion the positive [pole].[25]

One can divide this line into infinitely many points, so that in each, repulsion flees towards A and attraction towards B. Attraction will always attract the subsequent point and thus be the principle of *cohesion*.[26]

In the form of electricity (surface), the relationship of degree of the two forces is predominance of repulsion: it extends itself on all sides and thus forms a surface.

And if one must immediately assume that attraction works against it from all sides just as much as it extends itself, then the possibility of such an extension on all sides is still evidence of the predominance of repulsion.

[25] Günderrode's notes include a diagram here.
[26] Günderrode's notes include a diagram here.

19

Notes on Chemistry

Introduction

At the time Günderrode was writing, philosophy, including philosophy of nature,[1] was seen as closely connected with the sciences. Shared concepts and terminology in Günderrode's notes on chemistry and philosophy of nature reveal a concern with deriving characteristics of the physical world—including the properties of various substances and the basis for their reactions with each other—from an original, metaphysical starting point.

The first set of Günderrode's notes on chemistry likely summarizes ideas by the scientist, philosopher, and poet Henrik Steffens (1773–1845), who studied under Schelling at Jena. Günderrode's notes are probably taken from Steffens' 1800 paper "On the Oxidation- and Disoxidation Process of the Earth."[2]

The editor of the critical edition of Günderrode's works, Walter Morgenthaler, tentatively suggests that the source for the second set of notes may be a translation of A. F. Fourcroy's *System of Theoretical and Practical Chemistry* by the teacher, doctor, and chemist Christian Gotthold Eschenbach (1753–1831).[3] However, this volume mostly comprises tables of chemicals and their properties, and it is difficult to see parallels with Günderrode's notes. Antoine François, comte de Fourcroy (1755–1809) was a collaborator of the much more famous chemist Antoine Lavoisier (1743–1794) and a prolific popularizer of his theories. It is possible that the notes are from another text by Fourcroy or a different follower of Lavoisier.

---

[1] On the influence of *Naturphilosophie*, or philosophy of nature, on Günderrode's work, see the previous chapter, "Notes on Philosophy of Nature," and the introduction to "Idea of the Earth," also in this volume.

[2] Henrik Steffens, "Über den Oxydations- und Desoxydations-Prozeß der Erde. Eine Abhandlung vorgelesen in der naturforschenden Gesellschaft zu Jena," in *Zeitschrift für spekulative Physik*, ed. Friedrich Schelling, vol. 1 (Jena: Christian Ernst Gabler, 1800), 137–166. See Morgenthaler's comments in SW 3:341.

[3] SW 3:358. A. F. Fourcroy, *System der theoretischen und practischen Chemie. In Tabellen entworfen von A. F. Fourcroy*, trans. Christian Gotthold Eschenbach (Leipzig: Reinicke & Hinrichs, 1801).

Karoline von Günderrode. Anna Ezekiel, Oxford University Press. © Oxford University Press 2026.
DOI: 10.1093/9780190089177.003.0022

The account of "chemical affinity" in these notes relates to Günderrode's idea, articulated in "Idea of the Earth," "Letters of Two Friends," and "The Malabarian Widows," that entities are constellations of elements joined by a "law of affinity." At the time, chemical theory posited an "affinity" between certain chemicals, which caused those chemicals, when mixed, to combine with each other to form new substances. Günderrode used this idea of chemical affinities to fill out her claim that friends or lovers are attracted due to an affinity or harmony between the elements of which they are made.[4] It is likely that Günderrode's addition of "elements" and the more scientific-sounding elaboration of the "laws of attraction" in her later work stem from her study of recent developments in chemistry.

A similar adaptation of chemical theories to explain human relationships, especially the experience of love, was used much more famously by Johann Wolfgang von Goethe (1749–1832) in his novel *Elective Affinities*, published in 1809, three years after Günderrode's death. The German title, *Die Wahlverwandtschaften*, uses the German scientific term for this kind of chemical affinity. In Goethe's novel, the members of two couples each find themselves attracted to someone in the other pair, and eventually the original couples break up and the members form two new couples. Goethe read *Poems and Fantasies*,[5] which includes "The Manes," where Günderrode uses the "law of affinity" to explain attraction between human individuals. However, he cannot have read "Idea of the Earth" or "Letters of Two Friends," which spell out Günderrode's claims about the "elements," as these were not published until many years after her death. Still, it is interesting to see Günderrode working on similar ideas a few years earlier than Goethe, independently deriving features of her metaphysics and account of human relationships from contemporary theories in chemistry.

Notes on Chemistry

Dr. Steffens

The chemical activity of the earth decomposes in two continual processes: oxidation (acidification) and disoxidation (de-acidification). Volcanoes are the

---

[4] For details on this aspect of Günderrode's work, see the section on metaphysics in the general introduction to this volume, as well as the pieces "The Manes" and "The Malabarian Widows" and their introductions, also in this volume.

[5] Goethe, *Goethes Briefe an Eichstadt*, 87, 130.

main workshops of oxidation. The combustible materials suck in the air penetrating the crater, the oxygen in which the oxidizable materials ignite, and so causes the monstrous fires which pour this stream of oxidized material out over the earth, and at the same time breathe out the other part of the sucked-in air, azote. But water and air also induce constant oxidation, insofar as oxidizable materials suck the oxygen out of both.

Fourcroy[?]

Chemistry teaches us the inner properties of bodies, determines the quantity and characteristics of their constituent parts, shows us the means of separating these and combining them again.

The objects of chemistry are all bodies that one can enclose in vessels. All chemical operations may be reduced to two: decomposition (analysis) and composition (*synthesis*).

There are two methods of decomposition. The *simple* [method] is when we obtain a body in its totally pure constituent parts and the composition of these completely produces this body. These constituent parts are called *reagents*. The compound (analysis) is the most common. Through this, we obtain the constituent parts in new conjunctions. These are called *products*.

All bodies in nature have two forces, *attraction and repulsion*. But the force by which the basic components of the body themselves are held together and have more or less of a connection is called the *force of cohesion*.

The force of attraction which occurs between the basic components of two different bodies is called *chemical affinity*. It is distinguished from *cohesion* by the fact that it occurs between the similar, but not identical, parts of two separate bodies, while the latter only takes effect between the identical parts of these bodies.

Only bodies whose parts are related to each other may be chemically decomposed and compounded. For mechanical decomposition this affinity is not needed, in fact it is not even decomposition but only a division, in that it only *separates* the parts of the bodies but does not dissolve them. A chemical *composition binds* the constituent parts of the body; a *mechanical* [composition] only *mixes* them.

But there are *closer* and further degrees of affinity. Chemists mostly use this diversity of degrees of affinity in their analyses. If, *e.g.,* I have *chemically bound* the related *bodies A* and *D*, and now *want to separate* them again,

I must proceed thus: I add body B (which is more closely related to A than A and D are to each other); immediately A and D will separate; A and B will unite, due to their greater affinity, and D will fall to the ground as a *precipitate*, or, if it is intrinsically lighter, float up or evaporate as gas.[6]

---

[6] Günderrode's notes continue with details of the chemical properties of phlogiston, luminiferous material, electricity, air, water, and minerals. Phlogiston (*Wärmestoff*) and luminiferous material (*Lichtstoff*) were hypothetical substances used in the seventeenth and eighteenth centuries to help explain chemical processes such as combustion.

20

Notes on the Early German Romantics

Introduction

Early German Romanticism was an extremely influential literary and philosophical movement that developed among a group of young intellectuals in Jena around 1796. Central figures of early German Romanticism included the poet, philosopher, and mining surveyor Friedrich von Hardenberg (1772–1801), usually known by his pen name Novalis, the philosopher and translator Friedrich Schlegel (1772–1829), and the editors and translators Caroline Schlegel-Schelling (1763–1809) and Dorothea Veit-Schlegel (1764–1839). The Jena circle also involved many other influential philosophers, poets, novelists, literary critics, editors, and translators, as well as physicists, theologians, and anthropologists.[1]

One of the central features of early German Romanticism was the claim that the methods of science, philosophy, and literature (especially poetry) should be integrated to create forms of writing and speaking that engaged both the feelings and the mind. This "living philosophy" would, the Romantics thought, inspire people to actively explore the world emotionally and intellectually. Work by the Romantics often focused on feelings, intuitions, and personal experience, and advocated ways of living that authentically expressed one's own subjectivity. This focus was not intended as a rejection of scientific methods, but as a counterweight to what the Romantics saw as an overemphasis on science and empiricism in their contemporary culture. The Jena Romantics were also committed to sociable forms of doing philosophy, which they called *Symphilosophie*. This took the form of lively conversations in the salons run by Veit-Schlegel as well as co-authored

---

[1] These included (among others) Friedrich Schlegel's brother and Caroline Schlegel-Schelling's husband, August Wilhelm Schlegel (1767–1845), a poet, translator, and scholar of Indian ideas and cultures, the poet Ludwig Tieck (1773–1853), who edited a posthumous collection of Novalis' work, and the philosopher and physicist Johann Wilhelm Ritter (1776–1810). The philosopher Friedrich Wilhelm Joseph Schelling (1775–1854) and the poet Friedrich Hölderlin (1770–1843) are also often considered early German Romantics. For Schelling's influence on Günderrode's philosophy, see the notes on philosophy of nature and their introduction, translated earlier in this volume.

Karoline von Günderrode. Anna Ezekiel, Oxford University Press. © Oxford University Press 2026.
DOI: 10.1093/9780190089177.003.0023

works, including many of the fragments published in the Schlegels' journal *Athenaeum*.[2]

Günderrode's notes on the early German Romantics were probably taken between 1802 and 1804. They include fragments from the 1802 edition of Novalis' writings and three issues of the *Athenaeum*, excerpts from Schlegel's 1799 text "On Philosophy: To Dorothea," and a brief, slightly altered quotation from his "Speech on Mythology." Günderrode's transcriptions are mostly faithful to the originals, but there are a few differences, including some that may indicate deliberate modification. These differences, as well as the source for each fragment, are noted below in footnotes.

Günderrode's notes on "On Philosophy" mostly comprise near-quotes and paraphrases, sometimes summarizing long paragraphs of the original. The notes are highly selective and do not follow the order of Schlegel's text, with interesting implications for understanding the development of some of Günderrode's ideas and their differences from Schlegel's work. Günderrode's excerpting downplays the gender dualism at the heart of Schlegel's philosophy while retaining his claim that philosophy and poetry are necessary for both men and women.[3] Günderrode skips the start of Schlegel's text, which reflects his views on the differences in how men and women relate to language. She also omits most of his claims about religion, including his association of women with religion and spirituality.

Günderrode's notes focus instead on points that seem almost incidental in Schlegel's text, but were obviously important to her. These include the claim that "infinite being and becoming divides itself into and engenders that which we call God and nature" and "the thought of the universe is one and all; but there seems to be a certain fluctuation between individuality and universality."[4] The first of these quotations is followed in Günderrode's

---

[2] The Jena period of Romanticism ended after Novalis' death in 1801 and the departure of Schlegel-Schelling with Schelling, her third and last husband, in 1803. However, the ideas of the early German Romantics continued to influence philosophy and literature, in particular with regard to ideas about subjectivity, authenticity, and the expression of emotions and inner experiences. New forms of Romanticism followed, including the "high Romanticism" (*Hochromantik*) of the Heidelberg circle, which began in Heidelberg around 1806. Central figures in this movement included Günderrode's friend Bettina Brentano-von Arnim (1785–1859), Brentano-von Arnim's brother Clemens Brentano (1778–1842), her husband Achim von Arnim (1781–1831), and other poets, editors, linguists, and writers, including famous folklorists the Brothers Grimm. Owing to Günderrode's interest in the early German Romantics and her strong influence on figures such as Brentano-von Arnim and Clemens Brentano, her work forms an important link between early German Romanticism and Heidelberg Romanticism, and she is often herself described as part of the "Heidelberg Circle."
[3] Christmann, *Identitätsgewinn*, 79–80.
[4] Interestingly, Günderrode omits the next sentence in Schlegel's text: "You see, that would result in a kind of theogony and cosmogony" (KFSA 8:59).

notes and (after a couple of lines and a paragraph break) Schlegel's original by a promise to "show you only what is general and indispensable in the spirit of the individual sciences." Günderrode's closer juxtaposing of these claims suggests a possible derivation of scientific knowledge from access to more universal, divine truths, which is not implied in Schlegel's original. This slight but significant adjustment results in a text that recalls Günderrode's later notes on philosophy of nature. The latter begins with a summary of the emergence of the universe of finite forms from an "absolute," or a unity of matter and form, before deriving general laws of nature and specific natural phenomena from the processes that drive this emergence.[5]

Günderrode quotes only one sentence from Schlegel's "Speech on Mythology," but this text presents several other ideas that also appear in her writing. To give just one example, Schlegel's claim that modern poetry lacks a unifying principle such as (he asserts) is found in ancient poetry is echoed in Günderrode's comparison of modern and ancient poets in "Letters of Two Friends." The fact that Günderrode excerpted "Speech on Mythology" indicates that she read Schlegel's text and reveals a possible source for some of her ideas.

In addition to the notes translated here, Günderrode excerpted an untitled poem by Novalis, beginning "Deeply moved by holy goodness . . . ," that was published as part of the editor's note attached to the posthumous, 1802 publication of Novalis' *Henry of Ofterdingen*. This suggests that Günderrode may have read Novalis' novel as well.

Notes on the Early German Romantics

Novalis

A union contracted even for death is a wedding that gives us a companion for the night. Love is sweetest in death; for lovers, death is a wedding night of sweet mysteries.

---

[5] For details, see Günderrode's notes on philosophy of nature, translated earlier in this collection. Further explanation of Günderrode's metaphysics can be found in the introduction to the notes on philosophy of nature, the translation of "Idea of the Earth" and its introduction, and the section on metaphysics in the general introduction to this volume.

Is it not clever to seek a sociable resting place for the night?
That's why it is clever when someone loves those who have died.

Novalis[6]

Fragments from the *Athenäum*

The object of history is the becoming real of all that is practically necessary.[7]

As a transitory condition, skepticism is logical insurrection; as a system it is anarchy. Skeptical method would therefore be about the same as insurgent government.[8]

Sense that sees itself becomes spirit; spirit is inner sociability, soul is hidden amiability. But the actual vital force of inner beauty and perfection is disposition [*Gemüt*]. One can have a little spirit without soul, and much soul with little disposition. But the instinct of moral greatness that we call disposition need only learn to speak to have spirit. It need only stir and love to be fully soul; and when it is mature, it has the sense for everything. Spirit is like music of thoughts; wherever there is soul, the feelings also have the outline and form of noble proportions and charming coloration. Disposition is the poesie of sublime reason, and through its unification with philosophy and moral experience emerges that nameless art which grasps confused, fleeting life and forms into an eternal unity.[9]

The first impulse of morality is opposition to positive legalism and conventional justice, and a boundlessly irritable disposition. Add to that the intensity and clumsiness of youth, and excesses are unavoidable, the uncalculated consequences of which often poison someone's whole life. So it happens that the populace believes to be criminals those who, for truly moral people, are among the rarest exceptions.[10]

---

[6] Novalis, *Schriften* (1802), 2, 497. Novalis' original second sentence ends "for lovers death is a wedding night, a secret of sweet mysteries"; in Günderrode's notes, "a secret of" (*ein Geheimniß*) is scored out.

[7] KFSA 2:178 #90. Ten of the first 11 fragments translated here are from "Athenaeum Fragments" ("Athenäums-Fragmente," in *Athenaeum* 1.2 [1798], KFSA 2:165–255). The eleventh is from Novalis' collection "Pollen" ("Blüthenstaub," in *Athenaeum* 1.2 [1798]; Novalis, *Schriften*, vol. 2, 412–484).

[8] KFSA 2:179 #97.

[9] KFSA 2:225–226 #339.

[10] KFSA 2:248 #425. Günderrode has made minor changes to the text.

Transcendental is what is, should be, and can be this high . . . [11]

Universality is mutual saturation of all forms and all substances. It achieves harmony only through the union of poesie and philosophy: even the most universal, most complete works of isolated poesie and philosophy seems to lack the final synthesis. Right at the goal of harmony they stop, uncompleted. The life of universal spirit is an interrupted[12] chain of inner revolutions; all individuals (the original, eternal ones) live in it. It is a true polytheist and bears the whole of Olympus within itself.[13]

For us, returning into oneself means abstracting from the external world (voluntarily removing it from consciousness, detaching it from it), for spirits, analogically (by similarity), *earthly life* means *an inner contemplation* (insofar as one sees everything in oneself and oneself in all things), an immanent (inner) action. Thus earthly life springs from an original reflection* (reflection of impressions which objects make upon us) a primitive (initial) going into, collecting within, oneself, that is as free as our reflection. Conversely, spiritual life in this world springs from a breaking through of that primitive reflection (by stepping out of the circle of the representations that have arisen in us through objects). In turn, spirit unfolds itself, goes out of itself again, again partially sublimates that reflection (cancels out the forms that induced those impressions) and in this moment it says "*I*" for the first time. (It distinguishes its actual essence from mere representations insofar as it cancels them out and steps out of them.)[14]

　　* Reflection in fact means deliberation (considering). Deliberation may perhaps even be reducible to a reflection of the impressions that objects make upon us. We receive impressions through the objects, our thoughts reflect the impressions back upon the things and give them a form determined by the impression. This form is the representation of them that we posit in ourselves. The word "consider" means nothing other than a thinking about forgone impressions.

---

[11] KFSA 2:237 #388.
[12] Günderrode writes "interrupted" (*unterbrochne*) rather than "uninterrupted" (*ununterbrochne*); this may have been accidental.
[13] KFSA 2:255 #451.
[14] Novalis, *Schriften* 2:431 #45. Günderrode adds emphasis, explanations in parentheses, and the explanatory note beginning "Reflection in fact . . ."

Mathematics is, as it were, a sensual logic: it relates to philosophy like the material arts music and plastic relate to poesie.[15]

If every infinite individual is God, then there are as many gods as ideals. Also, the relationship of the true artist and the true human being to their ideals is definitely religion. If this inner religious service is the goal and business of one's whole life, one is a priest, which everyone can and should become.[16]

Can something be characterized otherwise than as individuals? Is something that, at a certain given standpoint, cannot be multiplied further not just as good a historical unity as something that cannot be further divided? Are not all systems individuals, just like all individuals, at least in kernel and by tendency, are systems? Is not all real unity historical? Are there not individuals that contain whole systems of individuals within themselves?[17]

Eternal life and the invisible world are to be sought only in God. All spirits live in him; he is an abyss of individuality, the only infinite fullness.[18]

The understanding, says the author of the Speeches on Religion,[19] only knows of the universe; if imagination reigns, then you have a God. Quite right: the imagination is the human organ for divinity.[20]

The human being is nature's creative retrospection on itself.[21]

The human being is free when it has produced God or made God visible, and thereby becomes immortal.[22]

---

[15] KFSA 2:232 #365.
[16] KFSA 2:242 #406.
[17] KFSA 2:205 #242.
[18] KFSA 2:257 #6. The remaining fragments translated here are from Schlegel's "Ideas" ("Ideen," in *Athenaeum* 3.1 (1800); see KFSA 2:256–272).
[19] I.e., Schleiermacher and his *Über die Religion*.
[20] KFSA 2:257 #8.
[21] KFSA 2:258 #28.
[22] KFSA 2:258 #29.

God is everything that is simply original and highest, and therefore the individual itself to the highest power.[23] But are not nature and the world also individuals?[24]

Every relation of the human being to the infinite is religion, namely the human being in the complete fullness of its humanity.[25]

So Fichte is supposed to have attacked religion?—If the essence of religion is an interest in the supersensible, then his whole teaching is religion in the form of philosophy.[26]

In religion it is always morning and the light of dawn.[27]

That which constitutes a free human being as such, that to which the unfree human being relates everything, is their religion. There is a deep sense in the expression that this or that is someone's God, or idol, and in other such [expressions].[28]

All philosophy is idealism, and there is no true realism other than that of poesy.[29]

Friedrich Schlegel, *On Philosophy: To Dorothea*[30]

Not the vocation of women, but their nature and situation, is domestic. The latter often entangles them so much in the necessities of [household] economy that they do not become conscious of their divine origin. And if they ever lift themselves out of the flow of commonness then it usually only happens when they love more strongly than is approved of by domestic

---

[23] The idea of *Potenz* ("potency") relates to the mathematical operation of exponentiation, or "raising to the power of x," and was an important concept in early German Romanticism. The ideas of raising to an infinite power ("x to the highest power") and squaring (e.g., "the poetry of poetry") were used particularly frequently.

[24] KFSA 2:261 #47.

[25] KFSA 2:263 #81.

[26] KFSA 2:266 #105.

[27] KFSA 2:269 #129.

[28] KFSA 2:271 #147.

[29] KFSA 2:257 #96.

[30] KFSA 8:41f.

morality. And because women's lifestyle has the propensity to limit their spirit ever more narrowly, women should carefully cultivate their aptitude for religion (their sense and capacity for the infinite and holy, for all love), and they cannot arrive at this religion without philosophy. Philosophy and poesie are the only saviors from commonness and narrowness; therefore they are indispensable to women.

In order to initiate you into philosophy, I would first remind you of the whole of humanity and elevate your feeling for this to thought. Then I would show you how this infinite being and becoming divides itself into and engenders that which we call God and nature. Then I would show you only what is general and indispensable in the spirit of the individual sciences. I would connect all this to your most individual opinions. But the infinity of the human spirit, the divinity of all natural things, and the humanity of the gods would remain the great unity in all the variations.

Poesie joins spirit with nature in friendship and entices heaven to earth with its magic. It is more natural to women than philosophy, for, however unsaintly they are, they still hold youthful senses sacred, and this poesie of life is natural to them. Poesie ornaments the earth, it is more inclined towards [the earth], but philosophy is more sacred, more closely related to the divine, and therefore more indispensable to women.

A person's own sense and will is their most sacred thing, and the most human; whether they belong to one sex or the other is more accidental and insignificant. The sex difference is a good institution of nature, but only an externality of human existence, and therefore should be subordinated to higher laws. Masculinity and femininity, as they are usually taken, are impediments to humanity that one must seek to mitigate, so that the individual entity can find wider limits within which to move.

The female organization is oriented to the purpose of maternity, therefore artists prefer the masculine figure, because it exists more for itself, for its own sake, and seems to be completed in itself. Art and poesy hate the appearance of what is useful, they love what exists for itself, and take egoism under their wing. But the female figure is more human: in it, the spiritual and animal are more closely and more tenderly merged. –

To me, the thought of the universe is one and all; but there seems to be a certain fluctuation between individuality and universality, the pulsebeat of higher life.

Schlegel

Friedrich Schlegel, *Speech on Mythology*

It is the essence of spirit to determine itself, and to emerge from itself in eternal change, and to turn back to itself, and thought is nothing other than the result of such an activity.

21

Notes on Schleiermacher

Introduction

Günderrode's notes on the work of theologian, philosopher, and biblical scholar Friedrich Schleiermacher (1768–1834) were likely taken between 1802 and 1804. The notes titled "On Religion" are on the second speech, "On the Essence of Religion," in Schleiermacher's influential 1799 text *On Religion: Speeches to Its Cultured Despisers.*[1] In this work, Schleiermacher aimed to identify new grounds for religious belief that were not based on traditional Christian dogma or supposedly rational proofs, rejecting models, such as Kant's, that justified religious beliefs in terms of their value for morality. Instead, Schleiermacher identified the basis of religion in feeling and in a person's intuition of the infinite.

Günderrode occasionally quotes verbatim, but mostly paraphrases or reformulates selected points from Schleiermacher's much lengthier piece. Her notes capture Schleiermacher's central claims that religion is a third, separate area of human experience alongside the speculative or theoretical ("metaphysical") and practical ("moral") realms, and that it is based on intuition and feeling—specifically, intuition of the infiniteness of the universe and of the manifestation of this infinite in every individual part of the whole. Consistent with this grounding of religion on an individual's intuitions, Schleiermacher maintains that religions vary according to a person's imagination. However, what is essential to all religions (he claims) is the feeling for the infinite. On this basis, Schleiermacher argues that the ideas of God and of personal immortality as it is usually conceived are not essential to religion. These claims are reflected in Günderrode's notes.

Schleiermacher's ideas have clear parallels in Günderrode's work, most obviously in "Story of a Brahmin," which similarly makes religion a matter of individual intuition of the infinite and claims that this teaching is at the heart

---

[1] Friedrich Schleiermacher, *Über die Religion. Reden an die Gebildeten unter ihren Verächtern* (Berlin: Johann Friedrich Unger, 1799).

Karoline von Günderrode. Anna Ezekiel, Oxford University Press. © Oxford University Press 2026.
DOI: 10.1093/9780190089177.003.0024

of all religions. Günderrode, however, creates a stronger distinction between the "human" and "spiritual" realms than is allowed by Schleiermacher. For Schleiermacher, humanity, as embodied in each individual human being, is the paradigmatic place in which the infinite can be intuited.[2] By contrast, in "Story of a Brahmin," Günderrode claims that, while self-reflection is neces- sary to intuit the infinite, the "human" realm is essentially that of morality, rather than religion or spirituality.

Günderrode's notes themselves also show some differences to Schleiermacher's original. For example, Günderrode's statement that "you must not observe the individual, but rather humanity, as an ocean of surging forces" is not found in Schleiermacher's text.[3] Perhaps more signifi- cantly, Schleiermacher ends with the ambiguous promise that, after we have annihilated our individuality "we can talk more about the hopes that death gives us"; he adds that genuine immortality is "in the midst of finitude, to be one with the infinite and eternal in a moment."[4] In her notes, Günderrode changes this to a certainty of immortality through union with the whole: "If you coalesce with the universe like this, then there is no death for you; you be- long to the infinite." This is a central idea in Günderrode's work, as discussed in the general introduction to this volume: on her account, individuals die, but they live on in a literal sense, taking on altered forms as part of the whole and as new individuals.

The second set of notes is a loose summary of the first chapter of Schleiermacher's *Soliloquies*.[5] Unlike most of Günderrode's notes, this sum- mary presents the ideas in the third person, as belonging to someone else; it seems to be a relatively straightforward attempt to present Schleiermacher's ideas in a condensed form.

In this chapter, Schleiermacher distinguishes the busy "outer world" of actions and interactions from an "inner" life of contemplation. He advocates a new kind of ethics as inward, spiritual activity oriented toward oneself and a spiritual community (instead of outward activity aiming at concrete achievements). Prompted by the onset of a new century (the *Soliloquies* were published in 1800 and subtitled "A New Year's Gift"), Schleiermacher argues that this shift brings with it an altered relationship to time: specifi- cally, it enables the experience of the infinite within time. Schleiermacher

---

[2] Schleiermacher, *Über die Religion*, 49.
[3] Christmann, *Identitätsgewinn*, 83.
[4] Schleiermacher, *Über die Religion*, 132–133.
[5] Schleiermacher, "Die Reflexion," in *Monologen*, 5–30.

contrasts this form of immortality with belief in life after death. These ideas all appear in Günderrode's summary, but largely in her own words. The contrast between an "inward" and "outward" life and the relationship of these two forms of life to one's community are important in Günderrode's work, appearing in "Story of a Brahmin," *Muhammad, the Prophet of Mecca*, *Magic and Destiny*, and the short collection of reflections beginning "Excellence is a whole...."

Notes on Schleiermacher

On Religion

Religion is not *metaphysics* nor *morals*. It does not desire, like the *former*, to bring opinions about the highest being into a chain of conclusions and determine the nature of the universe; nor, like the *latter*, to develop a system of duties from the nature of human beings and their relationship to the universe. Religion is not speculative like metaphysics nor practical like morals: its essence is not thinking nor acting, but intuition and feeling. Intuition of the universe is its essence. Every being that emerges from the infinite fullness of the universe and presents it to us is this universe acting upon us. To let oneself be suffused by these influences in childlike passivity, and so to accept everything individual as a part of the whole, everything limited as a presentation of the infinite—that is religion. It [religion] lives in infinite nature, the symbol of which is multiplicity and individuality. And because everything finite is, as it were, cut out of the infinite, to [religion] everything finite is, at the same time, something infinite, which only exists as finite through the determination of its boundaries.—But because religion has neither laws nor formulas nor systems, each individual will have their own religion, their own intuition of the universe, *which is a whole again, a manifold infinite effect of the universe*. When the ancients worshipped as divine and gave names and temples to a particular way of being and acting, that was religion: they had grasped an act of the universe and designated its character like that. To present all incidents as actions of a god is religion, because it expresses a relationship to an infinite whole.

We first arrive at this standpoint of the intuition of the universe by contemplating natural laws: their unity in multiplicity, their *order* and their *disorder*, which indicates even greater relationships, unknown to us, than the *former.* But we arrive at this intuition most beautifully by contemplating humanity. In [humanity], the universe has revealed itself most vividly, and in your own mind you will recognize all its phenomena, for all the elements of humanity are in each human being. But you must not observe the individual, but rather humanity, as an ocean of surging forces moved here and there and mingled by the breath of life. The onesided critique of morals disappears here, everything is in its rightful place, if not in the individual then as a whole.—*For someone to whom* humanity and the universe are equivalent, religious intuition ends here, but religion itself *wants to be infinite, seeks an infinite object for its contemplation.* It seeks a higher character in human beings than their humanity, which it could relate immediately to the universe, and humanity, which is itself something movable and cultivable, appears to it as just a single form, a presentation of the universe.

Whether someone adds a god to this intuition of the universe depends on the course of their imagination. God is *not everything* in religion but *one thing.* The universe is *everything.*

Subsequently, even here [in this world], strive to annihilate your individuality and to live in one and all, strive to be more than yourself, so that you lose little when you lose yourself. If you coalesce with the universe like this, then there is no death for you; you belong to infinity. That is the immortality of religion.

Soliloquies

In the chapter "Reflections," the author differentiates world and spirit. He calls "world" the throng of outer actions, the community of spirits insofar as they affect each other and have formed the mass.[6] He calls "spirit" the *inner* operations of spirit, which, independently of the world, time and necessity, neither show these externally nor are subjected to them; which exist for themselves and are not subjected to any laws, but are free. These operations, which he calls *inner* doing, are eternal. Divinity is revealed in them: in them, in self-contemplation alone, is the true being of freedom, which a sensual

---

[6] This is a summary of Schleiermacher's claims regarding humanity's actions to master and form or shape the "raw mass" of nature (*Monologen*, 32). Schleiermacher presents this activity as belonging to the "outer world" but as indicating the presence of human "spirit," which is needed to form this material.

[person] does not understand.—They seek the immortality that lies in the inner doings of spirit, in self-contemplation, after the end of time (even if it is right next to time). They plant it in the shadow-world, because to them inner doing appears as a shadow of outer action. They delude themselves that the intuition of divinity dwells there, free from the limits of time.

22

Notes on Hemsterhuis

Introduction

Günderrode's notes on the Dutch philosopher and author François Hemsterhuis (1721–1790) were taken from his dialogue *Simon, or the Faculties of the Soul*,[1] sometime after 1803. The notes seem to be based on the original French text rather than the German translation that was available at the time, and begin in French before being repeated and continuing in German. Since the French and German versions in Günderrode's notes differ slightly, both are translated below, and the point where she switches language is indicated in a footnote.

The four "faculties of the soul" mentioned in the title of Hemsterhuis' work are the will, the imagination, the intellect, and the "moral organ." Hemsterhuis claims that human beings were endowed with these faculties by various divine figures: God (or Jupiter) provided the will, Prometheus gave us imagination and intellect, and Venus Urania (the embodiment of spiritual love) gifted us the moral organ. Central points from *Simon* are contained in Günderrode's brief notes, including the outline of these faculties and their origins, the close association of the moral organ with love, and Hemsterhuis' claims regarding the historicity, plasticity, and moral perfectibility of human nature. For Hemsterhuis, human beings are not created complete but are successively gifted with various faculties which it is their task to use and develop.[2] Hemsterhuis also gives an account of what he calls the moral organ, which he claims is the means by which we can come to both resemble and have knowledge of God. However, he maintains that humanity does not currently have a fully developed moral organ, but only its seed or germ. A crucial task for human beings, therefore, is to develop this organ.[3]

---

[1] *Simon, ou des facultés de l'ame* [1787], in *Oeuvres Philosophique de M. F. Hemsterhuis*, vol. 2 (Paris: H. J. Jansen, 1792). Günderrode's notes start at page 227.

[2] Laure Cahen-Maurel, "Philosophical Paths: The Legacy of Hemsterhuis' Dialogues in the Age of German Romanticism," in *The Dialogues of Francois Hemsterhuis, 1778–1787*, ed. and trans. Jacob van Sluis and Daniel Whistler (Edinburgh: Edinburgh UP, 2022).

[3] Dormann, *Kunst des inneren Sinns*, 118.

Karoline von Günderrode. Anna Ezekiel, Oxford University Press. © Oxford University Press 2026.
DOI: 10.1093/9780190089177.003.0025

Hemsterhuis' "moral organ" has parallels to Günderrode's idea of an "inner sense," which features in "Story of a Brahmin" and "The Manes." In the latter, Günderrode writes: "This inner sense, the deepest and finest organ of the soul, is totally undeveloped in almost all people and only there in seed form." For Günderrode, the inner sense is an "organ of knowledge" that allows us to recognize our interconnection with others.[4] In "Story of a Brahmin," this inner sense appears as the voice of conscience and at the same time the voice of nature and the divine; it reveals the underlying unity of all things and allows a person who listens to it to develop their connection with others, nature, and the infinite. These ideas, including the emphasis on harmony with others and the universe as a whole, are broadly in line with Hemsterhuis' thought in *Simon*.

Hemsterhuis was a strong influence on the popular idea that knowledge of the world and the divine, and our relationship to these, can best be developed by following an "inward path."[5] This is an important idea for Günderrode, appearing in "Story of a Brahmin," "Excellence is a whole . . . " and, perhaps most clearly, "The Wanderer's Descent." Hemsterhuis' influence on numerous thinkers whose work Günderrode also studied, including Johann Gottfried Herder, Friedrich Schleiermacher, Friedrich Schlegel, and Novalis, makes it difficult to determine which of his ideas influenced Günderrode directly and which came to her indirectly through other sources.[6] Either way, the short excerpt from *Simon* in Günderrode's notes indicates the importance of this thinker for the development of her philosophical ideas.

Notes on Hemsterhuis

He [Jupiter] created an essence susceptible to possible sensation and capable of action and the difference between this essence and that of Jupiter is that Jupiter acts immediately, while the other needs means to sense and act. To act he adds the force of will and the power of acting. Prometheus also adds

---

[4] Dormann, *Kunst des inneren Sinns*, 119.

[5] Cahen-Maurel, "Philosophical Paths"; Dormann, *Kunst des inneren Sinns*, 119.

[6] For example, Hemsterhuis is known to have influenced Schleiermacher's emphasis on conscience and the "inner voice," which also appears in Günderrode's work. For more on Schleiermacher's thought and its influence on Günderrode, see the previous chapter on Günderrode's notes on Schleiermacher. Hemsterhuis' influence on Herder, Novalis, and other Romantic thinkers of the time (including Günderrode) is the topic of the 2022 edition of the journal *Symphilosophie* (*Symphilosophie: International Journal of Philosophical Romanticism* 4: *Cosmic Web: Hemsterhuis among the German Romantics* [2022]).

this receptacle of all the sensations, imagination,[7] from which tubes go to the sensory tools in order to receive impressions there –

He [God] created a being that was receptive to all impressions, with the capacity to act, and the difference between this being and God consisted in the fact that God receives impressions and acts immediately while this creature needed means to do so. To this gift he also added will and ability, so that it [the creature] possessed the means to act. Prometheus added this receptacle of impressions, perceptions and ideas that is called imagination, but because he feared the representations it contained might become confused, he stole the heavenly spark of the understanding, to order what the imagination provided. These creatures, gifted with receptivity, activity, imagination and understanding, were not bound to each other by any bond; they waged war against each other and heaven, but Venus Urania descended to earth, and love and harmony with her.

The will is neither means nor organ, but the basis of activity. If it is not determined as this or that will, then it is an indeterminate willing dominated by outer or inner impressions.

The imagination retains what it receives and presents it again.

At first, the understanding only has intuitions of things, which are provided to it by the imagination, but as soon as it has developed the capacity to combine, compare and separate the ideas, it is called reason.

The moral organ has two instincts. According to the first, the soul is thoroughly passive: it receives impressions, love, hate, envy, desire, pity, wrath etc. According to the second it is active: it judges, modifies, riles up or soothes the sensations, and processes them, just as the understanding processes what fantasy provides it, or dictates a direction to the will, by virtue of which the will becomes sensible and consistent. Similarly, the moral organ judges whether the will is in accord with the right and virtuous, for just as contradiction is abhorrent to the understanding, what is wrongful is abhorrent to moral feeling. Imagine a person whose will is self-active,[8] whose moral organ is neglected, and whose too-lively will does not use this organ as a touchstone for what is right and wrong; add a strong imagination and great understanding to that, and you have the aptitude for great vices and crimes.

---

[7] Until this point, Günderrode's notes are written in French; here, mid-sentence, she switches to German.

[8] The term "self-active" (*selbsttätig*) is a key concept in German idealism, especially for Fichte and Schelling, and refers to a kind of activity that originates from itself, i.e., an activity that is unconditioned.

23

Miscellaneous Notes

Introduction

This section includes short notes from several sources. The notes begin with a "philosophical dictionary" and definitions of terms relating to Günderrode's philosophical studies, especially those undertaken with her friend Susanne von Heyden in 1804. These are followed by a series of philosophical and literary quotations.

The notes beginning "Reason and understanding . . . " are in Heyden's handwriting. Their source is unknown; they may be original ideas by Günderrode and Heyden or a summary of something they had read or heard. One possibility is that they take their starting point from a note written in 1800 by the local minister at Butzbach, Johann Georg Diefenbach, which is preserved among Günderrode's study materials. Diefenbach's note begins: "You do not err; only you must hold on to the distinction of the new [. . .] philosophers, especially Kiesewetter's, between *reason* and *understanding*. The understanding is concerned with the *conditioned*, or with given matter; reason with the *condition* through which the *conditioned* is, or with the *unconditioned*."[1] The first paragraph of the passage translated below has similarities to Diefenbach's note, but then takes a different direction.

The first set of quotations from November 1799 to summer 1801[2] is from Jean Paul Friedrich Richter's novel *Hesperus*,[3] although Günderrode often modifies the wording. Richter (1763–1825), usually referred to as "Jean Paul," was an eccentric but widely read author, specializing in humorous, satirical, and fantastical themes. *Hesperus* is a strange and complicated text, with some similarities to a *Bildungsroman*: it is presented as a "biography" and follows the efforts of a young man to realize his ideal on earth. However, the idea of

---

[1] SW 3:335.

[2] These notes also included excerpts from a popular volume of philosophical quotations (J. A. Neurohr and Johann Hugo Wyttenbach, *Aussprüche der philosophierende Vernunft. . .* [Jena: J. G. Voigt, 1797]). These are not translated here.

[3] Jean Paul Friedrich Richter, *Hesperus, oder fünfundvierzig Hundsposttage: Eine Lebensbeschreibung*, 3 vols. (Berlin: Matzdorff, 1795).

Karoline von Günderrode. Anna Ezekiel, Oxford University Press. © Oxford University Press 2026.
DOI: 10.1093/9780190089177.003.0026

Bildung or personal development is undermined by Jean Paul's emphasis on the contradictions of human existence, especially the gap between ideals and reality. These themes are reflected in the passages quoted by Günderrode.

The second set of notes, taken between summer 1804 and early 1806, seems to record things Günderrode had read or heard in conversation. They include summaries and paraphrasings of ideas from Kant and individuals noted only by their initials, including acquaintances of Günderrode's such as the writer Clemens Brentano, the jurist Karl Friedrich Savigny, and (possibly) Günderrode's sister Charlotte. Details on possible sources are given in the footnotes.

Miscellaneous Notes

Philosophical Dictionary and Other Definitions

Philosophical Dictionary

intellectual	spiritual
transcendental*	sublime, supersensual
intelligence	spiritual force, essence
rational	of the faculty of cognition
rational knowledge	what one knows a priori
empirical knowledge	what one knows from experience
tendency, goal, purpose,	striving to move oneself
antithetical	oppositional
category	classification according to genera
imperative	thoroughly commanding, ordering
pragmatic	lawful
ethics	morals
symphilosophy	collective philosophy [*Gesamtphilosophie*], philosophy together [*mit-philosophie*]
incitement	stimulation
amelioration and deterioration	improvement and worsening
discursive	of concepts
intuitive	through intuition
esoteric	secret
exoteric	public
antinomy	opposite, contradiction of laws

dynamic	doctrine of force
immanent	an inner effect, effect in ourselves
genesis	emergence
concrete	what is compounded from manifold things
abstractum	a completely general [thing], beyond all particulars
corollary	additional
to diverge	to move off from something
to converge	to *simultaneously* incline towards something else, or diverge.
integer	complete
causality	interaction, relationship of cause and effect

* also called unity of what is different, or the unity of the objective and subjective, or[4]

(Reason and Understanding...)

Reason and understanding, the internal and external pole of the I [*Ichheit*]. The understanding has one pole in itself as perceiving, the other in external things as what is perceivable. The more possibilities of conjunction with external objects there are in the understanding, the more syntheses. An understanding, the internal pole of which was versatile enough to synthesize with all visible things, would be the most real, for it would impart to the I the clearest knowledge of external things. It would find the right means for every course of action, since it would only join together what is homogeneous. Maladroitness is a lack of *extensivity* of the internal pole of the understanding, when it has more perceivable than perceiving [things] and therefore shoves many objects into one perception. By doing so, something confused and uncertain emerges. The purer the synthesis of what is perceived with what is perceiving, the more determinate [is] my knowing.

Reason has both its poles in itself. One appears to it internally as what is to be perceived, the other as perceiving. The product of their synthesis is the idea.

An I whose representing pole, reason, has great *extensivity* will be very productive.

[4] The note breaks off suddenly here

If the *intensity* of the perceiving poles of both the understanding and reason predominates, it will give rise to *egoism* in the noble sense, [while] *extensity* [will give rise to] production.

Mathematical Definitions

Arithmetic is the science of the discontinuous, or numerical sizes, of the succession of magnitudes the norm of which is time.

Geometry is the science of the continuous, or spatial sizes; but these are again to be measured by numerical size.

Other Definitions

As soon as I say nature *is*, I assert its infinite duration, for if something *is* it cannot also *not be*; if it came to an end it would no longer be: *being* and *not being* are contradictions.[5] Passing away is a future not-being, therefore if nature is, it will always be.

Primal knowing is the divine principle itself. Philosophy, as the science of all sciences (in which they are all contained, as the principle of all science), is the approach to this absolute knowing. Learning means seeking the divine; knowing means grasping it.

Notes from Jean Paul, *Hesperus*

Like the earth, human beings go from west to east, but it seems to them they go with it from east to west, from life into the grave.[6]

It is hard to gain virtue, freedom and happiness on earth, but it is even harder to disseminate them. The wise receive everything from themselves, fools everything from others. The free must free the slaves, the wise think for the fools, the happy work for the unhappy.[7]

Oh, what must we all have lost, if pictures of blessed days extract nothing from us but sighs? Oh peace, peace, you evening of the soul, you quiet

---

[5] These notes may relate to work by Schelling, perhaps his *Vorlesungen über die Methode des akademischen Studiums* (SW 3:334). Alternatively, they could be Günderrode's own claims.

[6] Dogpostday 14 in Jean Paul, *Hesperus* 1:331.

[7] Dogpostday 2 in Jean Paul, *Hesperus* 1:55–56.

Hesperus[8] of the tired heart, that always remains beside the sun of virtue—when our insides already melt away with tears before your gentle name. Oh, is that not a sign that we seek you but do not have you?[9]

The whole second world, the whole Elysium, God himself, appear to you in no place but within yourself. Be great enough to scorn the earth; become greater to esteem it.[10]

In human beings there is a great wish that will never be fulfilled: it has no name, it seeks its object, but it is not anything you call it nor any of the joys. It comes back when, on a summer night, you look to the north or towards far mountains, or when moonlight is upon the earth, or the sky is starry, or when you are very happy. This great monstrous wish uplifts our spirit, but with pain: *oh! we will lie down here thrown upright like epileptics*. But this wish, to which nothing can give a name, our strings and tones name to the human spirit—the longing spirit then weeps more intensely and can no longer contain itself, and cries in wailing ecstasy between the tones: yes, I am lacking everything you name...[11]

At the evening gate of this century is written: Here goes the way to virtue and wisdom; just like at the evening gate to Cherson stands the sublime inscription: Here leads the way to Byzantium.[12]

Infinite providence, you will make the day dawn. –

But the twelfth hour of the night still contends; nocturnal birds of prey streak by, the ghosts clatter, the dead perform their tricks; the living dream.[13]

Friendship can desire merits, but philanthropy [can desire] only human form. For that reason we all have such a cold, changeable philanthropy, because we mix up people's value with their rights, and want to love nothing in them but their virtues.[14]

---

[8] In Greek mythology, Hesperus is the evening star (i.e., Venus, when it appears in the evening).

[9] Dogpostday 8 in Jean Paul, *Hesperus* 1:166.

[10] Dogpostday 8 in Jean Paul, *Hesperus* 1:196–197.

[11] Dogpostday 19 in Jean Paul, *Hesperus* 2:85–86.

[12] Byzantium is an old name for Istanbul. Cherson (Chersonesus) was an ancient Greek colony on the Black Sea coast. The inscription mentioned here was on the west gate to the city, facing the sunset, hence the description "the evening door."

[13] Foreword, Seven Requests, and Conclusion in Jean Paul, *Hesperus* 1:10.

[14] Dogpostday 37 in Jean Paul, *Hesperus* 3:242–243.

The disrupted equilibrium of one's own forces makes the individual person miserable. The inequality of citizens, and that of the peoples, makes the earth miserable.[15]

When someone has nothing more to love, then they embrace the gravestone of their love, and pain becomes their beloved.[16]

The long sleep of the dead closes our scars, and the shortness of life our wounds.[17]

With the inequality of the peoples in power, wealth, culture a general storming from all corners of the compass can only end with an enduring calm.—But a ghost remains from midnight, which reaches far into the times of light: war. But the claws on the heraldic eagle grow until they curve up and make themselves useless. –[18]

The whole earth must *one day* become a single state, a Universal Republic: philosophy must endorse war, misanthropy, in short all contradictions with morals as long as there are still two states. –[19]

It is better for the whole to voluntarily suffer for the sake of one member than the latter to suffer, against its fair vote, for the whole. [...] One must prefer the greatest physical evil to the smallest moral one, to the smallest injustice.[20]

The wild encroachments into the wheel of time, which is driven by many small wheels, shift it out of place more than they accelerate it. Hang on the weight of the clockwork, which drives all the wheels, i.e.: be wise and virtuous, then you will be great and innocent, and build the city of God without the mortar of blood and without the building blocks of skulls.[21]

No calm and coldness is worth anything but those that are acquired—human beings must be capable of and powerful in passion.[22]

---

[15] Sixth Leap Day in Jean Paul, *Hesperus* 2:244.
[16] Dogpostday 20 in Jean Paul, *Hesperus* 2:105.
[17] Dogpostday 20 in Jean Paul, *Hesperus* 2:110.
[18] Sixth Leap Day in Jean Paul, *Hesperus* 2:244–245.
[19] Dogpostday 32 in Jean Paul, *Hesperus* 3:97.
[20] Dogpostday 32 in Jean Paul, *Hesperus* 3:98.
[21] Dogpostday 32 in Jean Paul, *Hesperus* 3:99–100.
[22] Dogpostday 33 in Jean Paul, *Hesperus* 3:120.

With more precise calculation, we find our distance from virtue, like that from the sun, only greater; and improvement only cancels out the crass errors, not the fine pricks of conscience.[23]

If only I always sacredly maintained the courage to sacrifice myself: then I would need nothing greater, for the greater only sacrifices stolen goods. Destiny can sacrifice centuries and islands to favor millennia and parts of the world, but human beings [can sacrifice] only *themselves*.[24]

This is why the earth is darkened every day, like cages for birds, so we can more easily hear the higher melodies in the dark.[25]

Without continuity of memory, the continuity of my *I* is no such thing: as soon as I forget my present I, then indeed some stranger could be immortal instead of me.[26]

Life is a sleep, an oppressed, torrid sleep. Vampires sit upon it, rain and wind fall upon the sleeper, and in vain he seeks to awaken.[27]

Notes from Summer 1804 to Early 1806

If the German language continues to be as cultivated as now then we will soon have no more good poets. Determinacy in all parts is a perfection of languages; but this determinacy limits the poet in the choice of attributes for his images, for in a fully cultivated language what is appropriate to each object is already determined, and the poet may no longer choose.[28]

Two things fill the mind with ever increasing admiration as frequently as one's meditation deals with them: the starry sky above me, and the moral law within me.—Kant.[29]

---

[23] Dogpostday 35 in Jean Paul, *Hesperus* 3:185f.

[24] Dogpostday 44 in Jean Paul, *Hesperus* 3:392.

[25] Dogpostday 38 in Jean Paul, *Hesperus* 3:269.

[26] Dogpostday 38 in Jean Paul, *Hesperus* 3:287–288.

[27] Dogpostday 39 in Jean Paul, *Hesperus* 3:311.

[28] Günderrode originally prefaced this quote with "In a conversation about language, Professor S. once said:" but crossed this out. "Professor S." may refer to Savigny (Hopp and Preitz, "Umwelt. III," 317–318).

[29] Translation adapted from Immanuel Kant, *Critique of Practical Reason*, trans. Werner S. Pluhar (Indianapolis: Hackett, 2002), 203 (AA 1, V:161). Günderrode quotes Kant loosely.

A traveler was shown the coronation cloak of the German Kaiser in Nuremberg; in the hem he found an Arabic inscription, previously taken for decoration, with the approximate content: This cloak is for the invincible ruler of the orient, who Allah will long sustain, Saladin. The attached date corresponded to the time in which Sultan Saladin lived. –[30]

In their painting, the Chinese have neither shadow and light nor perspective. Of shadows they say they are changeable and accidental, [and] may therefore not be presented in a painting as enduring. And perspectives are only a deceit of the eye that understanding must improve and not indulge.[31]

When, in the clefts of the earth, iron, sulphur and water come into contact, they ignite, and because heat extends the air, these, along with the equally elastic flame, seek an exit. If they find this they spit fire; if they do not find it an earthquake occurs.[32]

Wind or storm occurs when the equilibrium of the air is cancelled out. E.g., if the air in one region is very extended and thin due to warmth, then the denser and heavier air in another region presses against the lighter air until they have mixed; the wind then abates.[33]

Why do we long for a better life? A human being should arise thankfully from the table of nature like a sated guest, and rest and die.

There are people who, it seems, only set life in flight with their wings [Schwingen]; whose silent effects we only perceive in memory, as there are infinitely tender songs that we do not hear when they come from the lips, that must first be grasped from their echo and expressed again before we perceive them.   C. B.[34]

---

[30] Based on real events between 1796 and 1800. The cloak was made in 1133/34 in Palermo for King Roger the Second of Sicily (Hopp and Preitz, "Umwelt. III," 318). Saladin was born in 1137 and lived in North Africa and the Middle East. Günderrode may have been noting an idea for a story loosely based on real events.

[31] Hopp and Preitz ("Umwelt. III," 319) suggest this quote may be a paraphrase from Joachim von Sandrart, *Teutsche Academie der Bau-, Bildhauer- und Mahler-Kunst* (1675).

[32] Morgenthaler suggests this may be a summary of claims in Kant's *Geschichte und Naturbeschreibung der merkwürdigen Vorfälle des Erdbebens welches an dem Ende des 1755sten Jahres einen großen Teil der Erde erschüttert hat* (1756), AA 1, I:429–462 (SW 3:333–34).

[33] Morgenthaler suggests this may be a summary of claims in Kant's *Neue Anmerkungen zur Erläuterung der Theorie der Winde* (1756), AA 1, I:489–504 (SW 3:333–334).

[34] The initials "C. B." in this quote and the next refer to Clemens Brentano. The quotations are not found in Brentano's published works and are presumably from letters or oral communication (Hopp and Preitz, "Umwelt. III," 319–320).

We cannot associate with, watch and imitate the life of beautiful people, for it is not the individual, but the friendly inner connection, which is there without struggling for this connection. We can *never* become like that, for this beauty dwells so very much in itself that it can never become an example.

C. B.

The demand of the moralists that we only be sure that our actions are moral, without further considering their consequences, seems excessive to me. If it were so, we could stop at the mere thought, but the action as such has the purpose of producing a change outside us; it is natural that we consider whether this change (the consequence of the act) is also something good. For if merely the thought that was the basis of the action is good, but not also the change that it brought about, then it was no more a good thought than a good action.

C. G.[35]

Poesie is transformation of ideas into bodies, formation of the ideal in the real. Philosophy also transforms bodies into ideas, return of the real into the ideal.[36]

---

[35] Hopp and Preitz note that this kind of argument against the moralists, but not this direct quote, is found in the work of the philosopher Christian Garve (1742–1798). Alternatively, they suggest this could be a verbal quote from Günderrode's sister Charlotte (who, at this point, had been dead for at least three years) or her friend Carolina von Glauburg ("Umwelt. III," 320).

[36] Hopp and Preitz suggest this statement may be based on Schelling's work ("Umwelt. III," 321).

PART 3
LETTERS

24

Günderrode's Letters

Introduction

Letters have long been used to study the thought of philosophers, with prominent examples including Spinoza's letters, correspondence between Karl Marx and Friedrich Engels, and letters between René Descartes and Elisabeth of Bohemia. In Günderrode's case, it has been argued that there is an "indissoluble connection" between her letters and published writings and that her letters are "a genuine, indeed possibly the most important, part of her literary work."[1] The philosophical value of Günderrode's letters is clearest with regard to her claims about personal identity and friendship, but they are also relevant to her views on death, gender, creativity, memory, and time.

Günderrode's contemporaries were prolific letter writers: it was common to send and receive correspondence with every post. Letters were often meant to be shared with other members of the recipient's household or an even wider circle; correspondence by notable figures or that were thought to have particularly high scientific, literary, moral, or philosophical merit might even be published. For women in particular, letters were a means of participating in intellectual debates, allowing them to reach beyond the restrictions of their household and local acquaintances to communicate with a wider social network, including on philosophical topics.

Through her letters, Günderrode participated in an intellectual network despite her relative seclusion in a convent.[2] She was a frequent correspondent and, as with her philosophical studies, undertook letter-writing as a sociable activity. She often dictated letters or wrote them with friends, using her correspondence to involve other people in her engagement with philosophy and

---

[1] Christa Bürger, "Aber eine Sehnsucht war in mir, die ihren Gegenstand nicht kannte ...' Ein Versuch über Karoline von Günderrode," *Metis* 2 (1995): 58.

[2] Jordan R. Lavers, "The Epistolarity of a Social Network: Simulating a Romantic Network Community in Letters by Karoline von Günderrode," in *Nineteenth Century Literature Criticism* 338 (2017): 149–171.

Karoline von Günderrode. Anna Ezekiel, Oxford University Press. © Oxford University Press 2026.
DOI: 10.1093/9780190089177.003.0028

literature and her works in progress. She sometimes enclosed drafts or finished poems; these are a valuable source for her unpublished writings. The letters also include correspondents' responses to their reading and record the sharing of books and other materials.

Unfortunately, many of Günderrode's letters have been destroyed, often deliberately. Fearing a scandal due to his role in triggering Günderrode's suicide, Günderrode's lover Georg Friedrich Creuzer destroyed their correspondence that was in his possession. This included almost all the letters from Günderrode to Creuzer and as a result only ten or so of these remain; by contrast, around 120 of Creuzer's letters to Günderrode survive.[3] Some letter writers at the time collected their correspondence and promoted its circulation; not only did Günderrode not do this, but some of her letters include instructions to their recipients to destroy them. Clearly, Günderrode did not intend her correspondence to be read by a wider public.

Nonetheless, Günderrode's letters are an important source not just for her biography but also for certain areas of her philosophy, especially in relation to friendship and the nature of the self. The letters translated here have been selected and excerpted to include Günderrode's claims on these topics, as well as passages that are often cited by commentators. The latter have tended to be used to build a picture of Günderrode as depressive, restless, escapist, solipsistic, and showing suicidal ideation for years before her death. In particular, Günderrode's letters around the time of her sister Charlotte's death in the fall of 1801 are frequently cited as revealing longing for death and a conflicted sense of self. Her letters describe the misery of sitting with a dying person and the consolation of reading together. In this context, Günderrode's descriptions of the pleasure of being "able to soar in a beautiful sublime fantasy world" and the misery when "the blessed dreams dissolve" seem like normal responses rather than distinctive character traits.

Other of Günderrode's remarks ostensibly about herself can be read, not primarily as claims about herself at all, but as indicating her conception of what it is to be a self in general. This model, which has been called "momentary," "catastrophic," and "fragmentary,"[4] is unconventional, and presents the self as changing radically from one moment to the next. For example, Günderrode writes to her friend Carl Friedrich Savigny that "my essence is uncertain, full of fleeting phenomena that come and go changeably" and to

[3] Weißenborn, *Ich sende Dir*, 32.
[4] Bohrer, "Identität als Selbstverlust"; Ezekiel, "Narrative and Fragment."

Savigny's future wife, Kunigunde "Gunda" Brentano, "sometimes I have no opinion of myself at all, my self-observations are so fluctuating."

While some readers have taken these claims to suggest that Günderrode was unable to create a stable identity for herself,[5] other letters clarify that they are general claims about personal identity. Günderrode explicitly applies this model of a radically changeable self to others, including Gunda, Gunda's brother Clemens, and Savigny. For example, she writes to Clemens "It often seems to me as if you had many souls; when I begin to like one of these souls, then it departs and another steps into its place." The fact that Günderrode discussed this claim with Clemens is significant: Clemens Brentano is known for developing an unconventional and influential conception of personal identity, which, as Karl Heinz Bohrer has argued, has similarities to Günderrode's.[6] It is likely that a mutual influence obtained between Günderrode's and Clemens' ideas of the self.

Günderrode also sketches a model of ideal interpersonal relationships, or friendship, in her letters. According to Günderrode, friends should participate in each other's interests, revealing their innermost thoughts and feelings and reflecting these back again in an honest but positive way. Thus, she writes to Charlotte, "I want to share everything with you that I know and have learnt," and to Gunda, "Every interesting piece of knowledge, feeling and experience, if someone else doesn't share it with me, is a mountain that separates me from the person with whom I'd like to join." In sharing and reflecting each other's feelings and ideas, Günderrode claims, friends help endow each other's changeable self with a degree of stability and, hopefully, affirmation: "I love inordinately to behold myself again in others; for I hope the other will let me see a more beautiful image than I see myself."

Consistent with the idea of a self that changes from one day, or one moment, to the next, Günderrode claims that friends must continually renew their engagement with each other. She writes to Brentano-von Arnim: "It seems as if you've completely forgotten my way of being and foisted a strange image upon it"; and to Clemens that she feels he is writing to someone else rather than her, or that he has put a "wig" on her that does not fit. She links these points to the changeability of the self: "I don't know if I would speak the way you read my letter, but it seems to me, oddly, that I listen to how I speak and my own words seem almost stranger to me than those of strangers. Even

---

[5] Burwick, "Liebe und Tod," 209.
[6] Bohrer, "Identität als Selbstverlust."

the truest letters are, in my opinion, only corpses: they describe a life that inhabited them and [...] the moment of their life is already past."

It is clear that Günderrode was often disappointed in her friendships, and Gunda Brentano was a particular target of annoyance. She complains to Gunda, who had not been writing often enough or in a way that Günderrode approves, that "I strike tones and always hear only the same monotonous sounds; it almost makes me lose patience that new tones don't alternate with those that have already died away." In contrast to Günderrode's ideal of a friend, Gunda, she accuses, is superficial, uninterested in cultivating her capacities, and—just as important—in encouraging Günderrode to develop her own: "you don't demand any virtue of me that I don't have."

Günderrode also takes issue with Gunda's fatalism ("don't say your cold *it must be so*") and her disparagement of the world as "muck" (*Dreck*). These points are important because Günderrode is sometimes said to espouse fatalism and to have developed her metaphysical claims, especially regarding the dissolution of individuals in the whole after death, in response to a desire to turn away from the world.[7] These claims are contradicted in her letters.

Gunda was a wealthy socialite who did not share the intellectual interests of many of her social circle; she was also a romantic rival of Günderrode's regarding Savigny, whom Gunda married in 1804. Günderrode's letters to Gunda are increasingly harsh; this evidently stems from feelings of rejection as much as jealousy. It is apparent that Günderrode desperately wanted a closer relationship with Gunda, whom she initially admired. The later letters to Gunda and Savigny show her efforts to salvage a close relationship with both of them. She also refers in more detail to her ideals for communication and for responses from a friend with whom one can share everything, exhorting Savigny to answer her sincerely, not out of politeness: "answer your friend without any consideration—that is, really like a friend."

Günderrode's later letters to Savigny, Creuzer, and Creuzer's wife Sophie also emphasize the importance of sincerity. To Creuzer, she writes "I must give myself to you not partially, but always my self," and to Sophie "I have always written to C[reuzer] without deliberation and hidden none of my feelings from him." She tells Creuzer that she is "sincere towards" Sophie. The latter claim is, perhaps, questionable: parts of Günderrode's correspondence with Creuzer were written in Greek to keep them secret from

---

[7] Burdorf, "Sehnsucht," 53; Weißenborn, *Ich sende Dir*, 35. For details on Günderrode's metaphysics, see the section on metaphysics in the general introduction to this volume.

Sophie, and Günderrode persistently tried to persuade Creuzer to commit to her romantically, or at least to come to some sort of accommodation with Sophie that would allow Günderrode to remain in his life. Once again, the letters show Günderrode attempting to navigate a love triangle that eventually excluded her.

Famously, Günderrode's relationship with Creuzer ended in disaster. Clemens involved himself, as did Savigny, who was supporting Creuzer financially, each attempting to persuade both parties to end the relationship.[8] Creuzer loathed Clemens and urged Günderrode to avoid the Brentano family completely.[9] The result was that Günderrode severed ties with them, including Gunda and Clemens' sister Bettina Brentano-von Arnim, who had been a close friend and correspondent since they met in 1801. As Günderrode's biographer Margarete Lazarowicz notes, of Günderrode's friends, Brentano-von Arnim was perhaps the one most interested in the kind of relationship with Günderrode that Günderrode claimed characterized true friendship.[10] The younger woman was devastated by the termination of their relationship and by Günderrode's death. In 1840, she published a volume of her edited correspondence with Günderrode,[11] and scraps of the letters from the "Günderode" figure in this volume can be identified in actual letters from Günderrode. These are often modified: Brentano-von Arnim's book was not intended as a faithful record of their correspondence but as a work of literature. As a result, these letters are not necessarily reliable indications of Günderrode's own claims.

Of Günderrode's actual letters to Brentano-von Arnim only a few remain, and one has been translated here. This letter contains further indications of Günderrode's model of a transitory and radically changeable self. Günderrode here makes an especially interesting claim about biographies, which she argues always present only a partial and one-sided account of an individual's personality and life. This is broadly consistent with early German Romantic ideas about narrative, especially narrative self-construction, as a creative, provisional exercise that artificially connects events to give a semblance of coherence and meaning.[12] Günderrode emphasizes the inadequacy of such attempts: "the complexity of human existence always remains

---

[8] Lazarowicz, *Porträt einer Fremden*, 314–318, 331.
[9] Lazarowicz, *Porträt einer Fremden*, 330, 359.
[10] Lazarowicz, *Porträt einer Fremden*, 349, 366.
[11] Brentano-von Arnim, *Die Günderode* (Grünberg: W. Levysohn, 1840).
[12] Novalis, *Schriften*, 2:580 #242.

unattained." On one level, this seems like an obvious statement: of course no biography can include everything about a person. However, in the context of Günderrode's claims about friendship and the self, it is possible that Günderrode meant to compare this inadequacy of narrative to the truer perception of an individual that a friend can have, if they make a genuine attempt to earnestly share in their friend's experiences.

Günderrode's letters to Gunda, Savigny, Clemens, and Creuzer can give an impression of unrelenting personal disappointment in those closest to her. However, she also maintained more positive relationships, including with her friends Christian and Elisabetha Nees von Esenbeck, Susanne von Heyden, and Claudine Piautaz, the Brentanos' well-educated housekeeper. Few of Günderrode's letters to these individuals have survived; however, it is clear from their numerous replies that she remained in active correspondence with them until her death.

A letter to Piautaz is included in the translations below, and shows Günderrode making a self-conscious effort to provide a literary and conceptually interesting description of her surroundings. She reflects on the interaction between the imagination and its environment, arguing that, rather than being stimulated by beautiful surroundings, creativity emerges best when "it finds no outer objects," so that it must produce things itself. She considers the different emotional states one can experience and, consistent with her "momentary" account of the self, the centrality of time to these experiences: "I don't believe one can have two states at the same time; I believe they must be consecutive (however small the sections of time may be)." She relates this idea of time to her studies of Kant: "I learnt that one can't have intuitions of the outer senses without the characteristics of time and space, and no intuition of the inner sense without the characteristic of time." Alone among Günderrode's letters, it seems she may have intended to rework this one to include in her published writings. In addition to stylistic differences to the rest of her correspondence, the later part of the letter includes two sets of reflections—on dying and the notion of sin, which she relates to a Kantian morality of rational control over one's actions—that are repeated in "Letters of Two Friends." Günderrode also enclosed two draft poems with this letter, one beginning "In Proud Arcs" and the other titled "The Mourner." A revised version of "The Mourner" was published in *Poems and Fantasies* as "The Mourner and the Elves."

As well as their importance for understanding Günderrode's philosophy, Günderrode's letters give indications of her writing process, including the ways she navigated input from friends and critics. For example, her letters to Clemens show her efforts to keep him at arm's length, both personally and in his assumed role as intellectual mentor. Günderrode was not interested in being "one of Clemens' pupils";[13] in response to his feedback, she tells him "Don't give me any more advice; I always have to laugh at this part of your letter." Her description to Savigny of Nees von Esenbeck's efforts to influence her play *Muhammad, the Prophet of Mecca*, which she has deflected, also shows her resisting male interference and the imposition of patriarchal restrictions on her writing.

While this introduction points to some of the philosophically interesting aspects of Günderrode's letters, these are still to be investigated thoroughly and compared in detail to work on related issues by her contemporaries. In particular, it will be exciting to deepen our understanding of Günderrode's conception of the self and idea of friendship as they are presented in her letters, especially in relation to the metaphysics, ethics, ideals for community, and claims about reincarnation, love, and consciousness that she develops in her published writings.

Letters

To Karoline von Barkhaus, 4 July 1799

I left you reluctantly yesterday, and in a fierce struggle with myself about whether or not I should reveal the state of my heart to you. I longed for the solace of being able to pour out my heart into yours, and yet a secret fear, the roots of which I can't explain to myself, held me back. It would be easier, I thought, to reveal myself in writing. This thought became a decision, which still remains in my soul.

At first glance Savigny already made a strong impression on me. I tried to hide it from myself, and persuaded myself that it was merely sympathizing with the gentle pain that his whole being expresses, but soon, very soon, the increasing strength of my feelings instructed me that what I felt was passion. I hardly knew how to contain my joy when you wrote to me in your last letter that S would come with you to Wilhelmsbad.—I wanted to be angry with myself that my heart would give itself so quickly to a man who is probably

---

[13] Sophie von La Roche, Letter to Sophie Mereau, 22 July 1805, SW 3:160.

entirely indifferent to me, but it is so, and my only solace is in seeking the kindest sympathy in you, dearest. I don't know how you'll take my perhaps too hasty confidence, for with this step I haven't asked my reason, only my heart, which is wholly inclined toward you. I beg you, tell me soon that I haven't lost anything in our friendship by doing this.

[...] I embrace you in my thoughts. Don't forget me. All the best to your good mother and sister Sophie.

Karoline G.

I beg you, burn this letter.

To Karoline von Barkhaus, 17 July 1799

[...] So far I've also read a lot of Herder's *Ideas for a Philosophy of the History of Humankind*. This book is a true consolation to me in all my pain: I forget myself, my sufferings and joys in the weal and woe of all humanity, and in such moments I seem such a small, insignificant point in creation that my own affairs don't seem worth any tears or an anxious minute. It's only a pity that this feeling doesn't last long; soon afterwards my own distress again demands all the sympathy that previously I could and wanted to give only to humanity. It's very sad to have to observe how egoism stalks us everywhere, and is often closest to us where we believe it furthest from us.

To Karoline von Barkhaus, 14 February 1800

[...] How do I live? Often unsatisfied with myself. I can't actually love any of those who surround me closely here (don't be angry with me because of this); I can't imagine any love without harmony of sentiment, and that's impossible here. And often—I can't deny it to a friend like you—often I feel bitterness against these people when I see that they have so little feeling for what interests me. When the first storm of irritated sensation has passed, then I easily appreciate how impossible it is, given the whole state of affairs, for these people to think and feel like I do. It hurts me deeply, but I commit the injustice all over again, for I can't command my sentiments. I say to myself a thousand times that it's egotistical to only love people with the same sentiments, and yet it stays the same. I resign myself to compassion, only I can't love these alien creatures . . .

Write soon

Your Karoline

To Charlotte von Günderrode, 27 August 1800

Dear Lotte,

I won't see you when the others come, I know that and accept that it must be so; but I can hardly wait to see you. I have a thousand things to say to you that only Lotte should know. Certainly you don't love me as I love you; your image is drawn before my soul and your weaknesses, which, when I'm annoyed with you, often arouse me to impatience and sharpness, seem as small and insignificant to me as atoms. I want to share everything with you that I know and have learnt. Seek solace, love and harmony in your soul. I beg you, Lotte, when I'm with you again, learn to bear my weaknesses lovingly, don't let it annoy you when I point out yours, for you know I'm impatient with nothing so much as the weaknesses of beloved people. I beg you, do everything possible so that our beautiful harmony will never be disturbed.

Write soon

Your Karoline

To Gunda Brentano, 11 August 1801

How weird the first days of a stop in a strange place are: the bonds that tied us to the previous stop are severed for the present; it's as if they step into the background of sensation, and the state until one has accustomed oneself to one's new surroundings is thoroughly unpleasant. There's an emptiness that one wants to thrust from oneself; at least, so it seems to me. Every interesting piece of knowledge, feeling and experience, if someone else doesn't share it with me, is a mountain that separates me from the person with whom I'd like to join. It often seemed like that regarding you, but I didn't know whether I should try to get rid of the mountain between us, for I often thought you'd be indifferent to seeing me as I am. You know how difficult it is for self-love to show someone else something common in oneself.

I was often (I flatter myself) a true mirror to you, in which you could con-template yourself; yes, I cast the image I received back to you with greater sincerity; but never yet have I contemplated myself in you—tell me, how is that? I don't always like to show myself (I've said so before), but when I have showed myself, I love inordinately to behold myself again in others; for I hope the other will let me see a more beautiful image than I see myself. Or rather, sometimes I have no opinion of myself at all, my self-observations are so fluctuating. In general it's totally incomprehensible to me that we have no consciousness other than perception of effects, never of causes. All other knowledge seems to me (when I think of this) not worthy of knowledge, as long as I don't know the cause of the knowledge, my faculty of knowledge. To me, this ignorance is the most unbearable lack, the greatest contradiction. And I think if we really ever enter the borders of a second life, then one of our first inner phenomena would have to be that our consciousness would grow larger and clearer; for it would be unbearable to drag this limitation into a second life.

I had many questions to ask you, e.g., whether Clemens had written? how you are? whether Klötchen[14] is there again? Only the suspicion that you might take questions to be a means of extorting your answers doesn't let me simply do so. In this, I surrender to the favor and disfavor of your moods, for I know, simply by the fact that they are yours, that they are lovable children with beautiful bright wings.

Probably it will be much longer than I thought till I see you: my sister Lotte is very sick, she can't live much longer, and I can bring her pleasure for these few days by my being here. I've never seen anyone as ripe for death as she is; her course has ended, in her own assessment too, for her soul is so formed that it will never develop happily outwards, no-one will ever draw her gaze away from her interior, and this interior has blossomed and borne its fruit (only in and for itself). Now nothing more can grow in her other than death and annihilation; happily, physical death comes to help her.

How do you find the following definition? "Anger is impatient love, not for the object about which one is angry, but for its opposite."

I had other things to say to you, but I can't; another time, if I'm still thinking of it or it still seems interesting to me.

Karoline.

---

[14] A diminutive for Claudine, here Claudine Piautaz, housekeeper for the Brentanos.

To Gunda Brentano, 19, 22, 23 August 1801

19th

Yesterday I was so sad; if I had written to you, Gunda, it would have yielded several pages full of mere whining. I felt so constricted externally, so upset internally. I have so very little time for myself, cannot say now I want to do this, then that; I must watch for and seize any moments for myself, and when they come I don't enjoy them. Nothing makes me happy. I'm in indeterminate pain, I'm in the most wretched state: that of not-feeling, of muffled cold slogging along. In this state I hate myself. It's essential to the life of my soul that some idea enthuse me, and this is often even the case, but it must always be something new, for I drink from the nectar cup so intemperately, until I have slurped it all up; and when it's empty, that's unbearable.

From time to time, my sister reads passages from Godwi[15] to me, and I like it better like this. It's wonderful that almost all spiritual pleasures are increased by sharing; with material things the opposite happens. Giving and becoming richer through giving! It's most wonderful, yes, I think it contains a refutation of materialism.

22nd

I left you with strange feelings on Wednesday. From Gunda one must not expect indulgence, mercy, support, I thought, and it's true: anyone who entrusts their fortunes to you trusts the shifting sea. You're only a spectacle; one must enjoy you, and not more, for you're truly a beautiful multifarious play suited for beholding. Anyone who takes you otherwise doesn't understand you, anyone who wants you otherwise harms the pleasure they could enjoy in viewing you. It's certainly so: with respect to you I will accustom myself more and more to observation.

23rd

I've no desire to write at all today, dear Gunda, I only ask you to write to me.

Karoline

My sisters send greetings to you, and I to Klötchen.

---

[15] Clemens Brentano's 1801 novel *Godwi, oder Das steinerne Bild der Mutter.*

To Gunda Brentano, 29, 30 August 1801

29th

I received your letter last night. —But forgive me! I can't retract my judgment about you, for I didn't only find you like that in Wilhelmsbad. No, you've always seemed like that to me, just more distinctly and clearly then. Admittedly, I should also take into consideration the lines you wrote me. I would be at a loss to judge you, for a completely different spirit to Gunda's flows through them: I wouldn't believe they were from you at all, if I didn't know that you were sick, and because of that perhaps your forces are a little less effervescent and instead softer and more relaxed.

It's an ugly failing of mine that I can so easily lapse into a state of not feeling, and I'm glad of anything that drags me out of this. Yesterday I read Ossian's "Darthula," and it had such a pleasant affect on me: the old wish to die a hero's death seized me with great intensity; it seemed intolerable to me to still be alive; even more intolerable to die a peaceful and common death. I had already often had the unfeminine wish to throw myself into, to die in, the wild thick of a battle. Why was I not a man! I have no sense for feminine virtues, for a woman's happiness. Only the wild, great, glorious pleases me. It's a deplorable but incorrigible discrepancy in my soul, and it will and must remain so, for I'm a woman, and have desires like a man, without manly strength. That's why I'm so changeable, and so at odds with myself.

30th

[. . .] When I saw you for the first time, you struck me in a very impressive way; that is, I got it into my head to make a good impression on you too; I was dumb, abashed and forced in your presence, out of fear of displeasing you. But when I learned you were not unfavorable to me, then for several days I was drunk with proud pleasure.

Farewell; let me hear soon that you are well.

Karoline

Gunda, you'll laugh over this letter; even to me it seems so disconnected and confused.

To Gunda Brentano, 4, 5 September 1801

4th

You put me in a bad position by not wanting to write to me like a person who has fallen in love with their echo; or, if I were to be really particular about it, much more serious, of course the echo is deaf to all questions, all pleas, but one can still imagine one hears an answer from it; and I can never do that with you. Suggest this to Clemens so he doesn't hold back from writing to me. If you don't, if you continue to keep your pen idle, then I have nothing of you but a memory, which may not look at all like your so-called I (if I see it again) any more, for you're changeable, doubly changeable: out of natural propensity, and out of coquetry, which anyway, as you say, is also natural.

Clemens says you're sick; I seriously believe you are. But I know I can never contribute anything to your recovery; I can only live and act as it occurs to me to do, and deal with nothing. I can't deal with people I like, because I'm too candid, too intimate with them; [nor with] those I can't stand, because I'm not considerate and too sluggish, yes often even too intense. And I find it difficult to have an effect on you.—Also, I believe you won't recover.

5th

I'm happy that you're so free to not be limited by others' opinions or by a certain anxiousness which is so established in many people. You let yourself live by the mood of the moment; and you also, I believe, do so with those around you; at least I feel so good with you because you don't demand any virtue of me that I don't have; because you don't make me worry that I can't have this or that perfection. That's very convenient, and also, according to your system, good, for it must be so; but that being good depends on the truth of your system; otherwise it's bad, for it cuts the flight feathers of our spirit in two forever; that's also why I hate it.

Greet the good Klötchen; and don't speak so much about your illness in front of her, otherwise your talk will be a second illness for the good soul.

I beg you don't be annoyed with me.

Karoline

To Gunda Brentano, 20, 21 October 1801

20th

I don't know, Gunda, whether I should tell you anything about myself, because I can almost certainly assume that you can't take an interest in what I'd like to tell you about me. The onesidedness of our correspondence also stirs up unpleasant feelings in me. I strike tones and always hear only the same monotonous sounds; it almost makes me lose patience that new tones don't alternate with those that have already died away.—You almost become too strange to me to usher you into the most essential parts of my inner world; nonetheless, you're a guest one may not leave standing outside the door. A great quandary. I thought you could be led into a not-too-distant compartment and the actors (thoughts, fantasies, feelings) allowed to perform for you, without letting you come behind the curtains, especially not to see the deepest workings.—But I can't do that, Gunda, at least it's too difficult for me. I must either close the theater altogether or unveil what is deepest too.

21st

Gunda I'm impatient and in a bad mood, in short totally ugly and disfigured. I must sit almost the whole day beside the sickbed, and with a patient whose spiritual forces are so worn out that not a single gratifying expression is heard from them. No, I can't tell you how impatient I am, and how very much I hate this impatience at the same time, without being able to overcome it. I succumb to myself, I'm inwardly totally miserable. Advise, help me, and don't say your cold *it must be so*, or at least let's spin dreams around this dire theme.

A little while ago I was able to soar in a beautiful sublime fantasy world, in Ossian's half-dark magical world. But the blessed dreams dissolve; they seem like love potions, they intoxicate, exalt and then disappear: that's the misery and wretchedness of all our feelings. It's no better with thoughts; it's also easy to overthink a thing to the point of staleness.—A pygmy age, a pygmy generation is performing now, very well in its way.

Minchen[16] sends greetings, and Klötchen; me too.

Karoline

---

[16] A diminutive for Wilhelmine, presumably in this case Günderrode's sister Wilhelmine.

To Gunda Brentano, 24 November 1801

You made me very happy by coming here, for Gunda, in all seriousness, I thought I was completely forgotten by you, my letters to you too burdensome. Only the latter thought was unpleasant for my pride; the other was no less than gratifying, but I felt it with a certain resignation, which may have arisen from feeling how little I am to you. I also know I must be tolerant, out of self-love, for I myself am fickle, easily become cold towards those who are long absent—and yet it's an ugly admission; I don't want to finish it here. I wonder, Gunda, why you don't sacrifice something in order to maintain, or reclaim, Clemens' love; to me it seems so sweet to be loved by excellent people; to me it's the most flattering proof of my own value. I'm too weak against these too seductive flattering voices: they can make me unfaithful to myself. Often and in vain I've resisted myself. The failure of such resolutions (a sad experience of my life) is a triumph of your system, which I very much begrudge you.

Certainly, Gunda, you're missing out due to Clemens' distance, I feel it for you so surely, and fear it will hurt you twice as much later if you don't change this unpleasant relationship.

My life is so empty, I have so many boring, blank hours. Gunda, is it only love that pours life and feeling into this dull emptiness? Or are there other feelings that do this? There is a void here in my soul; in vain I seek to fill it, in vain to reason it away. Art can only proliferate through nature, with nature; without it, it can do nothing. I began to feel early—I fear I used up my faculty for feeling early; I'm left with only the benchmark of what was there before, and the idea: I stand between the two and can achieve neither. And even now, as I describe this state to you, I feel it less than I perceive it.

Even friendship denies me its happy deceptions. People in whom I saw the sense and love for interesting objects and a certain striving for them would often become my friends, because for me communication is a need. But soon I would exhaust the interest I shared with them, and find I had exhausted them too; they only had the strength to think, feel, what has already been thought, already felt; but to connect what was distinctive to them, and special, to this generality, to create new opinions of things within themselves— nature denied them this ever-streaming abundance of spirit. In such cases one must grow tired, or always give the other so much that one doesn't realize how little one receives. I couldn't do the latter; I often became cold towards my friends, and neither their love nor their other perfections could make me forget this shortcoming. And all too often they also lacked the patience and strength to bear me as I am. So friendly relationships usually brought me more pain than joy. And even if I were to find a friend who was everything that I wished, I'd find myself unworthy of them; and for me, bliss itself would have thorns.

Karoline

To Gunda Brentano, 30 December 1801

[...] Your claim that everything in the world is *muck* seems totally dire; as long as I still have breath I will dispute you about that. Your reviews[17] are entirely too vicious for me. Not once do you spare the cosmos. You won't have spared me at all since I've been here. You'll have committed treason against me, at least. I know what one can expect from you. I'm like a bold sailor; I entrust myself to the stormy sea.—I must forcibly restrain myself, I could muster ten pages full of blasphemies against you. [...]

To Gunda Brentano, June 1802

You force me to consider my relationship to you, my feelings for you—now listen to what I must tell myself. You know I'm well-inclined towards you, that I like to be with you, but you also know that I simply cannot delude myself about your failings, far less love them. I've often told you what I condemn in you, what I must forego with you because you either don't have the aptitude for it or because this aptitude is stifled in you. But I also complain about much in you that you could change, if an inertia, which I can't think of without impatience, and a limitless addiction to always finding yourself loveable, didn't prevent you from doing so. My heart always grows bitter or cold towards you when I see how everything good, how all impetus to improvement that you have now is not able to change this in you. I can be silent about these things, but I find them reprehensible, and the more demands you make on me the more vividly I feel how you should be different, for I have no patience at all for some failings, and least of all in people I want to love. And I want to love you, even if I don't love the person directly, but only

---

[17] Gunda has sent comments on books she has read.

the excellence. It always hurts me when someone robs me of my love, like you often rob me of my feelings for you and my faith in your future. See, as long as it stays like that I can't prefer you to everyone else, it's impossible; I must always love those who are better more than you.

I tell you this again so that you never delude yourself about me.—But I hope you'll bring a better existence with you from the springs of life in Wiesbaden;[18] until then, adieu.

K.

Tear up this page. When are you leaving?

To Clemens Brentano, 19 May 1802

It was a strange feeling when I read your letter, though I was thinking more than feeling, for it seemed to me, and still seems to me, as if your letter were not written to me at all. Thus I laugh at myself. But that I think so is not an artificial institution; it came like that all by itself.

Yes, I understand the moment in which you wrote to me; in general I've never gone further than understanding your moments a little. Of their coherence and undertone I know nothing at all. It often seems to me as if you had many souls; when I begin to like one of these souls, then it departs and another steps into its place, which I don't know and just stare at, surprised. But I don't think about all your souls at all, for one of them has my confidence, which is only a fearful child thrown onto the street. The child has now become much stupider and won't turn back. For that reason I also can't really write to you about me.

I read your letter to Bettina about truth and it made me very happy and at the same time richer by a few opinions, which were previously only dark and fluctuating to me.

Bettina will make off with this letter. I haven't seen her for a long time; she also didn't write to me as she promised.

I'm working hard and drawing again—in short, I'm following all your sensible suggestions.

Karoline

---

[18] The springs in Wiesbaden, like hot springs throughout Europe, were believed to have curative powers.

To Clemens Brentano [1803?]

I don't know if I would speak the way you read my letter, but it seems to me, oddly, that I listen to how I speak and my own words seem almost stranger to me than those of strangers. Even the truest letters are, in my opinion, only corpses: they describe a life that inhabited them and, whether or not they're like the living, the moment of their life is already past. But for that reason, it seems to me (when I read what I wrote a while ago) as if I saw myself lying in my coffin and my two Is stared at each other in amazement.

My trust was, admittedly, not a lovable child. It didn't know how to say beautiful things, so bystanders always whispered to it: child! be clever! don't go on like that. Then the child would become confused and clumsy, it didn't rightly know how to be clever and wavered back and forth. Can one hold this against it? But the child isn't headstrong; if it feels accepted kindly and gently at home, then it would rather turn around than linger longer on the street.

Don't give me any more advice; I always have to laugh at this part of your letter. I won't be able to use the word[19] any more; moreover, it reminds me of somersaults. I've never rightly understood what you wanted to say by that, it just seemed ridiculous to me without knowing why.

I know few people, and perhaps none completely accurately, for I'm very clumsy at observing others. Thus, if I understand you in one moment, I can't conclude anything from this about all the others. There may well be very few people who can do this, and I am not among them. Now, I think that it's good to observe you, and pleasant, but one should only want to observe you. Is this view true or false?

Karoline

To Carl Friedrich von Savigny, end July 1803

I am supposed to have done *you* wrong? *I* should repent?[20] Before I go to this extreme, I must first tell you how very naturally and humanly I made my judgment. In every life there are moments in which the present works more

---

[19] The relevant letter from Clemens has been lost, so we don't know which word Günderrode is talking about or what advice from Clemens she is resisting.

[20] Günderrode had written to Savigny, concerned that Gunda had told him she had feelings for him, to deny it; she asked him not to write again since she felt he did not like writing to her. Savigny replied that she was being unfair (Weißenborn, *Ich sende Dir*, 102–103).

powerfully than the past and the future, so I thought, and I thought, further, that you had been a little engulfed by the present like this. And I wouldn't find that so bad at all if it were possible to let oneself be so engulfed by this monstrosity for a short time that one's hearing and sight and various thoughts totally vanish. But as I said, it mustn't last too long, for there are so many things that might gladly be heard and seen. But oh heaven! How I have departed from you and our topic through comparisons that would better fit the Prophet Jonah[21] than you. I don't see how I can return to it with order and coherence. Advise me, or rather tell me, must a letter necessarily be written with order and coherence? If that were the case, I'd have to completely refrain from writing, because my head is missing a couple of organs and I have reason to suspect that it is those of order. I beg you, close your eyes to these natural failings.

I must also tell you that I now believe I did you wrong, for I have a great inclination to believe you, and I'd like to stop there, for well I see that no exact likeness of you exists in my judgment; I always find error and uncertainty. Moreover, believing is often nicer than seeing.—Therefore I believe—

Karoline

[...]

To Carl Friedrich von Savigny, 26 December 1803[22]

There are so many thoughts confused in my head that all want to turn to you; only first I want to see whether you even want to hear them. I've told you before, dear Savigny, how it's almost too much a need for me to express myself, when I'm very merry or sad or gripped by anything else unusual. I'm also often in conflict with myself and doubt myself, and seek another's judgment, someone else's approbation, in order to be happy in myself again. In such cases I then easily let myself be carried away, trusting someone who can't give me what's missing, misunderstands me or handles me clumsily. The state

---

[21] In the Hebrew Testament, God told Jonah to warn the inhabitants of Nineveh that he would destroy them if they did not change their ways, but instead Jonah fled by sea. God created a storm; the sailors realized this was Jonah's fault and threw him overboard where he was swallowed by a whale or large fish. After Jonah repented, God had the fish vomit Jonah onto the shore, from where he went to Nineveh and convinced the inhabitants to repent. Jonah's story is seen as (among other things) illustrating the futility of evading God; Günderrode is possibly referring to her previous accusation that Savigny was trying to avoid her.

[22] Part of a letter begun on the 25th.

within me that follows such an incident is the most adverse for me. I'd like to change that, would like to always speak with you about such things and write to you about them, can I? Are you not much too busy? I'm afraid you might listen to me and answer out of a kind of generosity that I wouldn't like to have, so don't do that; answer your friend without any consideration—that is, really like a friend.

Karoline

Günderrode and Gunda to Carl Friedrich von Savigny, 1, 3 January 1804

1st

Yes dear Savigny! I believe in Gundelchen's[23] excellence, and will gladly be entitled to you.[24] I find our new relationship very nice and free, but I'd like some visible bond to bind me to you, as if I were your brother, or Gundelchen's sister; I wouldn't find it nicer, but more secure. The relationships of kinship are so indestructible and no destiny can dissolve them. I'd like that, and it could make me much calmer and happier than I am now.

I can't write further without first confessing something. Yesterday evening I upset Gundelchen very much. She said.—but no, she shall write the whole thing to you herself. The feeling out of which I spoke has died forever: it doesn't even belong to me at all; it was a stranger that paid me an unwelcome visit; it will never find me again. Gundelchen is no longer sad about it at all, and not at all angry with me. And, what's more, she's not allowed to be, surely not?[25]

3rd

Gundelchen is so good to me.—I paint the future very precisely for myself, and even now flee to it when I don't feel right in the world. I usually carry around a quiet little chamber in my mind; in this I live a private, secluded, happy life, interested in or loving some person, an idea, a science, or an art, and, because I linger much too much in this cozy little corner, I'm stupid and strange with the world and people, and always remain too clumsy to treat

---

[23] A diminutive for Gunda (itself a shortening of Kunigunde).
[24] In a previous letter, Savigny told Günderrode that she would not just belong to him and Gunda (who were engaged) but be entitled to them (Weißenborn, *Ich sende Dir*, 113).
[25] A passage written by Gunda is omitted here.

them as one should. And if the little chamber is closed to me for a while, if I can't find it and live within it, then I'm very unhappy, and if I want to usher someone inside and they won't like it there, that can also be really painful for me. It always seemed to me as if I couldn't lead Gundelchen there, or it wouldn't be good for her and me there. Is that an error? Or is it true? And what's the cause of that? Tell me.

Karoline

To Carl Friedrich von Savigny, February 1804

My heart hasn't turned away from you, far less towards another mortal; no, I always think with great joy about the fact that in future I'll belong to you and Gunda, but for a few weeks it has seemed different to me than a couple of months ago. Gunda reproaches me, says I'm arrogant, love no-one and don't take an interest in anyone, but she's wrong, at least she greatly exaggerates: I'm not at all arrogant, for I lack the conviction that I'm excellent. I can only believe it transiently, and then not at all again. But do you know what it is, in fact? I can only tell you with great inanity that I'm writing a drama;[26] my whole soul is occupied with that. Yes, I think myself so vividly into it, become so at home in it, that my own life becomes strange to me. I have great aptitude for such an abstraction, such an immersion in a stream of inner observations and productions. Gunda says it's stupid to let oneself be ruled to such a degree by an art as small as mine; but I love this failing, if it is one: often it makes up for the whole world to me.

I should be firm and clear and warm. Indeed, it would be lovely if I were, but can I be? Don't you believe in the necessity of all things? I believe my essence is uncertain, full of fleeting phenomena that come and go changeably and without enduring, inner warmth. Nonetheless, I beg you, forgive me my inherent depravity.

Karoline.

---

[26] Günderrode's play *Muhammad, the Prophet of Mecca*.

To Claudine Piautaz, April 1804

All day I was not in the mood to write.

The region is so beautiful, so adventurous, but my wellspring of poetry has dried up. I thought I'd find a lot of material here. It's strange that the imagination produces the most when it finds no outer objects; then it creates objects itself, and forms them all the more carefully because they aren't foreign material but its own children. There's no poetry in enjoyment (reality kills the dream); only in longing: this calls forth in me another life to the real one. Whoever fully enjoys, whoever really lives and loves like that, how could they still want or be able to dream? Life will not be divided; one cannot wander in the underworld with the shadows and at the same time in the world of the living under the sun and with people.—I've often thought about it, but I don't believe one can have two states at the same time; I believe they must be consecutive (however small the sections of time may be).

How wonderfully we are intertwined with time. In logic I learnt that one can't have intuitions of the outer senses without the characteristics of time and space, and no intuition of the inner sense without the characteristic of time.[27] Very strange, that this is only just becoming a really clear concept to me. [...][28]

The rain pours down in copious streams, the wind howls on the plains and tousles the tops of the trees, damp mists rise up, grey mists shroud the mountains and embrace them with wet arms. I turn inward and create another world for myself. Light dreams float around me; my consciousness is lost in contemplation. It might be like this for a dying person: consciousness grows ever weaker and more interrupted; dreams envelop them ever more densely and merge with the forms of reality until these fade completely and the dreamer becomes dream. Clear consciousness is burdensome: it's always bound up with a thousand pains, it can't forget time and joins to earth and temporality with unholy bonds. For that reason, consciousness doesn't know eternity. But eternity is in dreams: there the calculations of time don't count; in dream is bliss, and all bliss is only dreamt—eternity is the land of dreams.

---

[27] A reference to Kant's theory of the pure or a priori forms of sensible intuition—space and time—without which human beings cannot have impressions of the world. According to Kant, human beings always organize information about things outside themselves both spatially and temporally, but experience their inner states (thoughts, feelings etc.) as temporal only.

[28] Günderrode here includes a poem about the Rhine, beginning "In Proud Arcs..." (SW 3:475).

Everything that was created was good, says Holy Scripture, so why not human beings? Why should they be otherwise than they are? Marvelous!— This fills me with sorrow. To butcher one's sensations and wishes on the altars of necessity or morality—they call that virtue. To kill oneself piece by piece is also virtue. To stand triumphantly over the ruins of one's own spirit, to be able to say "see here at my feet what I have slain, shackled, the site of the fires; my will is victor over them all"; this is the requiting feeling of the virtuous.[29]—Sad triumph!—I pity the murdered and the shackled, and I'd like to ask the victor: why did you do that?[30]

To Carl Friedrich Savigny, 31st May, 1st June, 1804

I can't tell you how unpleasantly strange everything seemed to me the first day here. I consoled my poor mind constantly that I would soon [be able to] complain to you, but for 24 hours that wouldn't help me at all. In the end I went to see Heiden,[31] and she was so happy to see me, and told me about so many pleasant things, that I felt very fond of her. I grew cheerful and calm, and am still, and will remain so, if alarming things don't happen.

Here they are firmly convinced that I am Tian,[32] and denials will not help at all. There's a review in the *Freimütige*[33] that I enclose here, because of how bad it is. A certain Mr. Engelmann, a private tutor here, is the author. I noticed immediately that the good man was a private tutor: his official air easily shows through the coarse weave.

I've already twice nearly written "*Du*" instead of "*Sie*,"[34] but because I didn't, it seemed the whole time as if the letter wasn't to you.[35] See how much your *falseness* embarrasses me—are you still false?[36] Tell me whether the magical ciphers I sewed into the flannel have worked or not?

---

[29] Cf. "Story of a Brahmin."

[30] The letter ends with a draft poem, "The Mourner." Günderrode published a revised version of this poem, "The Mourner and the Elves," in *Poems and Fantasies*, in the same year (SW 3:66).

[31] Susanne Maria von Heyden, née Heiden (1775–1845).

[32] One of Günderrode's pseudonyms.

[33] Review of *Poems and Fantasies* in *Der Freimüthige oder Ernst und Scherz*, 15 May 1804 (SW 3:61).

[34] Savigny has asked Günderrode to switch from the familiar "you" (*Du*), used with family, close friends, and lovers, to the formal "you" (*Sie*), because of his recent marriage to Gunda.

[35] Here, Günderrode uses the familiar "you" (*Du*) again.

[36] The words translated in this sentence as "falseness" and "false" are, respectively, *Fanschheit* and *fansch*. These are not in common use in German and I have translated them tentatively based on context.

Adieu Gundelchen, adieu dear Savigny, who am I?

Your Günderrödchen

1st June

[. . .] I must give the lie to the first page of my letter; today I'm melancholy. Your image stands before my soul surrounded by fog; even the fact that you explicitly forbade me to call you "*Du*" was meaningful, very meaningful. Something was missing. But through this it was made into a whole. But what am I complaining for? The one who erred is more in the wrong.

I almost wanted to cross out what I had written, but no, that would be untruthful.

To Carl Friedrich Savigny, June 1804

I have so much good to do that I almost can't get to the best: writing to you. I'm having Müller's history of Switzerland[37] read to me, I'm studying Schelling with the greatest diligence, and am working on a new drama. My life is now fulfilled through these things, and I am satisfied. [. . .]

Write to me with the outgoing post how one can win your love. I want to parody the well-known saying, "the race is not to the swift,"[38] and say that your grace is not to the excellent, which I don't believe, for otherwise, dear Savigny, you would have to be terribly in love with me, which I don't believe. Rather, it seems to me that I lay all my accomplishments modestly at your feet. But you step upon them as if they were paving-stones, but because you do it with great grace and very delicate feet, one puts up with this kind of thing.

I can't send you the letter from Nees,[39] I feel too sorry for my poor Muhammad. To Nees, he seems like a herm;[40] a muse wants to cover the unorganic feet with clothes, but a satyr mischievously pulls the cloth away and shows the unperfected figure to the public. He wants to express this idea in a foreword, because he finds it very political to express one's failings

---

[37] Johannes von Müller (1752–1809), a Swiss historian and politician.

[38] A reference to Ecclesiastes 9:11: "the race is not to the swift, nor the battle to the strong [. . .]; but time and chance happeneth to them all" (King James Bible online).

[39] Günderrode's friend Christian Nees von Esenbeck.

[40] A kind of statue, generally a bust (although it may include more of the torso than a bust) emerging from a plain, uncarved lower section.

oneself. As a consolation I must tell him that the worst parts will be crossed out, and the whole thing will appear under the title of a fragment.

Friendliest greetings to Gundelchen. Write to me soon, but properly; you know well what I mean by properly.

Adieu

Your Günderrödchen

To Clemens Brentano, 10 June 1804

Before I come to a serious treatment of your serious questions, I must urgently beg you to remove the dreadful wig you forced on me,[41] which I don't actually wear as it would very much restrict me. So, right at the start of my letter, away with it, so I can move freely.

How did I come up with the idea of having my poems published, you want to know? I've always had a murky inclination to do so, and rarely ask myself why or what for. I was very happy when I found someone who agreed to represent me to the publisher; easily, and not knowing what I did, I thus broke the barriers that separated my innermost mind from the world; and I haven't yet regretted it, for the longing is always new and vivid in me to express my life in an enduring form, in a figure that would be worthy of joining the most excellent, greeting them and being in community with them. Yes, I've always craved this community; this is the church for which my spirit has always made its pilgrimage on earth.

Because I want to be very sincere with you today, I must also tell you that I have no real relationship to you; if that can develop, that would make me happy. It would have to start from you. But if it cannot be, that would hardly trouble me. My connection to you is not friendship, not love; my sentiment therefore doesn't need any relationship—rather, it resembles the interest one can have in an artwork. But confused, misunderstood relationships could tarnish this interest for me.

Don't say any more that my essence is reflection or even that I'm mistrustful. Mistrust is a harpy that throws itself greedily upon the divine banquet of enthusiasm and sullies it with impure experience and common cleverness, which I've always scorned with respect to all worthy persons.

---

[41] In a letter to Günderrode, Clemens criticized *Poems and Fantasies* and added "it is as if a modern sage had found a pair of ancient, prophesying doves, poked out their eyes and put wigs on them" (SW 3:63).

Greet your wife most kindly from me; I'm also looking forward to seeing you and your child, who I imagine as very sweet. You made me very happy with the Ponce de Leon.[42]

To Friedrich Creuzer, 22 March 1805

Last Sunday I was at home alone all day. In the evening I had some chest pains, and I was not only very calm about it, but, I might almost say, deeply glad. I thought of all the oppressive circumstances around me, and the thought of perhaps soon being unchained from them was very desirable to me. At the same time I thanked destiny that it had let me live long enough to grasp something of Schelling's divine philosophy, and to intimate what I did not grasp, and that at least the sense for all the heavenly truths of this teaching had arisen in me before death. Then I thought of that passage in Sophocles: "Oh happy mortals, who, having seen these rites, wander to Hades; for it is their part alone to live on there."[43]

I also thought of you, and very profoundly, and looked forward to being with you; for I hoped you would also have to die soon. Then that sonnet you once gave me came to mind; I read it so moved I could have cried.

Afternoon

In the afternoon, your letter, which I had recently received, seemed so strange to me, and I could not rightly understand either its language or its look. It's so rational, so full of useful desires for deeds, and takes pleasure in life. But I have already lived many days in Orcus and only thought about wandering down there, soon and without pain, not only in thought, no; wholly and completely. I wanted to find you there, too, but you're thinking of other things. Even now, you're establishing yourself very well in life, and, as you say yourself, should the meaning of our union be "that we'll go gladly if nature calls us back"—we could have done that without having known each other. I meant it very differently, and if you meant nothing further, then you have very much mistaken me and I you, and you're not at all the one I mean. So explain yourself about that, so I know what I can hope from you. Friendship, as I meant it with you, was a union in life and death. Is that too serious for you? Or too irrational? Once, the thought of dying with me seemed very valuable

---

[42] Clemens Brentano's 1803 comedy *Ponce de Leon*.
[43] Retranslated from Günderrode's German.

to you, and, if you died first, of my being torn down with you. But now you have much more important things to think about, and I could also be useful in the world somehow. Then it would be a shame if you should be the cause of my early death. I must now follow your example and think about you like that. I don't understand this reasonableness.

Forgive me! I know how overwrought I am; my way of being must be starting to annoy you.

Do you know what the meaning of our union was? That I no longer[44]

To Friedrich Creuzer, 25, 26, 27 April 1805

25th

I had a strange dream last night that I can't forget. It seemed I lay in bed; a lion lay to my right, a female wolf to my left, and a bear at my feet! All half on top of me and sleeping deeply. Then I thought, if these animals wake up they'll be furious with each other and tear each other and me apart. I was terribly afraid and pulled myself gently from underneath them and escaped. The dream seems allegorical, what do you think of it? Since then it occurred to me what Heyden will write to you; my good spirit has departed from me; I wander around in strange planes; I'm inwardly restless and everything is strange to me. You yourself are strange to me, not due to sentiment, but to the cleft that I know lies between you and me, and I understood more clearly, it's as if I've been thrown out of my sweet homeland and am as little in my place among my own thoughts as I was tonight under the predators that the strange dream gave me as companions.

26th

Yesterday I was with Heyden. I wrote a couple of lines to you that were the imprint of my disquiet, for it isn't possible for me to hide anything from you, for I must give myself to you not partially, but always my self.

27th

The friend[45] was just here; he said he had often wanted to write to you, but it would be so awkward for him because he couldn't write what was really on

---

[44] The letter ends suddenly here.

[45] Günderrode sometimes referred to herself as "the friend," using the masculine form (*der Freund*), in order to disguise her professions of love for Creuzer in case Creuzer's wife found the letters.

his mind. I assure you, he's completely devoted to you. Tell me, how did you win him so? Concerning the rest of his life, I notice more and more that his heroic soul is more and more dissolved in love's tenderness and longing for love. This state is not good for a person who must live alone and may well never again be united with the object of his love. He can't stay focused on resignation for long; he often deceives himself about it—show him the impossibility, support me: your persuasions will work best. It's strange, but he possesses his beloved object so *wholly* in his thoughts that there are many moments in which he thinks that one could only think something so certainly and in so much detail if one day it would really be like one thought it. When such a paroxysm is over, he's always terribly sad. Tell me, how should I treat him? [...]

To Bettina Brentano-von Arnim, November 1805

I've written to you last, dear Bettina! But I believe you were already in Kassel when my letter arrived, so don't think I'm as lazy as you accuse. It seems as if you've completely forgotten my way of being and foisted a strange image upon it, for you say I would declare your pursuits to be doing nothing, and you're certainly wrong there. Everything that stimulates, refreshes and fulfills the mind is worthy of reverence to me, even if no monument to it remains in memory. Thus I've always read biographies with a peculiar joy, and in doing so it always appeared to me as if one could not invent a complete person; one only ever comes up with one side and the complexity of human existence always remains unattained, and to perceive this correctly has always given me a great interest in history.

I'll very glad to be with you in Trages, for I also really long for spring and am looking forward to seeing you and being around Savigny.

You say you love Clemens, and I can be genuinely well inclined towards the idea of him, but his real life seems so far from what I expect of him according to this idea that it's always a real annoyance to me. For this reason I can also never have a firm opinion of him.

Adieu, Bettina.

Karoline

To Carl Friedrich von Savigny, December 1805

Dear Savigny, to be entirely true to you I must say that at different times I have a very different confidence in you; often I could tell you almost everything, and then much less. On the whole, I'm actually inclined to presuppose a certain unfairness towards my deepest nature in you, and to this extent I have a clear limit to my confidence; but when I see you and you're so good and sympathetic to me, that touches me so much that I'm only very unclearly conscious of the previous boundary.

I've always written to Creuzer very calmly, indeed almost serenely. I'm also not restless, but not at all happy any more: that I must conceal so much from him robs me of him much more than my circumstances; I can't tell you how bitterly I feel that. But I promise you I'll always hide my longing and my pain from him. I see myself that it's necessary, and I can do it.

Adieu dear Savigny, tell Bettina I'll write to her right away.

Karoline

I wrote to Creuzer's wife; she answered me kindly.

To Sophie Creuzer, 5 January 1806

May I ask you, dear Sophie, to give the enclosed to our friend.[46]

Your letter prompts me to another confession: I have always written to C. without deliberation and hidden none of my feelings from him. As things stand, this intense destructive exchange of hopes, fears and wishes is now past, and I have nothing more to write to him in this way. But a melancholy, a deep despondency has remained, which rules my whole life and which is involuntarily expressed as soon as I speak the truth about myself, so it also intrudes in my letters to Cr. I would have to lie for it to be otherwise, but if in such painful utterances you see something disadvantageous for you, then I would even renounce this consolation and watch what I say even more. I think so much about your security and tranquility that I won't trust myself, but only your own remarks.

Adieu, dear Sophie.

---

[46] I.e., Creuzer.

To Friedrich Creuzer, late May 1806

Whatever you tell me seems like you feel pity, and want to console me and yourself with that for the trust you're stealing, but there's no consolation for that other than that this painful tension in you can't last. It seems your eyes are ailing badly; I feel your pain, and mine, too, that I won't be seen by you. I longingly anticipate the moment when the most delightful light will be given back to you.

Why do you call me "*Sie*,"[47] even in your most intimate letter?

I'm disconcerted that my letter aroused Sophie's concern: I don't talk any differently in it than how one should talk about a friend who is one in the full sense. I thought Sophie was capable of a friendship that was more than the capricious miscellany that's usually taken for it. Doesn't it seem like I always thought too much of her? I believe that unwillingly. What does she fear from me? I'm sincere towards her, that's why she's uneasy; of course she'd have reason for it if I hid slyly.

I can say: I've seen many beautiful bright points in Sophie's life. Why can't she join them together into a beautiful, enduring whole? Why must there be so many moments of petty mistrust, of egoistical unfounded anxiety amongst them? How can she at the same time trust and not trust, endorse our relationship one day and fear it the next? How can she love you so much that she can't forsake you at any price, and yet always complain about you to her acquaintances? By God, that's hard to understand! Even torture wouldn't force complaints about you from me, even if you behaved unfairly towards me.

I received the books from Mohr[48] the day before yesterday—thank you very much. I'm really interested in Heraclitus, even without any connection to you, but hush—I'm lying, I can't do otherwise;[49] I must bring everything into connection with you, otherwise it's dead to me. That's also the source of my deplorable sincerity towards you: I must tell you about everything I come across. [...]

---

[47] Creuzer has used the polite, formal "you" (*Sie*) instead of the familiar "you" (*Du*).

[48] Jacob Mohr was the publisher of Creuzer and Carl Daub's journal *Studien*, in which Günderrode's plays *Udohla* and *Magic and Destiny* appeared.

[49] This phrasing suggests a reference to Luther's legendary speech at the 1521 Diet of Worms, in which he refused to recant his heretical statements. He is said to have stated: "Here I stand. I cannot do otherwise."

Sources for the Translations

The most complete and accurate German edition of Günderrode's works is the critical edition edited by Walter Morgenthaler ("SW"). Due to the dismantling of the publisher, I was unable to track down the owner of the copyright for this edition. The translations of Günderrode's published writings and drafts are therefore based on Leopold Hirschberg's collection of Günderrode's works.[1] Where the text differs from SW this is indicated in footnotes.

"Idea of the Earth" and some of the notes on philosophy of nature are adapted with permission from Kristin Gjesdal and Dalia Nassar's *Women Philosophers in the Long Nineteenth Century: The German Tradition*. The remaining notes are based on Günderrode's manuscripts at the Universitätsbibliothek J. C. Senckenberg of the Goethe Universität in Frankfurt am Main and the Freies Deutsches Hochstift, Frankfurt.

There are multiple German editions of Günderrode's correspondence, which is in the public domain. The most complete is edited by Birgit Weißenborn.[2] Many letters can also be found in two articles edited by Max Preitz[3] and in Christa Wolf's 1979 edition of Günderrode's selected works and correspondence.[4]

Details of where to find the manuscripts of Günderrode's notes, as well as German transcriptions of the notes and letters translated in this volume, are included below.

Sources for Günderrode's Notebooks

Notes on Philosophy of Nature

(The True Idea of Materialism ...)
UJCS, Ms. Ff KvGünderrode Abt. 2, A2 fol. 76r–77v. Transcription SW 2:404–406.

(Nature is an eternal activity ...)
UJCS, Ms. Ff KvGünderrode Abt. 1, 132–138. Transcription SW 2:364–367; Hopp and Preitz, "Umwelt. III," 292–293.

Idea of Nature
UJCS, Ms. Ff KvGünderrode Abt. 2, A2 fol. 55r–59r. Transcription SW 2:398–403.

---

[1] Leopold Hirschberg, *Gesammelte Werke der Karoline von Günderode* (Berlin and Wilmersdorf: Bibliophiler Verlag, 1920–1922).
[2] Weißenborn, *Ich sende Dir.*
[3] Max Preitz, "Karoline von Günderode in ihrer Umwelt. I. Briefe von Lisette und Christian Gottfried Nees von Esenbeck, Karoline von Günderode, Friedrich Creuzer, Clemens Brentano und Susanne von Heyden," *Jahrbuch des Freien Deutschen Hochstifts* (1962): 208–306; Preitz, "Karoline von Günderode in ihrer Umwelt. II. Karoline von Günderrodes Briefwechsel mit Friedrich Karl und Gunda von Savigny," *Jahrbuch des Freien Deutschen Hochstifts* (1964): 158–235.
[4] Wolf, *Schatten eines Traums.*

(All things are…)
UJCS, Ms. Ff KvGünderrode Abt. 1, 139–199. Transcription SW 2:368–396; Hopp and Preitz, "Umwelt. III," 294–305.

Notes on Chemistry

Dr. Steffens
UJCS, Frankfurt, Ms. Ff KvGünderrode Abt. 1, 201–202. Transcription SW 2:397; Hopp and Preitz, "Umwelt. III," 306.

Fourcroy[?]
Freies Deutsches Hochstift, Frankfurt [hereafter "FDH"], Günd. 1, Hs. 8351, 3–4. Transcription SW 2:442–449 (here 442–443).

Notes on the Early German Romantics

Novalis
UJCS, Ms. Ff KvGünderrode Abt. 2, A4 fol. 206v. Transcription SW 2:275.

Fragments from the Athenäum
UJCS, Ms. Ff KvGünderrode Abt. 2, A2 fol. 67r–70v and Abt. 2, A4 fol. 199v. Transcription SW 2:413–417, 281.

Friedrich Schlegel, On Philosophy: To Dorothea
UJCS, Ms. Ff KvGünderrode Abt. 2, A4 fol. 196r–199r. Transcription SW 2:278–281.

Friedrich Schlegel, Speech on Mythology
UJCS, Ms. Ff KvGünderrode Abt. 2, A4 fol. 199r. Transcription SW 2:281.

Notes on Schleiermacher

On Religion
UJCS, Ms. Ff KvGünderrode Abt. 2, A4 fol. 199v–203v. Transcription SW 2:282–286.

Soliloquies
UJCS, Ms. Ff KvGünderrode Abt. 2, A2 fol. 91r–v. Transcription SW 2:287.

Notes on Hemsterhuis

FDH, Günd. 1, Hs. 8351, 37–38. Transcription SW 2:299–301.

Philosophical Dictionary

UJCS, Ms. Ff KvGünderrode Abt. 1, 81–83. Transcription SW 2:350–351; Hopp and Preitz, "Umwelt. III," 280–281.

(Reason and Understanding...)

UJCS, Ms. Ff KvGünderrode Abt. 2, A2 fol. 92r–v. Transcription SW 2:353–354.

Mathematical Definitions and Other Definitions

UJCS, Ms. Ff KvGünderrode Abt. 1 (from back), 13v and Abt. 1, 110 and 112. Transcription SW 2:352, 356, 257; Hopp and Preitz, "Umwelt. III," 289.

Notes from Jean Paul, *Hesperus*

UJCS, Ms. Ff KvGünderrode Abt. 1, 74–80. Transcription Hopp and Preitz, "Umwelt. III," 277–280.

Notes from Summer 1804 to Early 1806

UJCS, Ms. Ff KvGünderrode Abt. 1, 86–94. SW 2:355; Transcription Hopp and Preitz, "Umwelt. III," 281–284, 289.

Sources for Günderrode's Letters

To Karoline von Barkhaus, 4 July 1799. Preitz, "Umwelt. II," 162–163; Weißenborn, *Ich sende Dir*, 49–50; Wolf, *Schatten eines Traumes*, 153.

To Karoline von Barkhaus, 17 July 1799. Preitz, "Umwelt. II," 165–166; Weißenborn, *Ich sende Dir*, 53–54; Wolf, *Schatten eines Traumes*, 154–155.

To Karoline von Barkhaus, 14 February 1800. Weißenborn, *Ich sende Dir*, 62–63.

To Charlotte von Günderrode, 27 August 1800. Weißenborn, *Ich sende Dir*, 72.

To Gunda Brentano, 11 August 1801. Preitz, "Umwelt. II," 167–169; Weißenborn, *Ich sende Dir*, 75–76; Wolf, *Schatten eines Traumes*, 156–158.

To Gunda Brentano, 19, 22, 23 August 1801. Preitz, "Umwelt. II," 169–170; Weißenborn, *Ich sende Dir*, 77–78; Wolf, *Schatten eines Traumes*, 158–159.

To Gunda Brentano, 29, 30 August 1801. Preitz, "Umwelt. II," 170–171; Weißenborn, *Ich sende Dir*, 78–79; Wolf, *Schatten eines Traumes*, 159–161.

To Gunda Brentano, 4, 5 September 1801. Preitz, "Umwelt. II," 171–172; Weißenborn, *Ich sende Dir*, 79–81; Wolf, *Schatten eines Traumes*, 161–162.

To Gunda Brentano, 20, 21 October 1801. Preitz, "Umwelt. II," 172–173; Weißenborn, *Ich sende Dir*, 81–82; Wolf, *Schatten eines Traumes*, 162–163.

To Gunda Brentano, 24 November 1801. Preitz, "Umwelt. II," 173–175; Weißenborn, *Ich sende Dir*, 82–84; Wolf, *Schatten eines Traumes*, 163–165.

To Gunda Brentano, 30 December 1801. Preitz, "Umwelt. II," 175; Weißenborn, *Ich sende Dir*, 84–85; Wolf, *Schatten eines Traumes*, 165.

To Gunda Brentano, June 1802. Preitz, "Umwelt. II," 176; Weißenborn, *Ich sende Dir*, 89–90; Wolf, *Schatten eines Traumes*, 166–167.

To Clemens Brentano, 19 May 1802. Weißenborn, *Ich sende Dir*, 88–89; Wolf, *Schatten eines Traumes*, 210–211.

To Clemens Brentano [1803?]. Wolf, *Schatten eines Traumes*, 211–212.

To Carl Friedrich von Savigny, end July 1803. Preitz, "Umwelt. II," 186–187; Weißenborn, *Ich sende Dir*, 103–104; Wolf, *Schatten eines Traumes*, 177–178.

To Carl Friedrich von Savigny, 26 December 1803. Preitz, "Umwelt. II," 193; Weißenborn, *Ich sende Dir*, 112; Wolf, *Schatten eines Traumes*, 184–185.

Günderrode and Gunda to Carl Friedrich von Savigny, 1, 3 January 1804. Preitz, "Umwelt. II," 194–195; Weißenborn, *Ich sende Dir*, 113–115; Wolf, *Schatten eines Traumes*, 186–188.

To Carl Friedrich von Savigny, February 1804. Preitz, "Umwelt. II," 199; Weißenborn, *Ich sende Dir*, 119–120; Wolf, *Schatten eines Traumes*, 191–192.

To Claudine Piautaz, April 1804. Weißenborn, *Ich sende Dir*, 125–127.

To Carl Friedrich Savigny, 31st May, 1st June, 1804. Preitz, "Umwelt. II," 200–201; Weißenborn, *Ich sende Dir*, 141–142; Wolf, *Schatten eines Traumes*, 194–195.

To Carl Friedrich Savigny, June 1804. Preitz, "Umwelt. II," 202–203; Weißenborn, *Ich sende Dir*, 155–156; Wolf, *Schatten eines Traumes*, 196–97.

To Clemens Brentano, 10 June 1804. Weißenborn, *Ich sende Dir*, 151–152; Wolf, *Schatten eines Traumes*, 221–222.

To Friedrich Creuzer, 22 March 1805. Weißenborn, *Ich sende Dir*, 205–207; Wolf, *Schatten eines Traumes*, 253–254.

To Friedrich Creuzer, 25, 26, 27 April 1805. Weißenborn, *Ich sende Dir*, 215–217; Wolf, *Schatten eines Traumes*, 254–256.

To Bettina Brentano-von Arnim, November 1805. Weißenborn, *Ich sende Dir*, 268–269.

To Carl Friedrich von Savigny, December 1805. Weißenborn, *Ich sende Dir*, 285; Wolf, *Schatten eines Traumes*, 207.

To Sophie Creuzer, 5 January 1806. Weißenborn, *Ich sende Dir*, 293.

To Friedrich Creuzer, late May 1806. Weißenborn, *Ich sende Dir*, 321–322; Wolf, *Schatten eines Traumes*, 272–273.

Bibliography

Allingham, Liesl. "Countermemory in Karoline von Günderrode's 'Darthula nach Ossian': A Female Warrior, Her Unruly Breast, and the Construction of Her Myth." *Goethe Yearbook* 21 (July 2014): 39–56.

Anon. "Literarische Beitrag aus Frankfurt am Mayn." *Der Freimüthige oder Ernst und Scherz* 97 (15 May 1804): 385.

Arnim, Bettina [Brentano-]von. *Die Günderode.* Grünberg: W. Levysohn, 1840.

Arnim, Bettina [Brentano-]von. "Report on Günderrode's Suicide (1808/1839)." In *Bitter Healing: German Women Writers. From 1700 to 1830. An Anthology.* Ed. Jeannine Blackwell and Susanne Zantop, 455–472. Lincoln: University of Nebraska Press, 1990.

Arnim, Bettina Brentano-von. "Selections from *Günderode.*" Trans. Anna Ezekiel. In *Women Philosophers in the Long Nineteenth Century: The German Tradition.* Ed. Dalia Nassar and Kristin Gjesdal, 92–121. New York: Oxford UP, 2021.

Bär, Gerald. "'Ossian fürs Frauenzimmer'? Lengefeld, Günderrode, and the Portuguese Translations of 'Alcipe' and Adelaide Prata." *Translation and Literature* 22.3 (2013): 343–360.

Bär, Gerald. "Ossianomanie und Aeronautik. Karoline von Günderrode zwischen populärem Zeitgeist und kritischer Selbstbespiegelung." In *Noch Zukunft haben: Zum Werk Karoline von Günderrodes.* Ed. Frederike Middelhoff and Martina Wernli, 135–162. Berlin and New York: Springer, 2024.

Battersby, Christine. "Stages on Kant's Way: Aesthetics, Morality, and the Gendered Sublime." In *Feminism and Tradition in Aesthetics.* Ed. Peggy Zeglin Brand and Carolyn Korsmeyer, 88–114. University Park: Pennsylvania State UP, 1995.

Battersby, Christine. *The Sublime, Terror and Human Difference.* Oxford: Routledge, 2007.

Becker, Sabina. "Gelebte 'Universalpoesie'. Rahel Varnhagen und die frühromantische Gesprächs- und Geselligskeitskultur." In *Rahel Levin Varnhagen. Studien zu ihrem Werk im zeitgenössischen Kontext.* Ed. Sabina Becker, 17–52. St. Ingbert: Röhrig, 2001.

Becker-Cantarino, Barbara. "The 'New Mythology': Myth and Death in Karoline von Günderrode's Literary Work." In *Women and Death 3: Women's Representations of Death in German Culture since 1500.* Ed. Clare Bielby and Anna Richards, 51–70. Rochester, NY: Camden House, 2010.

Becker-Cantarino, B. and Jeanette Clausen. "Gender Censorship: On Literary Production in German Romanticism." *Women in German Yearbook: Feminist Studies and German Culture* 11 (1995): 81–97.

Bohrer, Karl Heinz. "Identität als Selbstverlust. Zum romantischen Subjektbegriff." *Merkur* 38.4 (1984): 367–379.

Brüggemann, Heinz. "Luftbilder eines kleinstädtischen Jahrhunderts. Ekstase und imaginäre Topographie in Jean Paul 'Des Luftschiffers Giannozzo Seebuch.'" In *Die Stadt in der europäischen Romantik.* Ed. Gerhard von Graevenitz, 127–182. Würzburg: Königshausen & Neumann, 2000.

Burdorf, Dieter von. "'Diese Sehnsucht ist ein Gedanke, der ins Unendliche starrt'. Über Karoline von Günderrode—aus Anlaß neuer Ausgaben ihrer Werke und Briefe." *Wirkendes Wort* 43.1 (April 1993): 49–67.

Burwick, Roswitha. "Liebe und Tod in Leben und Werk der Günderode." *German Studies Review* 3.2 (1980): 207–223.

Butzer, Günter and Joachim Jacob, eds. *Metzler Lexicon literarischer Symbole*. Stuttgart: J. B. Metzler, 2008.

Bürger, Christa. "'Aber eine Sehnsucht war in mir, die ihren Gegenstand nicht kannte ...' Ein Versuch über Karoline von Günderrode." *Metis* 2 (1995): 24–43.

Cahen-Maurel, Laure. "Philosophical Paths: The Legacy of Hemsterhuis' Dialogues in the Age of German Romanticism." In *The Dialogues of Francois Hemsterhuis, 1778–1787*. Ed. and trans. Jacob van Sluis and Daniel Whistler, 22–44. Edinburgh: Edinburgh UP, 2022.

Cahen-Maurel, Laure and Giulia Valpione, eds. *Symphilosophie: International Journal of Philosophical Romanticism 4. Cosmic Web: Hemsterhuis among the German Romantics* (2022).

Christmann, Ruth. *Zwischen Identitätsgewinn und Bewußtseinsverlust. Das philosophisch-literarische Werk der Karoline von Günderrode (1780–1806)*. Frankfurt: Lang, 2005.

Dormann, Helga. "Die Karoline von Günderrode-Forschung 1945–1995. Ein Bericht." *Athenaeum* 6 (1996): 227–248.

Dormann, Helga. *Die Kunst des inneren Sinns. Mythisierung der inneren und äusseren Natur im Werk Karoline von Günderrodes*. Würzburg: Königshausen und Neumann, 2004.

Eickenrodt, Sabine. *Augenspiel. Jean Pauls optische Metaphorik der Unsterblichkeit*. Wallstein, nd.

Engelstein, Stefani. "Sibling Incest and Cultural Voyeurism in Günderode's *Udohla* and Thomas Mann's *Wälsungenblut*." *German Quarterly* 77.3 (2004): 278–299.

Ezekiel, Anna. "Earth, Spirit, Humanity: Community and the Nonhuman in Karoline von Günderrode's 'Idea of the Earth.'" In *Romanticism and Political Ecology*. Ed. Kir Kuiken. Romantic Praxis Circle, 2024.

Ezekiel, Anna. "Introduction to *Hildgund*." In Karoline von Günderrode, *Poetic Fragments by Tian*. Ed. and trans. Anna Ezekiel, 39–55. Albany: SUNY Press, 2016.

Ezekiel, Anna. "Introduction to *Muhammad, the Prophet of Mecca*." In Karoline von Günderrode, *Poetic Fragments by Tian*. Ed. and trans. Anna Ezekiel, 121–151. Albany: SUNY Press, 2016.

Ezekiel, Anna. "Introduction to 'Piedro,' 'The Pilgrims,' and 'The Kiss in the Dream.'" In Karoline von Günderrode, *Poetic Fragments by Tian*. Ed. and trans. Anna Ezekiel, 87–103. Albany: SUNY Press, 2016.

Ezekiel, Anna. Introduction to *Poetic Fragments by Tian*. Ed. and trans. Anna Ezekiel, 1–38. Albany: SUNY Press, 2016.

Ezekiel, Anna. "Karoline von Günderrode, 'Musa.'" *Trail of Crumbs*, January 2021. Available at https://acezekiel.com/2021/01/19/karoline-von-gunderrode-musa/.

Ezekiel, Anna. "Metamorphosis, Personhood and Power in Karoline von Günderrode." *European Romantic Review* 25.6 (2014): 773–791.

Ezekiel, Anna. "Narrative and Fragment: The Social Self in Karoline von Günderrode." *Symphilosophie: International Journal of Philosophical Romanticism* 2 (2020). Available at https://symphilosophie.com/wp-content/uploads/2020/12/4_Symphilosophie-2_2-Ezekiel.pdf.

Ezekiel, Anna. "Revolution and Revitalisation: Karoline von Günderrode's Political Philosophy and Its Metaphysical Foundations." *British Journal of the History of Philosophy* 30.4 (2022/2020): 666–686.

Ezekiel, Anna. "Through Consciousness Parted from Dream: Alternative Knowledge Forms in Karoline von Günderrode." In *The Significance of Negation in Classical German Philosophy*. Ed. Gregory Moss, 163–180. Dordrecht: Springer: 2023.

Ezekiel, Anna. "Women, Women Writers, and Early German Romanticism." In *The Palgrave Handbook of German Romantic Philosophy*. Ed. Elizabeth Millán Brusslan, 475–510. Palgrave Macmillan, 2020.

Fichte, Johann Gottlieb. "[First] Introduction to the *Wissenschaftslehre*." In *Introductions to the Wissenschaftslehre and Other Writings (1797–1800)*. Ed. and trans. Daniel Breazeale, 7–35. Indianapolis: Hackett, 1994.

Figueira, Dorothy M. "The Dynamics of Exoticism: Herder's Epigram and Günderrode's Epitaph." In *The Exotic: A Decadent Quest.* Ed. Dorothy M. Figuiera, 21–28. Albany: SUNY Press, 1994.

Firchow, Peter. Introduction. In *Friedrich Schlegel's* Lucinde *and the Fragments.* Ed. Peter Firchow, 3–40. Minneapolis: University of Minnesota Press, 1971.

Fourcroy, Antoine François. *System der theoretischen und practischen Chemie. In Tabellen entworfen von A. F. Fourcroy.* Trans. Christian Gotthold Eschenbach. Leipzig: Reinicke & Hinrichs, 1801.

Friedrichsmeyer, Sara. *The Androgyne in Early German Romanticism: Friedrich Schlegel, Novalis, and the Metaphysics of Love.* Bern: Lange, 1983.

Galasso, Stephanie. "Form and Contention: *Sati* as Custom in Günderrode's 'Die Malabarische Witwen.'" *Goethe Yearbook* 24 (2017): 197–220.

Gersdorff, Dagmar von. *"Die Erde ist mir Heimat nicht geworden." Das Leben der Karoline von Günderrode.* Insel: Frankfurt, 2006.

Goethe, Johann Wolfgang von. *Goethes Briefe an Eichstadt. Mit Erläuterungen.* Ed. Woldemar Freiherrn von Biedermann. Berlin: Gustav Hempel, 1872.

Grier, Michelle. "Swedenborg and Kant on Spiritual Intuition." In *On the True Philosopher and the True Philosophy: Essays on Swedenborg.* Ed. Stephen McNeilly, 1–20. London: The Swedenborg Society, 2002.

Gudin de la Brenellerie, [Paul-Philippe]. "Sur le Globe Ascendant." *Journal de Paris* (28 August 1783): 989–990.

Günderrode, Karoline von. *Gesammelte Werke der Karoline von Günderode.* 3 vols. Ed. Leopold Hirschberg. Berlin and Wilmersdorf: Bibliophiler Verlag, 1920–1922.

Günderrode, Karoline von. "Karoline von Günderrode, 'Muhammad's Dream in the Desert.'" Trans. Anna Ezekiel. *Trail of Crumbs.* October 2021. Available at https://acezekiel.com/2021/10/18/karoline-von-gunderrode-muhammads-dream-in-the-desert/. Reprinted in Synkrētic no. 2 (June 2022): 133–144.

Günderrode, Karoline von. "Piedro." In *Poetic Fragments by Tian.* Ed. and trans. Anna Ezekiel, 106–111. Albany: SUNY Press, 2016.

Günderrode, Karoline von. *Poetic Fragments, by Tian.* Ed. and trans. Anna Ezekiel. Albany: SUNY Press, 2016.

Günderrode, Karoline von. *Sämtliche Werke.* 3 vols. Ed. Walter Morgenthaler. Frankfurt and Basel: Stroemfeld and Roter Stern, 1990–1991.

Günderrode, Karoline von. "On Fichte's *The Vocation of Humankind.*" Trans. Anna Ezekiel. In *Women Philosophers in the Long Nineteenth Century: The German Tradition.* Ed. Dalia Nassar and Kristin Gjesdal, 70–74. New York: OUP, 2021.

Halem, Gerhard Anton von. "Die Blume Oschaddi." In *Blüthen von Trümmern.* Ed. Gerhard Anton von Halem, 163–177. Bremen: Friedrich Wilmans, 1798.

Harries, Elizabeth Wanning. *The Unfinished Manner: Essays on the Fragment in the Later Eighteenth Century.* Charlottesville: UP of Virginia, 1994.

Hemsterhuis, François. *Simon, ou des facultés de l'ame* [1787]. In *Oeuvres Philosophique de M. F. Hemsterhuis.* 188–249. Vol. 2. Paris: H. J. Jansen, 1792.

Herder, Johann Gottfried. *Ideen zur Philosophie der Geschichte der Menschheit.* 4 vols. Riga: Hartknoch, 1784f.

Herrera, Hugo E. "Urgrund and Access to the Urgrund in Karoline von Günderrode's Discussion with the Thought of Friedrich Schleiermacher." *European Journal of Philosophy* 32.2 (2023): 378–393.

Hilliard, K. F. "Goethe and the Cure for Melancholy: 'Mahomets Gesang.' Orientalism and the Medical Psychology of the Eighteenth Century." *Oxford German Studies* 23 (1994): 71–103.

Hilliard, Kevin. "Orient und Mythos: Karoline von Günderrode." In *Frauen: MitSprechen. MitSchreiben. Beiträge zur literatur- und sprachwissenschaflichen Frauenforschung.* Ed. Marianne Henn and Britta Hufeisen, 244–255. Stuttgart: Heinz, 1997.

Hoff, Dagmar von. "Dramatisch Weiblichkeitsmuster zur Zeit der Französischen Revolution. Dramen von deutschsprachigen Autorinnen um 1800." In *Die Marseillaise der Weiber. Frauen, die Französische Revolution und ihre Rezeption*. Ed. Inge Stephan and Sigrid Weigel, 74–88. Hamburg: Argument, 1989.

Hölderlin, Friedrich. "An den Äther." In *Musenalmanach für das Jahr 1798*. Ed. Friedrich Schiller, 131–136. Tübingen: Cotta, 1797.

Hopp, Doris and Max Preitz. "Karoline von Günderrode in ihrer Umwelt. III. Karoline von Günderrodes 'Studienbuch.'" *Jahrbuch des Freien Deutschen Hochstifts* (1975): 223–323.

Kant, Immanuel. *Critique of Practical Reason*. Trans. Werner S. Pluhar. Indianapolis: Hackett, 2002. First published in German, 1788.

Kant, Immanuel. *Träume eines Geistersehers, erläutert durch Träume der Metaphysik*. Königsberg: Johann Jacob Kanter, 1766.

Kiesewetter, Johann Gottfried Karl Christian. *Grundriß einer allgemeinen Logik nach Kantischen Grundsätzen zum Gebrauch für Vorlesungen mit einer weitern Auseinandersetzung für diejenigen die keine Vorlesung darüber hören können*. Berlin: F. T. Lagarde, 1795.

Kiesewetter, Johann Gottfried Karl Christian. *Grundriß einer allgemeinen Logik nach Kantischen Grundsätzen zum Gebrauch für Vorlesungen begleitet mit einer weitern Auseinandersetzung für diejenigen die keine Vorlesung darüben hören können. Zweiter Theil welcher die angewandte allgemeine Logik enthält*. Berlin: F. T. Lagarde, 1796.

Koser, Julie. "Looking East: Cross-Cultural Encounters in Benedikte Nauberts *Walter von Montbarry*." In *The German Historical Novel since the Eighteenth Century: More than a Bestseller*. Ed. Daniela Richter, 15–44. Cambridge: Cambridge Scholars Publishing, 2016.

Krimmer, Elizabeth. *In the Company of Men: Cross-Dressed Women around 1800*. Detroit: Wayne State UP, 2004.

Kuzniar, Alice. "Labor Pains: Romantic Theories of Creativity and Gender." In *'The Spirit of Poesy': Essays on Jewish and German Literature and Thought in Honor of Géza von Molnár*. Ed. Richard Block and Peter Fenves, 74–88. Evanston: Northwestern UP, 2000.

Lang, Berel. "The Ethics of Style in Philosophical Discourse." In *Literary Form, Philosophical Content: Historical Studies of Philosophical Genres*. Ed. Jonathan Lavery and Louis Groarke, 219–234. Madison: Fairleigh Dickinson UP, 2010.

Lavers, Jordan R. "The Epistolarity of a Social Network: Simulating a Romantic Network Community in Letters by Karoline von Günderrode." In *Nineteenth Century Literature Criticism* 338 (2017): 149–171.

Lazarowicz, Margarete. *Karoline von Günderrode. Porträt einer Fremden*. Frankfurt: Peter Lang, 1986.

Lessing, Gotthold Ephraim. "Eine Duplik." In *Gotthold Ephraim Lessings sämtliche Schriften*. Ed. Karl Lachmann. Vol. 13, 19–90. Leipzig: Göschen, 1897.

Licher, Lucia Maria. *Mein Leben in einer bleibenden Form aussprechen. Umrisse einer Ästhetik im Werk Karoline von Günderrodes (1780–1806)*. Heidelberg: Winter, 1996.

Macpherson, James. *Fragments of Ancient Poetry, Collected in the Highlands of Scotland, and Translated from the Galic or Erse Language*. Edinburgh: Hamilton and Balfour, 1760.

Macpherson, James. *Morison's Edition of the Poems of Ossian, the Son of Fingal, Translated by James Macpherson, Esq., Carefully Corrected, and Greatly Improved*. 2 vols. Perth: R. Morison Jr, for R. Morison & Son, 1795.

Nassar, Dalia. "The Human Vocation and the Question of the Earth: Karoline von Günderrode's Philosophy of Nature." *Archiv für Geschichte der Philosophie* 104.1 (2021): 108–130.

Nees von Esenbeck, Christian. "Hamburg u. Frankfurt a. M., in Commiss. d. Hermannschen Buchh.: *Gedichte und Phantasien*, von Tian. 1804. 137 S. 8." *Jenaische Allgemeine Literatur-Zeitung* 163 (9 July 1804): 49–52.

Neurohr, J. A. and Johann Hugo Wyttenbach. *Aussprüche der philosophierende Vernunft und des reinen Herzens über die der Menschheit wichtigsten Gegenstände mit besonderer Rücksicht auf die kritische Philosophie zusammengetragen aus den Schriften älterer und neuerer Denker*. Jena: J. G. Voigt, 1797.

Ng, Karen. "The Idea of the Earth in Günderrode, Schelling and Hegel." In *The Oxford Handbook of Nineteenth-Century Women Philosophers in the German Tradition*. Ed. Kristin Gjesdal and Dalia Nassar, 527–548. New York: OUP, 2024.

Niehle, Victoria. "Die ästhetische Funktion des Raumes. Jean Pauls 'Des Luftschiffer Giannozzo Seebuch.'" In *Raumlektüren. Der Spatial Turn und die Literatur der Moderne*. Ed. Tim Mehigan and Alan Corkhill, 69–86. Bielefeld: transcript, 2013.

Norris, Benjamin. "Necro-ecology in Günderrode's 'Idea of the Earth': Life, Death and *Naturphilosophie* Beyond Schelling." *Idealistic Studies* 54.3 (2024): 283–303.

Novalis. *Schriften*. Ed. Friedrich Schlegel and Ludwick Tieck. Berlin: Realschule, 1802.

Novalis. *Schriften. Zweite, nach den Handschriften ergänzte, erweiterte und verbesserte Auflage in vier Bänden*. Ed. Paul Kluckhohn and Richard Samuel. 4 Vols. Stuttgart: W. Kohlhammer, 1960f.

Obermeier, Karin. "'Ach diese Rolle wird mir allzu schwer': Gender and Cultural Identity in Karoline von Günderrode's Drama 'Udohla.'" In *Thalia's Daughters: German Women Dramatists from the Eighteenth Century to the Present*. Ed. Susan Cocalis and Ferrel Rose, with Karin Obermeier, 99–114. Tübingen: Francke, 1996.

Obermeier, Karin. *Private Matters Made Public: Love and the Sexualized Body in Karoline von Günderrode's Texts*. Diss., University of Massachusetts Amherst, 1995.

Peter, Maria. "Zwischen Klassik und Romantik: Karoline von Günderrode." *Das Goldene Tor. Monatsschrift für Literatur und Kunst* 6 (1949): 465–473.

Plato. *Meno*. Trans. Benjamin Jowett. Upper Saddle River, NJ: Prentice Hall, 1949 [1871].

Preisendanz, Karl. *Die Liebe der Günderode. Friedrich Creuzers Briefe an Günderode*. Munich: R. Piper & Co., 1912.

Preitz, Max. "Karoline von Günderrode in ihrer Umwelt. I. Briefe von Lisette und Christian Gottfried Nees von Esenbeck, Karoline von Günderrode, Friedrich Creuzer, Clemens Brentano und Susanne von Heyden." *Jahrbuch des Freien Deutschen Hochstifts* (1962): 208–306.

Preitz, Max. "Karoline von Günderrode in ihrer Umwelt. II. Karoline von Günderrodes Briefwechsel mit Friedrich Karl und Gunda von Savigny." *Jahrbuch des Freien Deutschen Hochstifts* (1964): 158–235.

Raisbeck, Joanna. *Karoline von Günderrode: Philosophical Romantic*. Cambridge: Legenda, 2022.

Richter, Jean Paul Friedrich. *Hesperus, oder fünfundvierzig Hundsposttage. Eine Lebensbeschreibung*. 3 vols. Berlin: Matzdorff, 1795.

Riley, Helene M. Kastinger. "Zwischen den Welten. Ambivalenz und Existentialproblematik im Werk Caroline von Günderrodes." In *Die weiblich Muse. Sechs Essays über künstlerisch schaffende Frauen der Goethezeit*. Ed. Helene M. Kastinger Riley, 91–119. Columbia: Camden House, 1986.

Sandrart, Joachim von. *Teutsche Academie der Bau-, Bildhauer- und Mahler-Kunst*. City and publisher unknown, 1675.

Schärf, Christian. "Artistische Ironie und Fremdheit der Seele. Zur ästhetischen Disposition in der Frühromantik bei Friedrich Schlegel und Karoline von Günderrode." *Deutsche Vierteljahrsschrift für Literaturwissenschaft und Geistesgeschichte* 72.3 (1998): 433–462.

Schelling, F. W. J. "Allgemeine Deduction des dynamischen Processes oder der Categorieen der Physik." *Zeitschrift für spekulative Physik*. Vol. 1. Ed. F. W. J. Schelling, 100–136. Jena: Christian Ernst Gabler, 1800.

Schelling, F. W. J. *Bruno, oder über das göttliche und natürliche Princip der Dinge. Ein Gespräch*. Berlin: Johann Friedrich Unger, 1802. Translated by Michael G. Vater as *Bruno, or On the Natural and the Divine Principle of Things*. Albany: SUNY Press, 1984.

Schelling, F. W. J. *Einleitung zu dem Entwurf eines Systems der Naturphilosophie*. Jena: Christian Ernst Gabler, 1799.

Schelling, F. W. J. *Erster Entwurf eines Systems der Naturphilosophie. Zum Behuf seiner Vorlesungen*. Jena: Christian Ernst Gabler, 1799.

Schelling, F. W. J. *Ideen zu einer Philosophie der Natur*. Leipzig: Breitkopf und Härtel, 1797.
Schelling, F. W. J. *Vorlesungen über die Methode des akademischen Studiums*. Tübingen: Cotta, 1803 [1802].
Schlegel, Friedrich. *Friedrich Schlegel: Kritische Ausgabe seiner Werke*. Ed. Ernst Behler. 35 Vols. Munich: F. Schöningh, 1958–2002.
Schleiermacher, Friedrich. *Monologen. Eine Neujahrsgabe*. Berlin: Christian Sigismund Spener, 1800.
Schleiermacher, Friedrich. *Über die Religion. Reden an die Gebildeten unter ihren Verächtern*. Berlin: Johann Friedrich Unger, 1799.
Schrage-Früh, Michaela. "Subversive Weiblichkeit? Die Frau als Muse, Geliebte und Künstlerin im Werk Friedrich Schlegels und Karoline von Günderrodes." *Subversive Romantik* 24 (2004): 365–390.
Simpson, Patricia Anne. *The Erotics of War in German Romanticism*. Lewisburg: Bucknell UP, 2006.
Spalding, Johann Joachim. *Betrachtung über die Bestimmung des Menschen*. Expanded edition. Leipzig: Weidmanns Erben und Reich, 1768 [1748].
Steffens, Henrik. "Über den Oxydations- und Desoxydations-Prozeß der Erde. Eine Abhandlung vorgelesen in der naturforschenden Gesellschaft zu Jena." In *Zeitschrift für spekulative Physik*. Vol. 1. Ed. Friedrich Schelling, 137–66. Jena: Christian Ernst Gabler, 1800.
Takamura, David. "Illusion and Individuation in the Orientalisms of Arthur Schopenhauer and Karoline von Günderrode." *The German Quarterly* 96.3 (2023): 308–235.
Trop, Gabriel. "Arts of Unconditioning: On Romantic Science and Poetry." In *The Palgrave Handbook of German Romantic Philosophy*. Ed. Elizabeth Millán Brusslan. Palgrave Macmillan, 421–448. London and New York: Palgrave Macmillan Cham, 2020.
Wackenroder, Wilhelm Heinrich. *Phantasien über die Kunst für Freunde der Kunst*. Ed. Ludwig Tieck. Hamburg: Friedrich Perthes, 1799.
Wackenroder, Wilhelm Heinrich. *Werke und Briefe*. Ed. Gerda Heinrich. Berlin: Union; and Munich: Hanser, 1984.
Wägenbaur, Birgit. "'habe getaumelt in den Räumen des Aethers.' Karoline von Günderrodes ästhetische Identität." In *Frauen: MitSprechen. MitSchreiben. Beiträge zur literatur- und sprachwissenschaftlichen Frauenforschung*. Ed. Marianne Henn and Britta Hufeisen, 201–222. Stuttgart: Heinz, 1997.
Watanabe-O'Kelly, Helen. *Beauty or Beast? The Woman Warrior in the German Imagination from the Renaissance to the Present*. Oxford: OUP, 2010.
Weigert, Astrid. "Gender and Genre in the Works of German Romantic Women Writers." In *The Oxford Handbook of European Romanticism*. Ed. Paul Hamilton, 240–255. Oxford: OUP, 2016.
Weißenborn, Birgit, ed. *"Ich sende Dir ein zärtliches Pfand." Die Briefe der Karoline von Günderrode*. Frankfurt: Insel, 1992.
Wieland, Christoph Martin. *Agathodämon* [1796–1797]. In *C. M. Wielands sämmtliche Werke*. Vol. 32. Leipzig: Georg Joachim Göschen, 1799.
Wieland, Christoph Martin. "Die Aëropetomanie" [1783]. In *C. M. Wielands sämmtliche Werke*. Vol. 33, 105–130. Leipzig: Georg Joachim Göschen, 1840.
Wieland, Christoph Martin. "Die Aëronauten" [1784]. In *C. M. Wielands sämmtliche Werke*. Vol. 33, 131–191. Leipzig: Georg Joachim Göschen, 1840.
Willson, A. Leslie. *A Mythical Image: The Ideal of India in German Romanticism*. Durham, NC: Duke UP, 1964.
Wolf, Christa, ed. *Der Schatten eines Traumes. Gedichte, Prosa, Briefe, Zeugnisse von Zeitgenossen*. Munich: Deutscher Taschenbuch, 1997 [1979].

Index

For the benefit of digital users, indexed terms that span two pages (e.g., 52–53) may, on occasion, appear on only one of those pages.

"Adept, The," 18–19, 70n.13, 91–94, 103, 167
"Aeronaut, The," 14, 38, 146–50, 151–52
aesthetics, 10, 25–27, 45, 46–47, 52, 54, 58, 68, 127–39, 140–41, 142, 143, 145, 154, 235, 237, 273
   See also sublime, the
affinity, 11, 49–50, 63–64, 66–68, 221, 227, 228–29
   See also attraction; harmony; homogeneity
apocalypse. *See* revelation
"Apocalyptic Fragment, An," 10, 14, 15–17, 19, 34, 39–40, 48–49, 77–82, 151n.2
Arnim, Bettine von. *See* Brentano-von Arnim, Bettine von
attraction, 10–11, 31–32, 49, 53, 62–64, 68, 74, 97, 129, 130, 212–15, 216, 220–21, 222–23, 224–25, 227, 228–29
   See also affinity; friendship; love

Bildung. See self-development
birth, 10–11, 55, 61–63, 78, 81, 83, 84–85, 86, 90, 140–42, 143, 146–47, 149, 151–53, 157, 210, 219
   See also rebirth
Brahmin, 14–15, 22, 114, 115, 116, 124–26
   See also Hinduism; priest; "Story of a Brahmin"
Brentano, Bettina von. *See* Brentano-von Arnim, Bettina
Brentano, Clemens, 6, 7, 52–53, 231n.2, 254n.34, 261–65, 271, 273, 275, 276, 283–84
Brentano, Kunigunde (Gunda), 6, 7, 22–23, 24, 52–53, 260–62, 267–75, 278, 279
Brentano-von Arnim, Bettina von, 6, 8, 231n.2, 261–62, 263–64, 275, 286

"Cathedral in Cologne, The," 39–40, 140–41, 145
"Change and Constancy," 25–26, 36–37, 127, 128–31, 135–37

Christ, Jesus, 60–61, 78–79, 121–22, 133
Christianity, 55–57, 63n.20, 78–79, 112–13, 115–16, 118, 172n.19, 239
   Protestantism, 54, 58
   See also religion
colonialism, 21, 74–75, 166, 171–74
community, 3, 19–24, 25, 32, 67, 92, 112, 114, 116–17, 118–19, 124–25, 126, 128, 240–41, 242–43, 265, 283
consciousness, 12, 14–18, 46, 59, 60–61, 63, 69–70, 72–73, 77–82, 83, 84–85, 90, 115, 121–22, 124–25, 131–32, 137, 149, 151, 152–53, 210, 217, 224–25, 234, 236–37, 268, 280
   See also epistemology; intiution
Creuzer, Georg Friedrich, 5, 6–9, 28, 52–53, 56–57, 160, 172–73, 260, 262–63, 284–86, 287, 288
cultivation, 12, 31–32, 46, 49–50, 54, 58–59, 61–62, 63–64, 112, 115–17, 131–32, 236–37, 241–42, 253, 262
   See also self-development

"Darthula," 27–30, 158n.3, 160–61, 172n.18, 270
dead, the. *See* spirits of the dead
death,
   Günderrode's, 1–3, 5–6, 7–8, 27–28, 52–53, 160, 260, 263, 270, 284–85
   Günderrode's theory of, 12–17, 45–46, 49–50, 53–54, 60–61, 62–64, 66–68, 69, 70, 72, 74–76, 77–82, 83–84, 90, 102–11, 145, 146–47, 151–53, 154, 155, 189, 192, 268
   heroic, 28–29, 158–65, 189, 270, 272
   life after, 102–11, 240–41, 242 (*see also* rebirth; reincarnation; resurrection; transmigration of souls)
   and love. *See under* love
   union with loved ones after, 8–9, 11, 52–53, 74–76, 103–4, 232–33, 284–85
"Dream, A," 10, 14, 15–17, 48–49, 77–80, 82, 141

early German Romanticism. *See* Romanticism, early German
elements, 10–16, 20–21, 26, 31–32, 45–46, 48, 49–51, 53, 62–64, 67–68, 74, 76, 85, 88, 97, 104–5, 107–8, 167, 208–9, 214n.14, 216, 227, 241–42
epistemology, 17–19, 33, 53–54, 61, 62–63, 69–70, 83–90, 91–94, 95, 96, 98, 103, 105, 106–7, 110, 112–13, 119, 121, 122, 129n.4, 130n.5, 147–49, 167, 210, 216–17, 218, 224, 231–32, 235, 244–45, 248, 249–50, 268
See also consciousness; intuition
ethics, 10, 23–25, 26, 45, 127–39, 240–41, 248, 265
See also "Fragments on Ethics and Aesthetics"; morality; virtue
"Excellence is a whole. . .," 21–22, 24, 127–29, 131–33, 240–41, 245

Fichte, Johann Gottlieb, 1–2, 33n.69, 47, 48–49, 84–85, 116–17, 147–49, 205, 206–7, 210n.10, 236, 246n.8
fragment, 3, 10, 24, 25–26, 33, 38–40, 60–62, 127–39, 140–45, 230–31, 233–36, 260–61, 282–83
"Frank in Egypt, The," 18–19, 31–32, 36, 70n.13, 95–101, 116n.10, 173n.24, 209n.4
French Revolution. *See under* revolution
friendship, 11, 19–20, 22–23, 68, 72, 74, 97, 117, 131, 133, 237, 251, 259, 261–65, 266–67, 273–74, 277–78, 283, 284–85, 288
See also affinity; attraction; "Letters of Two Friends"; love

gender, 2, 26–32, 33–34, 74–75, 96–97, 104, 140–41, 148–49, 153–54, 158–65, 168–72, 208–9, 210, 231, 236–37, 259, 264–65, 270
German idealism. *See* idealism, German
German Romanticism. *See* Romanticism, early German
Goethe, Johann Wolfgang von, 1, 8–9, 60n.14, 75n.4, 96n.2, 167, 169n.7, 177n.29, 227

Hardenberg, Friedrich von. *See* Novalis
harmony, 10–12, 23–25, 26, 32, 45–47, 51, 65, 66–68, 72, 113, 116, 118–19, 120, 123, 128n.3, 137, 143, 145, 149, 150, 227, 234, 245, 246, 266–67
See also affinity; homogeneity
Hegel, Georg Wilhelm Friedrich, 47, 48–49
Hemsterhuis, François, 5, 17–18, 68–69, 205, 206, 244–46
Heraclitus, 5, 48–49, 288

Herder, Johann Gottfried, 5, 68, 116–17, 123n.19, 205, 245, 266
Hildgund, 27–28, 29–30, 95, 159–61, 170n.15, 172n.18, 174n.26
Hinduism, 15, 55–56, 60–61, 74–76, 115, 121–22, 168–74, 177, 179, 180–81, 189
See also Brahmin
homogeneity, 67–68, 71, 74, 222, 249
See also affinity; harmony
human vocation, 1–2, 14, 116–17, 119, 236–37

"Idea of the Earth," 10–17, 20n.34, 23–25, 26, 45–51, 52–54, 55–56, 63–65, 67–68, 104–5, 115, 127, 208–9, 227
See also organism
idealism, German, 9–10, 26–27, 38, 40, 47, 146, 147–48, 205, 210n.10, 236, 246n.8
Immortalita, 18–19, 36, 102–11
inner sense, 19, 22, 53–54, 60–61, 66–70, 72–73, 114, 116, 118, 121, 122–25, 141, 145, 245, 264, 280
See also intuition; moral organ
intuition, 33, 57–58, 69–70, 79, 100, 103–4, 109, 111, 114, 116–17, 120–23, 199, 210, 217, 230–31, 239–40, 241–43, 246, 248, 264, 280
See also consciousness; epistemology; inner sense
Islam, 112–13, 118, 121–22, 169–70, 176, 177, 181, 190
See also Muhammad, the Prophet of Mecca; "Muhammad's Dream in the Desert"; Prophet Muhammad

Jean Paul [Friedrich Richter], 148, 247–48, 250–53
Jesus Christ. *See* Christ, Jesus

Kant, Immanuel, 16–18, 23–25, 26–27, 60n.14, 67, 68–69, 83–84, 112–13, 114, 116–17, 147–49, 154, 205, 206–7, 253, 254, 264, 280
knowledge. *See* epistemology

"Letters of Two Friends," 10–17, 18–19, 23–25, 36, 39–40, 45, 52–65, 67–68, 74n.2, 104–5, 115, 127, 208–9, 227, 232, 264
love,
    and death, 8–9, 11, 53, 62–63, 74–75, 76, 103–4, 109–11, 126, 151–52, 160, 161, 163, 165, 232–33
    Günderrode's theory of (*see also* affinity; attraction; friendship), 11, 31–32, 68, 74, 76, 97, 126, 227, 266–67, 268, 271, 273, 280, 283

and knowledge, 18–19, 95, 100, 107, 121
Platonic, 24–26, 37, 46–47, 51, 65, 102–4,
109, 111, 127–39, 244, 246, 251, 266–
67, 273–75
romantic, 30, 32, 97, 160
"Love and Beauty," 25–26, 129, 134

Magic and Destiny, 7, 91–92, 127–28, 159,
166, 240–41
"Malabarian Widows, The," 11, 14, 31, 74–
76, 227
"Manes, The," 10–11, 14, 18–19, 21–22, 31,
36–37, 39–40, 48–49, 66–73, 127–28, 131,
227, 245
Melete, 1, 7–8, 45, 52–53, 74
metaphysics, 10–16, 19–20, 23–25, 26–27, 30–
32, 45–51, 55–56, 74, 77, 97, 104–5, 115,
142–43, 166, 167, 205, 227, 241
Mora, 27–28, 29, 36, 158–65
moral organ, 68–69, 244–45, 246
See also inner sense
morality, 3, 23–25, 34, 46–47, 48–49, 112–15,
116–17, 118–20, 121–22, 123–24, 169–70,
171, 233, 239–40, 241–42, 244, 248, 252,
253, 255, 264, 281
See also ethics; moral organ; virtue
Muhammad. *See* Prophet Muhammad
Muhammad, the Prophet of Mecca, 19–22, 29–
30, 38, 39–40, 95, 122n.17, 127–28, 166,
169n.7, 174n.26, 240–41, 282–83
"Muhammad's Dream in the Desert," 18–19, 92
music, 10, 25–26, 61–62, 104, 107–8, 123, 125,
132, 140–45, 158–59, 162, 163, 165, 175,
176, 184, 192, 200, 233, 235, 251, 254,
262, 272
Muslim. *See* Islam

Napoleon Bonaparte, 38, 95–96, 174n.26
Naturphilosophie. See philosophy of nature
Novalis, 1–2, 5, 17–18, 30–32, 35, 39, 67, 84–85,
96–97, 103–4, 140n.2, 205, 230–38, 245
See also Romanticism, early German

"Once I Lived Sweet Life," 14, 37–38, 151–57
organism, 10, 12, 16, 24–25, 26, 45–47, 49–51,
63–65, 212, 224
See also "Idea of the Earth"
Ossian, 27–28, 148–49, 158–65, 270, 272

philosophy of nature, 6, 40, 47–48, 115, 208–25,
226, 231–32
See also Schelling, Friedrich Wilhelm Joseph
Plato, 23, 24, 25–26, 60n.14, 103, 105, 129–30

Poems and Fantasies, 1, 7, 18, 66, 77, 83, 91, 95,
102, 127, 158, 227, 264, 283n.41
Poetic Fragments, 1, 7, 9, 39–40
priest, 57–58, 76, 91, 92–93, 121–22, 124–25,
133, 177, 178–79, 235
See also Brahmin
Prophet Muhammad, 22, 29–30, 38, 95, 121–
22, 178
See also Islam; "Muhammad's Dream in the
Desert"; *Muhammad, the Prophet of Mecca*
Protestantism. *See under* Christianity

rebirth, 15–16, 102, 140–41, 143, 151–53
See also birth; reincarnation; resurrection;
transmigration of souls
reincarnation, 14–16, 34, 46, 48, 78, 90,
115, 265
See also rebirth; resurrection; transmigration
of souls
religion, 13–14, 24, 54, 55–57, 58n.10, 60–61,
68–69, 73, 77, 78–79, 114–15, 116–17, 118,
121–25, 231, 235, 236–37, 239–43
See also Christianity; Hinduism; Islam; priest
resurrection, 63n.20, 140–41, 142n.6, 145, 189
See also rebirth; reincarnation;
transmigration of souls
revelation, 45, 53, 55–56, 57, 61–62, 63–64, 68,
69–70, 72–73, 77–82, 83, 120–21, 125, 202,
212, 241–43
See also "Apocalyptic Fragment, An"
revolution, 20–22, 166–202, 234
French Revolution, 29n.60, 95, 159
Richter, Jean Paul Friedrich. *See* Jean Paul
Romanticism, early German, 1–3, 5, 9–10,
30–32, 35–36, 37, 39, 54, 62n.17, 67, 80,
96–97, 103–4, 112–14, 115, 128, 130n.5,
140n.2, 142n.6, 146, 148–49, 154, 167,
230–38, 263–64
See also Novalis; Schlegel, Friedrich

Savigny, Carl Friedrich von, 4, 7, 253n.28, 260–66,
276–79, 281–83, 287
Schelling, Friedrich Wilhelm Joseph, 1–2, 5,
15, 35, 36, 47–49, 104–5, 205, 206, 208–25,
226, 246n.8, 250, 255, 282
See also philosophy of nature
Schlegel, Friedrich, 1–2, 5, 30–32, 35, 39–40,
54–55, 97, 140n.2, 205, 206, 230–38
See also Novalis; Romanticism,
early German
Schleiermacher, Friedrich Daniel Ernst, 5,
17–18, 21n.39, 67, 68–69, 116–17, 127–28,
205, 206, 235n.19, 239–43, 245

self-development, 3, 12, 14–15, 21–24, 31–32, 46, 48, 49–51, 55, 57–65, 68–69, 72–73, 96, 97, 112–17, 124–25, 128, 152–53, 178, 213, 218, 244–45, 246, 247–48, 268
  See also cultivation
spirit, 61–62, 133, 134, 143, 233, 234, 237, 238, 242–43, 251
  earth-, 50–51, 55, 60, 64
  eyes of. See inner sense
  of God, 78, 143, 219
  individual, 57–58, 59, 70, 98, 100, 116, 118–22, 143–44, 145, 188, 196, 217n.16, 234, 235, 236–37, 242–43, 270, 281, 283
  infinite, 13–14, 53–54, 55–56, 61, 115, 122, 124–25, 143, 216–17, 224–25, 234, 237, 273–74
  light-, 87
  as in mind, 30–31, 47, 50–51, 64, 70, 73, 82, 97, 123–24, 151, 153, 209n.4, 211–12, 217, 218, 224–25, 271
  of nature, 115, 121, 124–25, 209–10
  nature-, 56, 91, 93, 213–14, 219
  universal. See spirit, infinite
  voice of, 112, 116, 121, 125, 184, 245
  world-, 22, 116, 121–22, 125, 211
spirit world, 69, 100
spirits,
  of earth, 58–59, 83, 84–85, 88–90

of the dead, 66, 67, 69, 73, 80, 82, 116, 125–26, 162, 189
"Story of a Brahmin," 10, 13–15, 18–20, 21–22, 23–24, 31, 34, 36, 48–49, 91–92, 97n.6, 112–26, 127–28, 131, 170n.13, 239–41, 245
sublime, the, 26–27, 154, 248

transmigration of souls, 14–15, 46, 50, 64, 115, 124–25
  See also rebirth; reincarnation; resurrection

Udohla, 7, 19–21, 29–30, 36, 124n.23, 159, 166–202

virtue, 23–29, 36, 46–47, 51, 65, 72, 119–20, 127–39, 169, 180, 246, 250–51, 252, 253, 262, 270, 271, 281
  See also ethics; "Excellence is a whole"; morality
vocation, human. See human vocation

"Wanderer's Descent, The," 10, 18–19, 36, 83–90, 91–92, 103, 210, 245
Wieland, Christoph Martin, 48–49, 79, 148
women. See gender
world-spirit. See under spirit